Speech and Deafness

Speech and Deafness

A Text for Learning and Teaching

Revised Edition

By

Donald R. Calvert

Director, Central Institute for the Deaf
Professor of Audiology, Washington University

and

S. Richard Silverman

Director Emeritus, Central Institute for the Deaf
Adjunct Research Scientist of the Institute for Advanced Study
of the Communication Processes
University of Florida, Gainesville

Alexander Graham Bell Association for the Deaf
Washington, D.C.

The Alexander Graham Bell Association for the Deaf, Inc.
3417 Volta Place, N.W., Washington, D.C. 20007, U.S.A.

Library of Congress Catalogue Card Number 83-71360
ISBN 0-88200-153-1

PRE

To
Rae Calvert and Sally Silverman,
longstanding members of the
company of learners and teachers.

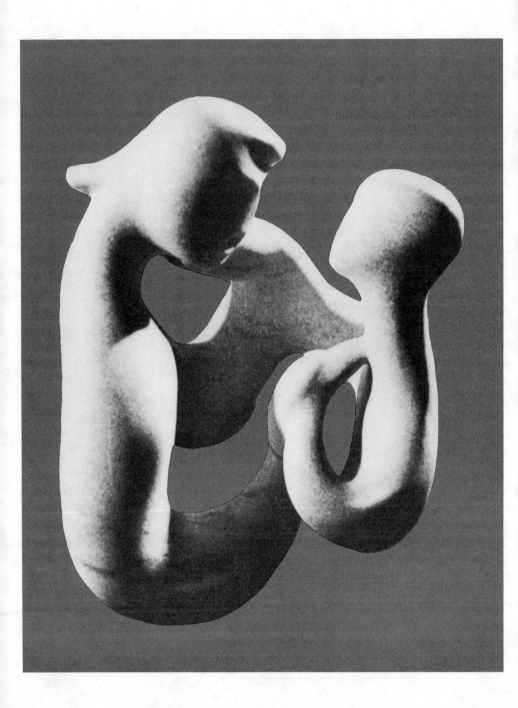

The awesome task for those of us engaged daily in teaching speech is to recapitulate for our deaf children the evolution of humankind's extraordinary and unique achievement—spoken language. Contemplate, if you will, the vast symbolic structures built by the human race and transmitted by sounds; what a feat, as Lewis Mumford points out in his "Myth of the Machine," of abstracting, associating, memorizing, recognizing, recalling, that at first must have demanded "strenuous collective effort!" No technological triumph surpasses its grandeur and its power.

S. Richard Silverman
The Volta Review, March 1974.

Sculpture Legend

The white marble sculpture, "Learners," that stands in the entry of the Central Institute School was created by Hillis Arnold of St. Louis, recalling his mother as his first teacher. It symbolizes the personal intimacy of teaching/learning speech, and its title reflects the perpetual learning about speech by both the children involved and by the adults, be they teachers, student-teachers, professors, parents, dormitory staff, or anyone in any way who lends support to this worthy endeavor.

Preface to the Second Edition

An indispensable requirement for effective teaching is the recognition that the responses of students govern the development of instructional practices. Our book constitutes an attempt to satisfy that requirement. It grows out of many years of experience in listening and reacting to students, colleagues, and deaf persons, and, in turn, develops our ideas and our suggestions for them about learning and teaching speech. In a very real and significant sense, all of us who have positive convictions about the value of communication by speech are members of a company of enthusiastic learners. In this spirit our book delineates a point of departure for continued learning rather than arrival at a final destination. It is a beginning, not an end. We predict with confidence that as we continue to learn, revision and elaboration will be inevitable. We would be disappointed if it turned out to be otherwise. Accordingly, this second edition constitutes an anticipated revision.

To all from whom we have learned we express our gratitude. Their "responses" stimulated and guided the preparation of the pages that follow. We are singularly indebted to our colleagues at Central Institute for the Deaf and elsewhere for their comments and recommendations during preparation of both editions. We thank especially those who contributed specific items as noted in the text. While our contemporaries contributed to the scope and currency of our writings, a special debt of gratitude is owed to our predecessors who pioneered and persisted in teaching speech to deaf children when hearing aids were only tubes and funnels, when the undertaking was more an intuitive art than a promising science, and when speech for most deaf children was only a distant dream.

We trust that those who benefit from the use of the material in this book will have the same rich satisfaction that its authors have had, not only in presenting the material but, perhaps more importantly, in contributing toward enabling a deaf child to acquire the precious skill of spoken language. This will be reward enough for our efforts.

St. Louis, Missouri   *Donald R. Calvert*
September 1983   *S. Richard Silverman*

Table of Contents

List of Tables

List of Figures

Introduction

Throughout the recorded history of the education of the deaf the desirability of equipping the deaf person with spoken language has seldom if ever been questioned. From the 16th and 17th centuries—which marked the period when literature about the education of the deaf began to emerge—through the period of the development of influential movements, to the present day, issues, values, and methods about teaching speech have commanded the interest and attention of writers, teachers, deaf persons, and observers of the field (154, 280). Of course, the continuing controversy about modes of communication that are emphasized in the education of the deaf persists, and, here and there, this causes variation in the significance that is placed on instruction in speech for the deaf. Nevertheless, none of the proponents of one or another view advocates elimination of teaching speech. We hope that what we have included in this book can be incorporated beneficially in whatever mode of communication is prominent in instruction and associated activities.

As we have said, teachers vary considerably in the emphasis they place on the teaching of speech, ranging all the way from teachers for whom the teaching of spoken language is a central focus to those whose attitudes toward teaching speech are crystallized in such comments as, "It's nice to do it, if you can get it, but don't spend too much time on it." This range of attitudes usually results in varying outcomes ranging from the production of intelligible speech to what amounts to just a string of unintelligible grunts or snorts. This last result discourages those who would spend more time on teaching speech. Attitudes which evolve into a spectrum of firmly held convictions seem to grow out of what in the modern managerial idiom we would call the *cost benefits* of teaching speech. These convictions have fed on themselves and—in many contexts where benefits in relation to expended efforts

1

have been judged, for whatever reason, to be insufficient—have unfortunately contributed to the denigration of the teaching of speech. In such situations there is very little reinforcement of attempts in classrooms, clinics, and homes—let alone in the general environment—to encourage or to improve speech by deaf persons.

Obviously the fact that we have undertaken to write this book underlines our conviction that the development of spoken language for deaf children and its improvement for deaf adults is worth every effort we can put forth. We are aware that even the best efforts may not ensure complete intelligibility of all deaf persons' speech in all situations, but as suggested in Figure 1, there are recurring communicating situations in which speech can be importantly functional. In a sense, the recurrence provides "auditory training" to the listener. The continuing aim should be the extension of the areas of understanding listeners. To reduce or abandon our best efforts in teaching speech to deaf persons is to deny them the opportunity for an achievement unique to man—the development of an acoustic code that enables a human being to communicate with his fellow human being in a distinctive way that is not possible through any other mode of communication.

Our aim in this book is to improve the competency of those who would take the teaching of speech to deaf children seriously, with the hope that their results may be improved. This, in turn, should reinforce their own efforts and consequently their own enthusiasm for the activity. In the pages that follow we have attempted to concentrate on the task of teaching and learning speech through the eyes of the person in whom the professional responsibility resides, namely the teacher, and, to some extent, supportive persons and parents. We have used the term "teacher" to apply to instructional personnel in schools and to speech pathologists and audiologists who are involved in programs for hearing-impaired persons.

What we have presented is based primarily but not exclusively on our own experience as teachers and as teachers of teachers. It is our chief credential for tackling the problem in the first place. This is essentially an "applied" book, though not a "manual." Its optimum use will be facilitated by continuing experience and direct application with students. We are not only aware, we are *convinced*, that a teacher's competence will be enhanced by her knowledge of the contributions to her task from related bodies of knowledge. We believe, however, that these subjects are adequately treated elsewhere in the professional and scientific literature. We have drawn on them only to the extent that they are directly and demonstrably relevant to developing speech in deaf individuals. Because indifference to the obvious, but essential, can be a pedagogical pitfall, we have here and there restated and condensed material from these sources as handy references or brief refreshers, some shamefully

elementary, for the teacher. The inclusion of fundamental anatomy and physiology and some conventional orthographic symbol systems are examples of
this. The point is that we wish to avoid being diverted from our main purpose
into exposition and even critical analysis of related areas, particularly since
we hope the sources contained in our bibliography accomplish this effectively.
Among the bibliographic items are some which we have selected for annota-

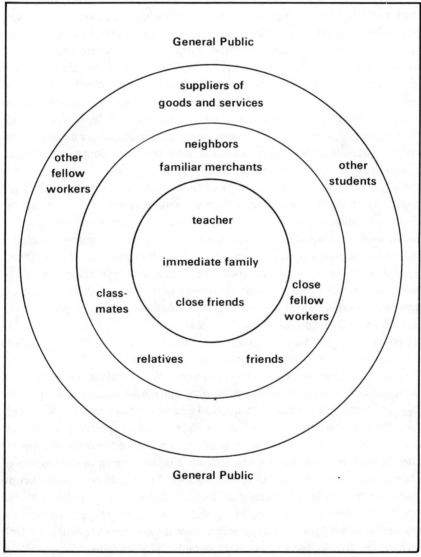

Figure 1. *Expanding groups of people with whom speech can be functional.*

tion to illustrate the kinds of helpful material available in the professional and scientific literature.

It would be presumptuous of us to state that we have treated our subject exhaustively. We have covered as much as we believe is pertinent, or necessary, to serve as *a point of departure* for a practitioner. We hope to enhance the teacher's *power to analyze the task of speech instruction and to plan procedures that follow logically from the analysis.* After all, children differ, environments differ, and teaching and instructional styles differ. The value of this book to the teacher will be commensurate with what she brings to the task by way of her own attitudes, knowledge, and skill. These stress an attitude that reflects a strong conviction about the worthwhileness of teaching speech to deaf persons; knowledge that underlines and strengthens the possibility for improvement in a teacher's ability, which should be a lifelong process, and building on a rational set of procedures applied to skilled instruction. Furthermore, all of this must be expressed in the context of the school in which the teacher practices her skills. This means that, in a school, we do *not* depend just on a designated specialist, helpful as such may be, to improve the speech of children, but rather that *every teacher is also a teacher of speech.* We cannot stress this point too strongly. We believe that attention to speech is not just a matter of something that is given for x number of minutes per day, but that it pervades all of the instructional procedures and activities.

We have searched diligently and extensively for an organizing scheme for this book that would by itself contribute to the achievement of its aim. After a good deal of cutting, pasting, modifying, eliminating, and adding, what follows represents our best current judgment. There is more than an expected amount of repetition and redundancy, as, for example, in the emphasis in different contexts on the use of residual hearing. This is deliberate in order to drive home our points, and it is also helpful for the teacher who may wish to pass over certain parts and plunge immediately into others.

Our text follows what we believe is an orderly, logical sequence. We start with *speech and its production,* refreshing our reader on anatomy, physiology, and some of the related acoustics. Then we consider *learning and teaching* speech, emphasizing general principles that lead to specific kinds of procedures and approaches. We then move on to a chapter on *using hearing for speech.* We have included this as a separate chapter because of the number of children in schools and classes for the deaf who have hearing levels that command recognition in the teaching of speech. Furthermore, it makes available results of research in the use of residual hearing, its relation to acoustic phonetics, and its practical application. Recent data from the Gallaudet College Center for Assessment and Demographic Studies indicate that 45% of hearing impaired children are reported to have hearing levels of 84 dB* or better in three speech frequencies. Incidentally, if the frequency of 250 Hz had been included in the calculation and a cut-off established at 90 dB, the numbers of children with hearing significant for speech development would be much greater.

We progress to the task of *developing speech,* and here we suggest "approaches" to the teaching of speech that encompass traditionally discrete but overlapping methods. Chapter V underlines the fundamental point that speech for deaf children must not only be developed, but must be *improved* and *maintained.* Chapter VI includes a detailed *analysis for instruction of* the *phonemes* and combinations of phonemes. Originally we had intended to include this in the Appendix, but it seemed to fit better here. Chapter VII completes the pedagogical sequence with some thoughts on what we have expressed throughout the book about *evaluating speech.* We hope that the *bibliography* and *suggested readings* will stimulate and add to the intellectual and professional sense of accomplishment the teachers derive from their work.

Throughout we have used the terms *deaf* and *hearing impaired* interchangeably. Agreement on the precise definition of these terms is still not universal. For convenience of style we have referred to the student as *he* and the teacher as *she.* We trust that activists in the "role of the sexes" movement will not treat our decision too harshly.

---

*Except where otherwise specified, all references to dB may be understood to be ANSI calibration.

CHAPTER I

Speech and Its Production

Speech may be studied from many points of view. It may be analyzed from a physical base, relating the body's vibrating and resonating systems to the frequency, intensity, and duration of the sounds of speech. Considered physiologically, the emphasis may be on interaction of muscles, cartilage, and bone, or on neurological activity such as excitation, transmission, integration, and response of the body's nervous system. Viewed psychologically, speech is concerned with personality, self-expression, and such processes as motivation, attention, perception, recognition, and memory. Speech also has an obvious socio-linguistic base as the prime vehicle for symbolically expressing meaning through language and as an important medium through which humans interact among themselves. How speech develops in individuals and how it has come to be one of mankind's distinctive achievements continues to command the attention and energy of investigators and practitioners.

For our purposes, as stated in the Introduction, we select material from those complex and richly stocked areas which are pertinent to our task. It is necessary that we organize our exposition around the analysis of those aspects of speech production that experience suggests are most useful in teaching children to talk. Various "models" for teaching and learning speech are now being investigated. Their validation and usefulness may result in changes in conceptualization of our task. For the present, however, we believe it is timely and pragmatic to organize our material in this chapter dealing with speech production around the primary factors influencing intelligibility. These are *articulation, voice,* and *rhythm.*

ARTICULATION

The process of shaping the breath stream from the larynx out through the mouth to form the speech sounds of language is called articulation. In talking, speech sounds do not follow one another as separate and distinct units like beads on a string. Nor do they flow forth in infinite variety, inseparable and unrecognizable. Each language has a finite number of speech sounds which recur within a limited range of variations.

Phonemes

The essential elements of these recurring sounds, recognized by listeners as the code signals which give meaning to speech, are called *phonemes.* Phonemes are abstractions, somewhat like an averaging, of those sounds which actually occur in connected speech (36). In the words *tea, cat, stay,* and *cattle,* we recognize a recurring common sound represented by the letter "t." We call this the phoneme t.* Yet in each of these words, the t is produced somewhat differently. In *tea,* the t is produced with the tongue tip on the gum ridge behind the front teeth and is exploded with audible breath just before beginning the vowel sound. The t in *cat* is typically a stop made without explosion or with very slight explosion of breath. In *stay,* the t stops the flow of breath but is not exploded as it is in *tea.* In *cattle,* the tongue remains on the gum ridge and the audible release is made laterally around the sides of the tongue. These and other variations of producing the phoneme t are called its *allophones.* These are phonetic variations in the place of articulation of the speech sounds within an utterance.

There are other common variations in the production of phonemes which may occur without changing meaning. The rhythm of speech may change the force with which a sound is produced to make its duration longer or shorter. In various regions of the world and among some cultural and ethnic groups where English is spoken, people speak with variations of the language called *dialects.* Dialects include variation in the production of some speech sounds, such as the southern United States "drawl" which lengthens and proliferates vowel sounds, or, as in the northeastern United States, the apparent omission of the r following a vowel as in *park.* Further variations are added in com-

---

*Throughout this book General American symbols, printed in boldface, will be used to represent phonemes. See Figures I-1, I-2 and I-3. (31)

paring the speech of those in cities and of those in rural areas of the same region. Of course, each speaker produces variations in speech sounds in his unique way, adjusting for the size and shape of his own speech mechanism.

Relation to meaning is an essential feature of the phoneme. When boundaries are exceeded in varying the production of a phoneme, it may be recognized as another phoneme (and thus change the meaning of a word) or not be recognized at all. For example, when the **t** sound is made with very little audible explosion where explosion is expected, listeners may recognize it as the phoneme **d** (try producing the word *tie* with no audible explosion of the **t**). When the **-i-** in *bit* is produced with the mouth open wide, the listener is likely to hear other vowel sounds such as the **-e-** in *bet* or the **-a-** in *bat*.

Orthographic Systems

To communicate about the phonemes of our language, we need a standard system of written symbols. In some languages, such as Spanish, the letters of standard spelling almost always have the same sound associated with them. But English is not so fortunate. It does not have a simple symbol-sound correspondence. Perhaps, this is because the English language developed from a mixture of the languages of Europe. Anglo-Saxon, derived primarily from Germanic dialects, was mixed with French and influenced by the Scandinavian languages of northern Europe, the Romance languages of southern Europe, and classic Greek and Latin. While this agglomeration of origins enhances our facility in expressing ourselves, its spelling and pronunciation follow no consistent set of rules.

Pronunciation which is not consistently predictable from spelling leads to problems. As we encounter a new word in print we determine its approximate meaning through the context of the words and phrases around it. We also formulate a probable pronunciation, using the rules of pronunciation and spelling we have learned inductively through our constant use of the language. But quite often we are aware that a new word can be pronounced several different ways because the rules of pronunciation we have learned are not absolute.

A major problem in English pronunciation is that the alphabet does not contain enough symbols to represent the phonemes of the language. English has an alphabet of only 26 letters to represent 43 sounds. The five letters which are called vowels (*a, e, i, o, u*) must represent 18 different vowels and diphthongs. The 21 consonant letters represent 25 different consonants. There is, for example, no special letter which represents the first phoneme in *church*. A number of other phonemes are represented in spelling by a combination of two letters as in *sh, th, wh* and *ng*.

A second related problem in English pronunciation is that the letters are not always pronounced the same way. While most consonant letters represent a single sound, none of the vowel letters exclusively represents a single sound. Note how pronunciation of the letter "o" changes in these words: *ton, top, told, tomb, woman, women.* However, some systematic pronunciation is evident. The 18 vowel sounds are more frequently represented by a single vowel letter, or by a particular combination of vowel letters, than by some other letter or combination of letters. Still a third problem in English pronunciation is that a single phoneme may be represented by a number of different letter combinations. The sound of **f**, for example, may be spelled "f " (*fir*), "ff " (*differ*), "ph" (*phone*), "gh" (*rough*) or "lf " (*half*).

We now consider some of the systems that address themselves to these problems (5, 31, 342).

The International Phonetic Alphabet: To avoid the spelling irregularities within a language, the differences in spelling from language to language, and the use of written characters other than Roman alphabet symbols in some languages, the International Phonetic Alphabet (IPA) was developed. The IPA includes a number of sounds which are not typically used in English, such as the bilabial fricative sound common in Spanish (*Havana*) and the fricative **r** sound common to Middle Eastern languages. It also provides for refined transcription with supplementary symbols describing particular variations in phoneme categories. The comprehensive and analytic features of this system make it especially useful for scholarly and professional communication about language and speech. (See Tables I-1 and I-2).

Visible speech symbols: Alexander Melville Bell and his son Alexander Graham Bell suggested a system of "visible speech" in 1894. In this system consonants are represented by four fundamental curves that relate to the "articulators," that is, to the back of the tongue, the top of the tongue, the point of the tongue, and the lips. The insertion of a short "voice" line in the bow of the curve changes a voiceless consonant to a voiced consonant. There is also a system for modifying a set of fundamental symbols to represent the vowels. This system is described in Bell's *The Mechanism of Speech* (11).*

Visual-tactile system: Dr. A. Zaliouk, late Director of the Institute for the Deaf in Haifa, Israel, devised a "visual-tactile system of phonetic symbolization" for teaching speech to the deaf. This system uses two categories of symbols: static and dynamic. The static symbols represent the hard palate,

---

*The numerals in parentheses here and throughout the text refer to numbered readings in the bibliography at the end of this book.

the tongue, the teeth, and the lips, all of which participate in various "articulatory positions." The dynamic symbols indicate movement (344).

Diacritical markings: Dictionaries use a system of diacritical markings (symbols attached to letters) to indicate pronunciation. Roman alphabet letters are used with special symbols attached to some of them to indicate their

Primary General American Symbol	IPA Symbol	Dictionary Diacritical Markings	Key Words
h	/h/	h	*had, ahead*
wh	/ʍ/	hw	*when, everywhere*
p	/p/	p	*pie, sip, stopped*
t	/t/	t	*tie, sit, sitting*
k	/k/	k	*key, back, become*
f	/f/	f	*fan, leaf, coffee*
th̰	/θ/	th̰	*thin, tooth, nothing*
s	/s/	s	*see, makes, upset*
sh	/ʃ/	sh̰	*she, fish, sunshine*
ch	/tʃ/	ch̰	*chair, such, teacher*
w-	/w/	w	*we, awake*
b	/b/	b	*boy, cab, rabbit*
d	/d/	d	*day, mud, ladder*
g	/ɡ/	g	*go, log, begged*
v̰	/v/	v	*vine, give, every*
t̰h	/ð/	t̶h̶	*the, smooth, bother*
z	/z/	z.	*zoo, size, lazy*
zh	/ʒ/	zh̰	*measure, vision*
j	/dʒ/	j	*jam, edge, enjoy*
m	/m/	m	*meat, team, camera*
n	/n/	n	*new, tin, any*
ng	/ŋ/	n͡g	*song, singer*
l	/l/	l	*low, bowl, color*
r	/r/	r	*red, bar, oral*
y-	/j/	y	*yes, canyon*
x	[ks]	x	*box, taxi*
qu	[kʍ]		*queen, liquid*

Table I-1. Consonant primary symbols of the General American Speech and Phonic System, International Phonetic Alphabet (IPA), and dictionary markings, with key words.

pronunciation. Common diacritical markings and dictionary symbols are shown in Tables I-1 and I-2.

Northampton symbols: At the Clarke School for the Deaf in Northampton, Massachusetts, dissatisfaction with the Bell symbols as a teaching device led Alice Worcester, a teacher, to develop symbols taken from the Roman alphabet, which she published in 1885. They were revised and organized into systematic charts in 1925 by Caroline Yale. The system reflects the pronunciation prevalent in New England (343).

The principle of the Northampton symbol system is to use as primary symbols either the alphabet letters most frequently used for particular sounds in speech (as **p, f, s, n**) or symbols which are not most common but almost invariably represent particular sounds when they occur in writing (as **k, ee, a-e** as in *name,* **aw** as in *law*). Numerous secondary symbols reflect the irregular relation between written letters and sounds. For example, "k" is the primary symbol for the **k** phoneme (as in *kind*). The letter "k" almost invariably

Primary General American Symbol	IPA Symbol	Dictionary Diacritical Markings		Key Words
oo	/u/	o͞o	ü	*boot, too*
-oo-	/ʊ/	o͝o	u̇	*book, could*
aw	/ɔ/	ô	ȯ	*awful, caught, law*
ee	/i/	ē		*east, beet, be*
-i-	/ɪ/	i	ĭ	*if, bit*
-e-	/ɛ/	e	ĕ	*end, bet*
-a-	/æ/	a	ă	*at, mat*
-o-	/ɑ/	â(r)	ȧ	*odd, father, park*
-u-	/ʌ/	u	ŭ	*up, cup*
-u-	/ə/	ə		*above, cobra*
ur	/ɝ/	er		*urn, burn, fur (General U.S.)*
a-e	/eɪ/	ā		*able, made, may*
i-e	/aɪ/	ī		*ice, mice, my*
oa	/ou/	ō		*old, boat, no*
oi	/ɔɪ/	oi		*oil, coin, boy*
u-e	/ju/	yo͞o		*use, cute, few*
ou	/aʊ/	ou		*out, loud, now*

Table I-2. Vowel primary symbols of the General American Speech and Phonic System, International Phonetic Alphabet (IPA), and dictionary markings, with key words.

represents the **k** phoneme, but it is not as commonly used to represent the sound **k** as is the letter "c" (as in *can*). However, the letter "c" may have the sound of $\overset{1}{s}$ (as in *city*) or of **sh** (as in *ocean*), as well as the sound of **k**. The letter "c" is therefore a secondary symbol for the **k** sound, but it also is used as a secondary spelling for the **s** sound. A system of diacritical numerals is also included to account for secondary and tertiary spellings, as well as to designate those symbols that occur for two or more speech sounds. An example is $\overset{1}{s}$, $\overset{2}{s}$, and $\overset{3}{s}$ to designate use of the **s** symbol for the different sounds in *boats, dogs,* and *measure,* respectively.

General American Symbols	IPA	Key Words	General American Symbols	IPA	Key Words
Stop Consonants			**Fricative Consonants**		
p	/p/	pie	**h**	/h/	he
b	/b/	by	**wh**	/ʍ/	why
t	/t/	tie	**f**	/f/	fan
d	/d/	day	ph		phone
k	/k/	key	**v**	/v/	vine
c(a)		cat	$\overset{1}{\textbf{th}}$	/θ/	thin
c(o)		cot	$\overset{2}{\textbf{th}}$	/ð/	then
c(u)		cut	**s**	/s/	see
g	/ɡ/	go	c(i)		city
Oral Resonant Consonants			c(e)		cent
			c(y)		cycle
y-	/j/	yes	**z**	/z/	zoo
l	/l/	lie	**sh**	/ʃ/	she
r	/r/	red	**zh**	/ʒ/	vision
w-	/w/	we	**Affricate Consonants**		
Nasal Resonant Consonants			**ch**	/tʃ/	chin
			tch		watch
m	/m/	me	**j**	/dʒ/	jam
n	/n/	no	-dge		edge
ng	/ŋ/	long	**qu**	[kʍ]	queen
n(k)		think	**x**	[ks]	box

Figure I-1. *General American Speech and Phonic Symbols: Consonants. Primary and secondary symbols with associated symbols of the International Phonetic Alphabet (IPA) and example words.*

General American Speech and Phonic Symbols: In order to reflect more closely the pronunciation used throughout most of the United States, and to reduce the complexity of secondary spellings and numerals that children have found difficult, as well as to improve the system for teaching speech, the symbols of the Northampton system were modified to form the General American speech and phonic system. Throughout this book we shall use the primary symbols of the General American system for phonetic transcription of phonemes. (31)

Figures I-1, I-2 and I-3 contain the General American symbols organized by their manner and place of production. Primary spellings are in bold type with secondary spellings just below, indented and in lighter type. The dashes beside some symbols indicate the common position of letters in relation to other letters. The **a-e** reflects that a consonant between *a* and *e* makes the letters associated with the sound /eI/ in *made*, rather than the /æ/ in *mad*. The **i-e** in *kite* and the **u-e** in *cute* also reflect intervening consonants. The **-i-, -e-, -a-** and **-oo-** suggest that these sounds are usually surrounded by consonants.

General American Symbols	IPA	Key Words	General American Symbols	IPA	Key Words
Front Vowels			Back Vowels		
ee	/i/	bee	**oo**	/u/	boot
ea		meat	ew		grew
-y		busy	**-oo-**	/ʊ/	foot
-i-	/I/	bit	oo(k)		book
-e-	/ɛ/	bet	**aw**	/ɔ/	lawn
-a-	/æ/	bat	ua		caught
Mixed Vowels			a(1)		walk
			-o-	/ɑ/	top
ur	/ɝ/	burn	ah		rah
er	/ɚ/	better	a(r)		car
-u-	/ʌ/	but			
	/ə/	upon			

Figure I-2. General American Speech and Phonic Symbols: Vowels. *Primary, secondary and tertiary symbols with associated symbols of the International Phonetic Alphabet (IPA) and example words.*

General American Symbols	IPA	Key Words	General American Symbols	IPA	Key Words
High Nucleus Diphthongs			Low Nucleus Diphthongs		
u-e	[ju]	cute	**oi**	/ ɔɪ /	coin
a-e	/eɪ/	made	oy		boy
ai		bait	**i-e**	/aɪ/	bite
oa	/ou/	boat	igh		fight
-o		no	**ou**	/au/	mouth
			ow		cow

Figure I-3.   *General American Speech and Phonic Symbols: Diphthongs. Primary and secondary symbols with associated symbols of the International Phonetic Alphabet (IPA) and example words.*

The numeral system, diacritical [1] and [2], is used consistently and exclusively to indicate the condition of voicing—[1] to designate a voiceless production and [2] to show a voiced production. The numerals appear above the primary symbols only to differentiate **th** as in *thin* from **th** as in *then*. But they can also be used to suggest the condition of voicing for other phonemes in relevant situations. Since errors of voicing are prevalent among deaf speakers, this simple code can be very useful to the teacher. For example, the voiceless production of **l** and **r** in blends with voiceless consonants can be indicated by writing *print, clay, free,* and *sleep.* To suggest the voiceless finish on final voiced fricative consonants, the teacher may write *leave.* When a voiceless fricative is given too much breath force between vowels, correction of the error may be indicated by writing the voicing numeral [2] as in *behind.* When a child produces a voiced/voiceless error, such as *die* for *tie,* the teacher can suggest the nature of the error by prompting the child with the written symbols *tie.*

Bracketed General American symbols suggest the influence of one sound upon the pronunciation of another. The letter *n* before *k* is usually pronounced **ng.** The *c* before *e, i,* and *y* becomes **s,** while before *a, o,* and *u* it is usually pronounced **k.** When *oo* is followed by *k* it is almost invariably pronounced **-oo-** rather than **oo.**

Table I-3 shows the correspondence between the spellings and vowel sounds of General American and Northampton symbols, based on a study of pronunciation of common words. The symbols on the left side are those which consistently represent a specific vowel sound (about 90% or more of the time).

The reader encountering a new word which includes one of these vowel letters or combinations of letters could be reasonably confident of the pronunciation. On the right side are spelling symbols which do not correspond very well. The spelling "ow," for example, can be pronounced like the vowel in *low* or the vowel in *cow* with almost equal frequency. The reader would be uncertain as to which would be the correct pronunciation. Other vowel spellings in the right column offer probabilities for predicting the correct pronunciation much better than by chance, although by no means perfectly.

None of the orthographic systems we have described satisfies all our needs for teaching speech. An ideal system of orthography would meet the following requirements: (1) The symbols would convey information about how to articulate the sounds (Bell's and Zaliouk's symbols), (2) The symbols would

General American and Northampton Symbols	Vowel Sound in Sample Word	Proportion of Time Symbol Occurs To Represent that Vowel Sound	General American and Northampton Symbols	Vowel Sound in Sample Word	Proportion of Time Symbol Occurs To Represent that Vowel Sound
a-e	make	100%	-a-	cat	83%
				table	13%
u-e	cute	100%			
			-u-	cup	73%
aw	law	100%		unite	24%
i-e	kite	99%	ea	meat	74%
				head	24%
oi	boil	99%			
			-e-	bet	70%
oa	boat	98%		be	30%
ee	beet	96%	ou	out	60%
				rough	35%
-i-	pin	91%			
	child	9%	oo	boot	59%
				cook	41%
ai	bait	90%			
			-o-	top	53%
au	caught	88%		told	40%
			ow	low	52%
				cow	48%
			o-e	home	34%
				come	66%

Table I-3. The proportion of times each of 19 alphabet spellings represents the designated vowel sounds in 7,500 common words (165).

be free of ambiguity (International Phonetic Alphabet), (3) The system would use the written symbols of the culture (General American), and (4) The symbols would be perceptually feasible (all that have been cited). Obviously some of these requirements are in conflict. We believe the General American system offers a pragmatic accommodation for our purposes.

Place of Production

Place of production of a sound refers to that part of the speech mechanism involved directly, prominently, and specifically in the production of sound. When we refer to the "speech mechanism," we are aware that the structures that are included in it serve biological needs as their primary function. We shall allude briefly to these functions and focus on their role as providing a place of articulation. Reference to Figure I-4 will help the student in this section.

Lips (*labio-, -labial*): Their primary function is to help contain food in the oral cavity. The lips can close to stop the breath stream as in articulating **p, b,** and **m**. By approximating the lower lip and upper front teeth, the breath stream is constricted for the production of **f** and **v**. Rounding the lips and changing the degree of opening contributes to the production of **w, wh**, and the vowel sounds.

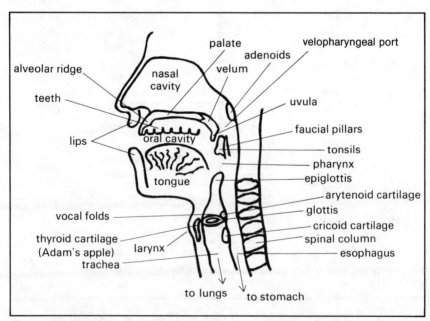

Figure I-4.   Diagram of structures used in speech production.

Teeth (*dento-, -dental*): Their primary function is to cut and grind in chewing food. In the growing child, structures change size, shape, dominant function, and relation to other elements. A good example is the developing dentition, shown in Figure I-5. The deciduous teeth, sometimes called the "milk" or "baby" teeth, erupt during a period of from 6 months to 2 years of age to include 20 teeth, 10 in the upper jaw (maxilla) and 10 in the lower jaw (mandible), arranged in symmetrical sets of 5 teeth on each side. Beginning from the midline, they are: central incisor, lateral incisor, canine (or eye tooth), first molar, and second molar. Beginning at about age 6 years, the deciduous teeth are replaced with 32 permanent teeth, 16 in the upper and 16 in the lower jaw, arranged in symmetrical sets of 8 teeth on each side. Beginning from the midline, these are: central incisor, lateral incisor, canine, first bicuspid (having two sharp points, sometimes called a premolar), second bicuspid, first molar, second molar, and third molar (or "wisdom" tooth). The sides of the tongue pressed against the molars help direct the breath stream toward the front of the mouth as in **sh**. The lower lip approximates the upper front teeth to constrict the breath stream for **f** and **v**; the tongue similarly approximates the upper incisors for the **th** and **th**. The approximated upper and lower front teeth provide friction surfaces for the **s, z, sh**, and **zh**.

Alveolar ridge (*alveolo-, -alveolar*): This is the gum ridge just behind the upper front teeth. The tongue presses against the alveolar ridge to stop the breath stream for the **t, d**, and **n**. Pressing the tongue point against the center of the ridge permits the breath stream to escape on both sides of the tongue for the **l**. The tongue tip approximates the alveolar ridge in formation of the **s** and **z**; the front of the tongue at a greater distance from the ridge forms the constriction of the breath stream for the **sh** and **zh**.

Palate (*palato-, -palatal*): This, sometimes called the "hard palate," is the structure separating the oral from the nasal cavity, extending from the alveolar ridge to the velum. Its primary purpose is to help contain food in the oral cavity and provide a hard superior (upper) surface for the process of swallowing. As the superior surface of the oral cavity, the palate contributes to vowel resonance. It helps to direct the breath stream toward the front of the mouth for consonant articulation. The back of the tongue presses against the back of the palate in the production of **k, g**, and **ng**. The tip of the tongue is lifted toward the palate, just behind the alveolar ridge, to help form the **r**.

Velum (*velo-, -velar*): The velum, sometimes called the "soft palate," is the structure just posterior to the palate. It raises to help close the velopharyngeal port, thus separating the oral from the nasal cavity. The *uvula* is an appendage extending inferiorly from the posterior midline of the velum. The

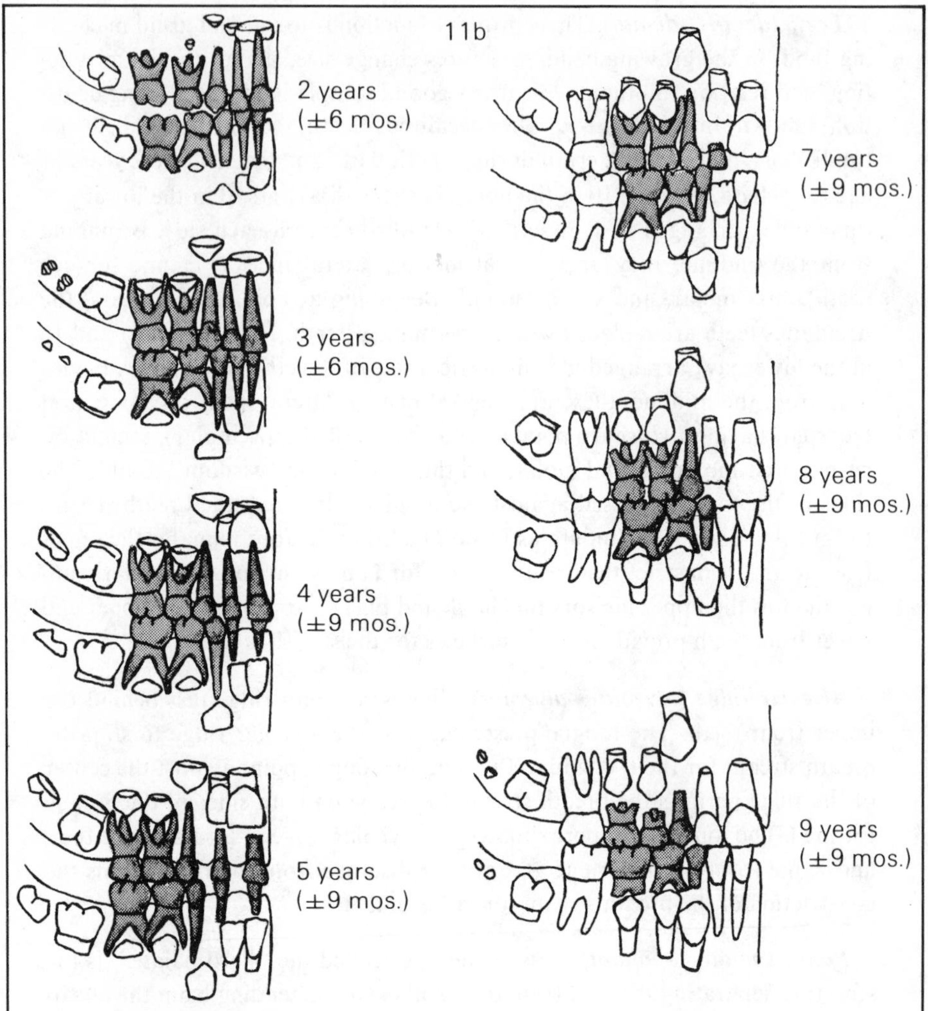

Figure I-5.   *Stages of children's dentition. Deciduous teeth are shown in dark tint, permanent teeth in white. From the chart, "Development of the Human Dentition," I. Schour & M. Massler. American Dental Association, 211 East Chicago Ave., Chicago, Ill. 60611.*

primary purpose of the velum is to keep food from entering the nasal cavity. The velum, by helping to close the velopharyngeal port, helps direct the breath stream to the oral cavity for articulation and for primarily oral resonances as in vowel sounds. When the velum is relaxed and the port opened, the breath stream can enter the nasal cavity for predominantly nasal resonance as in **m, n,** and **ng**. The back of the tongue presses against the back of the palate and front portion of the velum in the production of **k, g,** and **ng**.

Oral cavity (*oro-, -oral*): This cavity extends from the lips to the throat or pharynx. Its primary purpose is to contain food for chewing and swallowing. It can also receive inhaled and exhaled air but does not have the filtering and warming capacity of the nasal spaces. It acts as a resonating cavity for voice and channels the breath stream out the mouth for sounds other than **m, n,** and **ng**. Changes in its size and shape are largely responsible for articulation of speech sounds and their perceptual features.

Tongue (*lingua-, -lingual*): The tongue is a highly mobile muscular organ arising from the floor of the oral cavity. Its primary purpose is to direct food to the back of the oral cavity in the process of swallowing. Its five landmarks, the **point**, the **tip**, the **front**, the **middle**, and the **back**, are very important to speech sound articulation. Figure I-6 shows these landmarks as the very front edge of the tongue is narrowed or broadened to form the normal tip, the narrowed point, and the broadened front.

The tongue can narrow and point, as it does for the **l**, or it can present a broad front surface as it does in production of **sh**. Its tip and back sections can be elevated independently of each other. It can form a central groove to direct the breath stream as it does for **s**, or the tip can be elevated and drawn back (retroflexed) toward the middle of the oral cavity as in **r**. It can close off the oral cavity and quickly release compressed breath as it does in **t** and **k**.

Pharynx (*pharyng-, -pharyngeal*): The pharynx is posterior to the nasal cavity (the naso-pharynx), the oral cavity (the oro-pharynx), and, to a lesser extent, the laryngeal cavity (the laryngo-pharynx). The naso-pharynx and oro-pharynx are separated by the *velopharyngeal port* (which can be closed by the combined actions of the velum and uvula), the faucial pillars, the posterior wall of the pharynx, and masses of the tonsils and adenoids. The primary purpose of the pharynx is to direct food to the esophagus, and air to and from the trachea. It acts as a resonating cavity for voice and channels the breath stream to the oral and nasal cavities. Closure of the velopharyngeal port results in oral resonance and helps direct the breath stream to the oral cavity for articulation of speech sounds.

Nasal cavity (*naso-, -nasal*): Extending from the nostrils to the nasopharynx, the nasal cavity is primarily designed to receive inhaled air, filter and

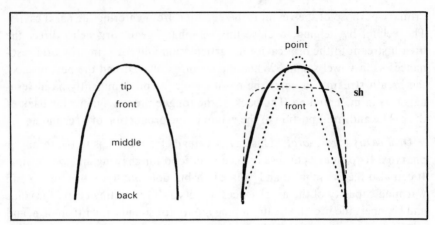

Figure I-6.   *Top view diagram of the tongue in its normal relaxed position (left) and in positions of a narow point and a broad front.*

warm it, and direct it toward the trachea. It also channels exhaled air. The nasal cavity contributes to vocal resonance and channels the breath stream out the nose for **m, n,** and **ng**.

Speech sounds may be described by their place of production, using the structures outlined above. For example, the **t** may be described as a lingua-alveolar sound (the tongue touches the alveolar ridge), the **f** as a labio-dental sound (the lip against the teeth), and the **th** as a lingua-dental sound (the tongue against the teeth).

Vowel sounds may be described by place of elevation of the tongue in the front of the mouth (as in **ee**), the back of the mouth (as in **oo**) or the middle portion of the mouth (as in **-u-**). Vowels may be further described by whether the tongue's elevation is high (as in **ee** and **oo**), low (as in **-a-** and **-o-** or midway (as in **-e-** and **aw**). Using the two parameters of place and height of tongue elevation, the place of production of vowels is plotted in Figure I-7. Of course, vowels are also modified by the degree of mouth opening and lip rounding.

Manner of Production

Another way of describing speech sounds is by the manner in which they are produced. The flexibility of our speech mechanism permits us to produce a surprising variety of noises. We shall consider four classes of the primary manner of speech sound production: *stops, fricatives, affricates,* and *resonants.*

Stops: These are sometimes called plosives or aspirates. The primary action in their production is an interruption of the breath stream by a closure

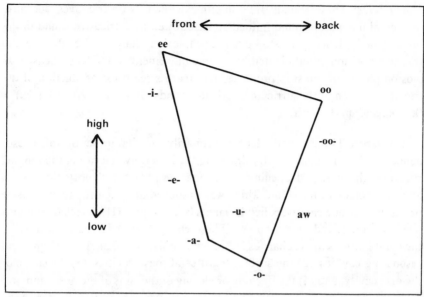

Figure I-7. *Vowel diagram showing relative tongue position, with place of tongue elevation in the mouth on the horizontal plane and degree of elevation on the vertical plane.*

within the oral cavity. Stop phonemes include **b, p, t, d, k,** and **g.** The stop action has two phases called the *closure* and the *release.* Both phases are important for the teacher to know about because some allophones of stop phonemes are made without the release phase. For example the **t** in *stop* is closed but not released with explosion, while the **t** in *top* is both closed and exploded. The rapid stopping of a preceding vowel sound by a stop consonant changes the resonance pattern of the vowel in a way unique for the position of closure of the stop, depending on whether it is at the lips (**p** and **b**), the alveolar ridge (**t** and **d**), or the velum (**k** and **g**), so that the alteration of the vowel gives the listener important information about the stop consonant that terminates it.

Fricatives: These sounds require constriction of the breath stream with audible friction for their production. They are formed by forcing the constricted air stream over the surfaces of the lips, teeth, tongue, alveolar ridge, palate, and velum. Fricative sounds include **f, v, th, th, s, z, sh, zh, wh,** and **h.** Friction may occur either with the unvoiced breath stream (as in **f, th, s, sh, wh,** and **h**), or with voicing (as in **v, th, z,** and **zh**). The term "sibilant" is sometimes applied to the **s, z, sh,** and **zh** sounds. Many other speech sounds include some degrees of friction in their production but are not dependent on friction for their perception.

Affricates: These sounds are sometimes called "stop-fricatives" because they combine a stop sound immediately followed by a fricative sound in the same syllable. During the stop portion (implosion phase) of the affricate, the fricative position is anticipated by tongue movement so that the release (explosion phase) of the stop produces the breath stream for production of the fricative portion of the affricate. Affricate sounds are **ch (t + sh)**, **j (d + zh)**, **x (k + s)**, and **qu (k + wh)**.

Resonants: These sounds depend primarily on alterations of voice resonance for their recognition. By dropping the lower jaw, elevating the tongue, rounding the lips, and opening or closing the pharyngeal port, the speech apparatus changes the sound which was produced at the glottis to emphasize bands of overtone energy, called **formants** (see Chapter III), which distinguish one resonant sound from another. These changes are effected physically by the combinations of (1) changes in the relative size of the pharyngeal and oral resonating cavities, (2) the surface textures of these cavities, (3) the shape of the oral cavity, and (4) the opening or closing of the ends of the nasal and oral cavities.

All vowels are resonant sounds with relative tongue elevation and position represented on the vowel diagram of Figure I-7. A number of consonants are also resonant sounds and are sometimes called semi-vowels, vowelized consonants, or liquids because of this characteristic. The resonant consonants are **m, n, ng, w-, y-, l,** and **r.** These consonant sounds usually have a second order designation based on their manner of production to distinguish them from vowel sounds. The **m, n,** and **ng** are designated nasals, since the oral cavity is partially closed off and the velopharyngeal port is opened to the nasal cavity for their production. The **w-** (as in *went*) and the **y-** (as in *you*) are called *glides* since they are of short duration and glide rapidly into the vowel sound which follows. The **l** is called a *lateral* since its position with the narrowed tongue point against the alveolar ridge forces emission of voice laterally around both sides of the tongue. The **r** is designated a *retroflex* sound because the tongue tip sometimes flexes toward the back of the oral cavity.

Another consideration in the manner of production of speech sounds is whether they are voiced or not. Those sounds which include voicing from the larynx are called *voiced* sounds. Those without voicing are called *voiceless* sounds, or sometimes unvoiced sounds. Occasionally the term "sonant" is applied for voiced sounds and "surd" for voiceless sounds. All vowels and over half of the consonants are voiced sounds.

Phonemes are conventionally categorized in descriptive terms, using the designations of voicing, place of production and manner of production. For example, the **t** is called a voiceless, lingua-alveolar stop sound; the **v** a voiced,

Manner of Production	Place of Production					
	Labio-Dental	Lingua-Dental	Bi-Labial	Lingua-Velar	Lingua-Alveolar	Lingua-Palatal
Stops			p b	k g	t d	
Fricatives	f v	$\overset{1}{\text{th}}$ $\overset{2}{\text{th}}$	wh	h	s z	sh zh
Affricates			qu ←——— qu	x ———→x	ch ——— ch j	ch ——— ch j
Resonants			m w-	ng	l n	r y-

Figure I-8. *Consonant sounds ordered by their manner and place of production.*

labio-dental fricative; the l a voiced, lingua-alveolar, lateral resonant, and the **qu-** a voiceless, lingua-velar, bilabial affricate. Figure I-8 categorizes consonant sounds by their manner and place of production. Recall that the General American symbols are arranged in Figures I-1, I-2 and I-3 according to place and manner of production for consonants, and by place of tongue arching for vowels.

Perceptual Features of Articulation

Another way to view speech production is by the information made available to our auditory, visual, tactile, and kinesthetic senses. To perceive and understand speech requires that the speaker produce acoustic information sufficient for the listener to hear and discriminate among sounds. The study of speech perception, though relevant to teaching speech, is beyond the scope of this book. Chapter III deals with speech perception as it relates to amplification of the acoustic parameters of the speech signal. In producing acoustic events through movements of the speech mechanism, the speaker also makes articulatory "gestures" of the lips, tongue, and jaw opening which can be seen by the listener-observer. This information can help the listener in understanding by "speechreading" as he listens. Some of the perceptual features of articulation provide internal feedback information which helps the speaker monitor his speech. Other features may be used by the teacher in her task because they have sensory instructional possibilities.

1. Internal Feedback Information

Pertinent to our purposes is the perceptual information in speech which is made available to the speaker through feedback from his own speech production. This internal feedback information, available through the auditory, tactile, and kinesthetic senses, is essential for the speaker to monitor his own speech production.

Auditory information: As we shall see in some detail in Chapter III, when we talk we produce acoustic signals which have varying features of intensity, frequency, and duration. These features are fed back to the normal speaker by sounds conducted directly through the bones of the skull and by sounds conducted through air into his ear. The severely hearing impaired person is limited to those air conducted sounds which his disordered hearing mechanism can transmit with the assistance of an acoustic amplifier. Even the most severely hearing impaired person seems to get some acoustic information fed back from his own speech with the use of a hearing aid. He may perceive only the presence or absence of sound, a cue to whether he produced voice or not. He may also perceive variations in intensity of sound, a cue to help in monitoring the loudness of his voice and to differentiate among speech sounds.

Speech sounds vary in intensity with a difference of about 30 decibels between the weakest sound and strongest. Strongest are the vowels and diphthongs, and the **w-** and **r-**. Next are the resonant consonants **m, n, ng, y-,** and **l.** In the next weaker group are the voiced fricatives **z, zh, th,** and **v,** the affricate **j,** and the stops **b, d,** and **g.** Then come the voiceless fricatives, affricates, and stops, the **sh, s, ch, x, qu, p, t,** and **k.** The weakest sounds are the voiceless fricatives **h, f, wh,** and **th.**

With only limited auditory feedback information, the speaker may receive important information about the duration of speech sounds, syllables, and phrases. This information can be of very great help in monitoring the suprasegmental rhythmic features of speech and apparently is very useful for the young deaf child in developing speech rhythm. Frequency feedback information is likely to be very restricted for a severely hearing impaired person. High frequency sounds of consonants are least likely to be available to him. Yet, he may be able to hear some differences in vowel formants which could help monitor his speech.

Tactile information: Another source of speech feedback information is that available to the sense of touch. Tactile information is especially important in helping a hearing impaired person maintain his speech. Tactile features offered by speech production include touching of parts of the speech apparatus, the perception of friction as air flow passes over the tongue, lips, or palate, and the perception of vibration associated with voicing (vibro-tactile) (2, 17). Those sounds offering the most tactile information are the voiceless stops **p** and **t** where strong contact is made by the lips and by the tongue and alveolar ridge, and the affricate **ch,** which includes the stop of the **t.** In the next group, where there is touching but the force of articulation is decreased, are the **b, d,**

m, l, n and **j**. In the third group are the voiceless fricative consonants marked by strong friction, including **wh, tḩ, f, s,** and **sh,** and the affricates **x** and **qu**. In the next weaker group are the **k, g,** and **ng,** which have contact in an area which gives little tactile feedback; the **h,** which has its friction between the velum and the back of the tongue; and the voiced fricatives **ţh, v, z,** and **zh**. In the weakest group for tactile information are the **w-, y-,** and **r,** the diphthongs, and the vowels.

Kinesthetic information: A third feedback sensation from speech production, kinesthesia, alerts us to the position of parts of the body without seeing them. This sensation is sometimes called "proprioception." The stimulus for kinesthesia is the stretching of muscle fibers as body parts move. Kinesthetic information, like tactile information, is important for monitoring speech. Although there is very little stimulus from movements of the velum and pharynx in closing the velopharyngeal port, movement of the lower jaw, the lips, and tongue provides considerable kinesthetic sensation. Those speech sounds whose production offer the most kinesthetic information are the lip rounding **aw, oo, w-, wh,** and **qu,** the lip retracted and wide jaw opening **-a-,** and the diphthongs **oi, ou, u-e,** and **oa,** which offer movement and lip rounding. In the next group are the diphthongs **i-e** and **a-e,** the occasional lip retracted **ee** and the wide jaw opening **-o-,** the **-oo-,** the voiceless stops **p** and **t,** the fricatives **sh** and **zh,** the affricates **ch** and **j,** and the retroflex **r**. In the third group are the **b,**

	Auditory	Tactile	Kines-thetic		Auditory	Tactile	Kines-thetic
h	1	2	1	v	3	2	3
wh	1	3	4	th	3	2	2
p	2	5	4	z	3	2	2
t	2	5	4	zh	3	2	4
k	2	2	2	j	3	4	4
f	1	3	3	m	4	4	3
th	1	3	2	n	4	4	3
s	2	3	2	ng	4	2	1
sh	2	3	4	l	4	4	3
ch	2	5	4	r	5	1	4
w-	5	1	4	x	2	3	2
b	3	4	3	qu	2	3	5
d	3	4	3	y-	4	1	3
g	3	2	1				

5 = *greatest information*
1 = *least information*

Table I-4. Estimated ratings of sensory feedback information for consonants.

	Auditory	Tactile	Kinesthetic
oo	5	1	5
-oo-	5	1	4
aw	5	1	5
-o-	5	1	4
ee	5	1	4
-i-	5	1	2
-e-	5	1	2
-a-	5	1	3
-u-	5	1	1
oi	5	1	5
ou	5	1	5
u-e	5	1	5
a-e	5	1	4
i-e	5	1	4
oa	5	1	5

5 = greatest information
1 = least information

Table I-5.   Estimated ratings of sensory feedback information for vowels.

d, y-, m, f, v, l, and **n.** In the next weaker group are $\overset{1}{\text{th}}$ and $\overset{2}{\text{th}}$, **s** and **z, k** and **x,** and **-i-** and **-e-.** In the weakest group are the **-u-,** the **h,** the **g,** and the **ng** sounds. Approximate ratings of sensory feedback information for speech sounds are shown in Tables I-4 and I-5.

2. Sensory Instructional Possibilities

In addition to the information which makes it possible for the listener to perceive speech and the feedback information which helps the speaker monitor his speech, speech production yields "by-products" which may be exploited by the teacher to provide sensory information in teaching speech.

Visual information: By showing the student his own production in a mirror and by drawing attention to her own model the teacher can present some visible features of speech sounds. These include mouth opening, lip rounding and protrusion, tongue or lips touching the teeth, tongue position inside the teeth, and the degree of jaw opening. Among the most visible speech sounds are the labial and dental consonants, the **m, b, v, f,** $\overset{1}{\text{th}}$, and $\overset{2}{\text{th}}$. Next are the diphthongs which move from one vowel position to another, vowels **aw** and **oo,** which involve maximum lip rounding, and consonants **w-, wh, qu, sh, zh, ch,** and **j,** which are also made with some lip rounding. In the third group are the consonants **t, d, n,** and **l,** which offer a view of the tongue just inside the teeth; the **y-, ee,** and **-a-** when they are made with some lip retraction; the **-oo-,** which offers some lip rounding; and the **-o-** made with wide jaw opening. In the next group the **-i-**, **-e-**, and **-u-** offer slightly different jaw openings, and the **s, z, r,** and **x** offer an obscured view of the front of the elevated tongue. In the least visible group of sounds are the lingua-velar stops **k** and **g**, the **ng**, and the **h**, which takes the shape of the vowel that follows it.

In addition to the natural visual gestures of speech production, other by-products can easily be converted to visual information by the teacher. By using such simple devices as a feather, flame, or strip of paper, the steady flow of air of fricatives or the explosion of air of plosives may be shown.

Tactile information: The vibration of voicing can be felt by the student's fingers on the lips, teeth, cheeks, nose, neck, throat, and under the chin near the base of the tongue. Voicing and the absence of voicing, and the difference between oral and nasal resonance can be thus distinguished (2). The difference between fricatives and plosives, comparing the steady flow of air to the explosion of breath, can be felt on the back of the student's hand. The difference between oral and nasal emission of air, as well as the amount, can also be felt on the back of the hand.

Coarticulation

The influence of adjoining sounds on individual phonemes is called coarticulation. This may affect production and perceptual features. For example, the place of production of **k** varies with the vowel sound which adjoins it. The point of elevation of the tongue for the **k** phoneme differs depending on whether the preceding or following vowel involves front tongue arching or back tongue arching, illustrated in Figure I-9. As the **k** is produced, its point of contact follows the position of elevation of the tongue for the adjoining vowel.

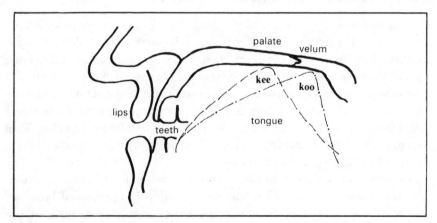

Figure I-9. *Relative position of contact of the tongue for stopping of breath for **k** preceding vowels **ee** and **oo**.*

Preceding or following **oo** the point of contact is the velum, while adjoining **ee** it is on the hard palate. The difference in place of tongue contact on syllables **koo** and **kee** results in predictable changes in the acoustic characteristics of **k**. Even though both **k** sounds are recognized as the phoneme **k**, coarticulation has made them slightly different acoustically. When a listener hears only the **k** sound in the syllable **kee**, the slight acoustic difference may be enough to tell him that it was the **ee** sound which followed **k**.

Similarly, when the vowel sound is the same in two syllables beginning with different consonants, as in **tee** and **kee**, the relative position of the tongue for contact on **t** and **k** influences the sound of the following **ee** so that it is slightly different in each syllable. Note, too, the difference in duration of the vowel **ee** in the words *eat* and *ease* as a result of the difference in the consonant following and terminating the vowel. The transitional and durational cues present in coarticulation give the listener important perceptual information about adjoining phonemes.

VOICE

A second major component of speech is voice. Producing voice, like articulating speech sounds, is a function we learn to overlay on structures fundamental to sustaining our bodies (28).

Production of Voice

Voice is produced by three actions: *respiration, phonation,* and *resonation.* These occur simultaneously and cooperatively. Together they produce changes in pitch, quality, and loudness of the voice.

Respiration: The raw material of speech is the breath stream produced in the process of respiration. The dome-shaped diaphragm moves downward at the center, reducing pressure in the chest cavity. In reaction, air rushes into the lungs, filling them as the rib cage expands. The oxygen of the incoming air is exchanged for carbon dioxide in blood vessels of millions of tiny air sacs of the lungs. The diaphragm relaxes and the air sacs empty into collecting *bronchial tubes* leading to paired *bronchi* which in turn lead into the *trachea.* The trachea directs the air through the glottis into the pharynx, nasal, or oral cavities, and out either the nose or mouth.

Respiration is accomplished by a complex interaction of muscles of the thoracic (chest) and abdominal (stomach) cavities. The process of bringing air into the lungs is called *inhalation* and that of evacuating the air is called *exhalation.* In normal breathing, the relative duration of inhalation and exhalation is about the same. But when speaking, the duration of exhalation in a single respiratory cycle is usually about 10 times as long as that of inhalation and may be as much as 50 times as long for practiced speakers. Since no more breath is used in speaking than in regular breathing exhalation, the extended duration of exhalation during speech reflects a remarkable economy in using the breath stream in order to sustain connected speech. This economy, realized by the efficient synergistic functioning of the respiratory muscles, larynx, and articulatory apparatus, apparently is learned.

Phonation: The process of the larynx acting on the exhaled breath stream to create voice is called phonation. The **larynx** (*laryngo-, -laryngeal*) is the complete structure of cartilage and muscles situated atop the trachea, the tube leading to the lungs. The primary purpose of the larynx is to stop food particles from entering the trachea and to expel them with coughing. Also, by closing off the trachea at the larynx, the air in the lungs keeps the thoracic cavity rigid as a help in elimination, childbirth, and heavy lifting.

At the anterior of the larynx, the *thyroid cartilage* forms the "Adam's apple" of the neck. The smaller *cricoid cartilage* rings the bottom of the larynx. Paired *arytenoid cartilages* rest on the cricoid cartilage, providing the paired vocal folds with highly mobile attachments at their posterior ends. The vocal folds, with assistance of laryngeal muscles and the arytenoid cartilages, serve to open and close the trachea at its port called the *glottis.* The laryngeal muscles relax to leave the glottis open, permitting free flow of the breath stream for breathing and for articulation of the breath consonants. These muscles close the glottis by tightly closing the vocal folds but may leave a small chink open between the arytenoid cartilages for the constricted breath stream of whispered speech. They can also close the glottis by lightly approximating the vocal folds so that they are parted by air pressure from the lungs, causing the rhythmic opening and closing of the glottis for phonation.

During phonation, the vocal folds follow this rhythmic cycle: closing of the glottis—increasing of air pressure beneath the glottis—bursting apart of the folds from the air pressure and emission of a puff of breath—closing of the folds again under constant muscle tension and with decreased air pressure. Air pressure beneath the glottis increases and the pattern is repeated. The resulting periodic puffs of breath give the sound of voice. The frequency of puffs of air from closing and opening the glottis determine the *fundamental frequency* of the voice. We can change the fundamental frequency of our voice by a complicated interaction of altering the tension, length, and mass of the vocal folds, accompanied by changing the sub-glottal air pressure.

When there is a considerable increase in the air pressure below the glottis, the vocal folds are forced farther apart during their close-open-close cycle. This increase in vocal fold amplitude is accompanied by an increase in the amount of air emitted and thus an increase in the perceived loudness of the voice. Since the vocal folds are forced farther apart for loud speech, there is also a greater consumption of air.

In addition to voice production, the larynx can contribute an articulated speech-like sound called a *glottal stop.* This sound, which has the IPA symbol / ʔ /, is used in some dialects in place of the medial **t** stop, as in *bottle.*

Resonation: In producing rhythmic closure of the glottis for the fundamental voice frequency, the vocal folds set up secondary vibrations (partials) of their parts which create sounds (overtones) higher than the frequency of the fundamental. These overtones usually are multiples of the fundamental called **harmonics.** If the fundamental voice frequency is 200 cycles per second, or **Hertz** (Hz), the harmonics would be 400 Hz, 600 Hz, 800 Hz, etc. These harmonics differ in their relative intensity, giving a distinctive quality to the sound of the fundamental frequency combined with its harmonics. The harmonics of voice are influenced by cavities of the vocal tract through which voice passes: the trachea, pharynx, oral cavity, and the nasal cavity. These cavities are set into vibration themselves by the flow of vibrating voice passing through them. In vibrating, they reinforce some harmonics of voice more than others, further modifying the overall sound of the voice. This process of modification is called *resonation.* The frequency with which these cavities vibrate and, thus, the harmonics which they emphasize depend on the size, shape, and surface texture of the cavities peculiar to each person. The combination of fundamental voice frequency, overtones of vocal folds, and characteristics of resonating cavities contributes to a complex sound relationship we refer to as *voice quality* or *timbre.*

Most English speech sounds are made primarily with oral voice resonance, that is, with the oral cavity open at the mouth and the velopharyngeal port closing off the nasal cavity at the pharynx. Nasal sounds **m, n,** and **ng** are the exceptions. However, even though the nasal cavity is closed at the pharynx, its resonance contributes to the sound of our voice. Recall how the voice sounds when the nasal cavity is stuffed up with a cold. When the velopharyngeal port is open for oral resonant sounds, the voice also sounds abnormal with open nasal resonance changing the sound. Nasal resonance is described as *hypernasality* (sometimes called open nasality) when the velopharyngeal port is abnormally open, and *hyponasality* (sometimes called closed nasality) when the nostrils are blocked making a closed cavity.

Perceptual Features of Voice

Voice produces a combination of auditory, tactile, and kinesthetic information which can be perceived by the listener and speaker.

Auditory information: Phonation produces the fundamental frequency which is heard as the pitch of the voice. The cycles of breath puffs and decreased pressure at the larynx are reflected in the acoustic measure of cycles/second or Hertz (Hz). The fundamental frequency of voice gradually decreases with age, until it rises again in old age. Adult males have a much lower fundamental than adult females. Some typical fundamental voice frequencies are as follows:

Infant hunger wails	512 Hz
Pre-adolescent child	265 Hz
Adult female	225 Hz
Adult male	125 Hz

Fundamental voice frequency for adults can vary from a low of 80 Hz for a male bass singer to over 1,100 Hz for a soprano.

Loudness of the voice, reflected in the physical dimension of intensity, can be altered by increasing the air pressure in the trachea below the glottis. Changes in loudness are used in rhythmic variations of speech, and to overcome background noise, to attract attention, and to adjust to distance. Average speech is about 65 dB sound pressure level (ranging from 60 to 70 dB), measured at about 39 inches (100 cm) from the speaker's mouth. Soft speech is about 45 dB and very loud speech reaches 85 dB. Average speech intensity levels for women are about 3 dB less intense than for men. At about one foot (roughly the distance from the lips to a body-worn hearing aid of the speaker), the average speech level can be 75 dB or greater. Because of a shadowing effect of the head, average speech reaching the ear of the speaker (about 6 inches from the speaker's lips) is not much more intense than that reaching the chest at 12 inches. This shadowing effect of the head is especially pronounced for high frequencies where there is a difference of as much as 7 dB (weaker) for a band of speech 2800 Hz to 4000 Hz reaching the ear, compared to the same speech sounds one foot directly in front of the speaker.

Resonation emphasizes certain overtones of the fundamental voice frequency which give the characteristic formant sounds of vowels. Vowel formants are discussed earlier in this chapter concerning articulation of vowels, and again in Chapter III. Resonation also emphasizes overtones which blend with the fundamental frequency to give perceived voice quality. The normal listener hears his own voice through an almost equal combination of bone conduction and air conduction. He is often very surprised when he hears his voice recorded to know how it sounds to other persons, because his voice sounds different when he hears it only through air conduction.

Tactile information: With voice production, vibration of the vocal folds and of the resonating cavities can be felt in various places on the chest, neck, and head. This vibro-tactile sensation is perceptible both to the speaker through his internal feedback system and to others through their fingertips. The difference between voicing and no voicing, for example, can easily be felt by the presence or absence of vibration. The difference between loud and soft voice can also be perceived by the difference in intensity of vibration, but subtle differences in voice intensity are hard to distinguish through tactile perception. Differences in very high and very low pitched voice can be perceived, but subtle differences in pitch are hard to perceive and may be confused with loud/soft differences. The *difference limen,* the smallest perceivable difference between two stimuli, is quite large for touch. Nasal emission of voice can be perceived by a combination of the place of vibration—especially noticeable on the nose—and generally increased vibration.

Kinesthetic information: Movements of the larynx or within the larynx can give kinesthetic sensations. In changing pitch of the voice, the larynx is raised and lowered giving some sensation of muscle activity. Increasing loudness of voice is often accompanied by increasing tension of the muscles of the larynx. Many of these sensations during speech are at an unconscious level for persons with normal hearing but may be of use to deaf speakers in monitoring their voice.

RHYTHM

Rhythm is often referred to as the prosodic, temporal, or patterned features of speech, or as the "melody" of speech. Speech rhythms are not directly analogous to singing, dancing, or other rhythmic bodily movements, nor are they similar to the common structured rhythms of music. Speech features are rhythmic in that they recur in patterns. Patterns differ from language to language with further differences in dialects and among individuals. Speech rhythm carries meaning, aids understanding, conveys emotional state, and expresses esthetic qualities.

Production of Rhythm

Rhythm features are produced by changes in voice and articulation, and usually by a combination of the two. Changes in intensity, frequency, and duration combine to produce varying "time envelopes" that constitute the fundamental cues for perception of rhythm.

The syllable: In studying articulation we used the phoneme as the basic analytic unit. For speech rhythm, the basic unit is the syllable. Phonemes are not presented to the listener in a haphazard order but occur coarticulated in clusters with consonants bordering vowels. These clusters are called **syllables**. In English the most common syllable cluster is a Consonant-Vowel-Consonant (CVC) combination; less frequently there is a CV or a VC pattern. Such clusters help in our recognition of each phoneme because of the transitional characteristics of consonant-vowel and vowel-consonant junctures which give important perceptual information. During speech, the muscles of the thorax and abdomen controlling exhalation show rapid repetitive pressure fluctuations corresponding to the duration of syllable clusters. The exhalation phase of respiration is marked simultaneously by individual pulses of breath imposed upon the steady exhalation of breath. This muscular action and resulting pulses of breath are the motor basis for syllable production.

Rhythm Features

Relevant to teaching speech are the features of *accent, emphasis, intonation, phrasing,* and *rate. Accent* involves the selection of one syllable to be stressed over other syllables within a word. *Emphasis* is gained by giving increased stress to a word in a phrase. *Intonation* is accomplished by changing pitch from syllable to syllable, rather than from word to word. *Phrasing* of connected speech ignores the boundaries of words and deals with syllable clusters. The *rate* of presenting phonemes to the listener is dependent upon the rate of articulating syllable units.

Accent: Accent is produced primarily by increasing voice intensity and by making stressed syllables longer, but some change in pitch also occurs. It is characteristic of English that every word of more than one syllable has a syllable stressed above the others. For words of several syllables, there may be both a primary accent and a secondary accent. Accent is so common to the English language that its misuse can severely hinder speech intelligibility. Try pronouncing these common words with the accent as indicated: *América, sylláble, ábove, intéresting, foundatíon.* In order for speech to be intelligible, accent must meet linguistic requirements.

Accent also has an effect on the pronunciation of speech sounds. Unaccented vowels in English lose their original vowel quality and are often pronounced as the -u- phoneme (*above, nation, cobra, telephone, waited*), but with reduced force of articulation reflected by the IPA symbol /ə/. Pronouncing vowels in unaccented syllables with their original vowel quality may actually interfere with intelligibility.

Accent is rarely phonemic in English, that is, it does not change meaning of a word, but it is sometimes used to indicate whether the word is a noun, verb, or adjective. For example, n. *rébel*/v. *rebél;* n. *cómplex*/adj. *compléx;* and adj. *pérfect*/v. *perféct.*

It is impossible to establish hard and fast rules for accent in English words, but some tendencies are helpful. There is a strong tendency for two-syllable words to have their accent on the first syllable. This is especially noticeable in the vocabulary used in the reading books of young children. But the accented syllable usually follows such common prefixes as *a-* (*above*), *be-* (*believe*), *re-* (*report*), *in-* (*intend*), *un-* (*unless*), *ad-* (*admire*), *ex-* (*extent*), and *de-* (*deport*). The accented syllable usually precedes suffixes such as *-tion* (*nation*), *-able* (*desirable*), *-ssion* (*commission*), and *-cious* (*delicious*). The *-ed* ending is rarely accented and the *-ing* ending never is.

Accent is not usually marked in English spelling as it is in some Spanish words, but it may be indicated for instructional purposes with a mark such as / *'* / either above the accented syllable or after the accented syllable if syllables are separated.

Emphasis: Emphasis refers to the stressing of a word or words within a phrase. Emphasis, like accent, is produced primarily by a combination of increased intensity and increased duration of syllables within the stressed word, with an accompanying change in voice frequency. It may even be achieved by pauses surrounding words. Emphasis does not have a regular pattern peculiar to the language as accent has, but is used to communicate speaker intent. For example, emphasis may be used to clarify by stressing a single word that reiterates a previous statement ("I mean we absolutely *cannot* finish the work on time."), to contrast with parallel structure ("They *walked* home but we *drove* home."), and to label something ("We call it a *hydrochronometer*."). Intended meaning determines which word is selected for emphasis. Try speaking the sentence, "My house is five miles down the road," several times and stress each word in turn. Imagine the context in which each of the words might be emphasized.

Emphasis affects pronunciation of speech sounds, too. The preposition *of* is so commonly deemphasized in phrases that its pronunciation /av/ usually becomes /əv/. The phrase "time to go" is commonly pronounced /taɪm tə goʊ/.

Intonation: Intonation refers to variations of pitch in connected speech as a function of time. Intonation patterns are described by the direction of pitch change, the degree of change, and by relative pitch levels. Absolute levels are extremely hard to specify, since individuals have different fundamental voice frequencies and have different habits of using more or less pitch variation in their speech.

Patterns of intonation are governed both by individual characteristics of talkers and by common usage of the language. We use common intonation patterns to give listeners a secondary level of language information without using additional words. To signal the end of a simple declarative statement, we commonly use a falling pitch on the last word of the statement as in, "I am going home." If there is more to follow after the last word of a phrase, we alert the listener to this by using a very slight drop in pitch or no drop at all, as in, "I am going home and I want you to be there." When we speak of a series of things, each item is given a slightly rising pitch until the last one, which has a falling pitch, as in, "We used the knives, forks, spoons, and plates."

When we ask a question and want the listener to give us a "yes" or "no" answer, we tell him this by using a rising pitch on the last word, as in, "Are you going home?" But when we want him to give us an answer other than "yes" or "no," we frequently end the question with a rising then falling pitch on the last syllables, as in, "Where are you going?" When a question requires a choice of named alternatives, intonation usage places a rising pitch on each alternate, just as it did on a serial statement, and a rising then falling pitch on the last word, as in, "Do you want a knife, fork, spoon, or plate?"

Intonation patterns are not marked in English spelling, but there are a number of ways of designating patterns for teaching purposes. Three common relative pitch levels can be indicated to the student with whole-sentence contour analysis, as in the following (90.14, 254).

Where are you | go | ing?   I am going home.

A fourth, higher level is reserved for expression of surprise.

My | good | ness!

Another system uses arrows showing direction of pitch change at certain points in a sentence, either after or above the critical syllables, as in,

Where are you going?   I am going home.

The relative degree of pitch change may be indicated by length of the arrow shaft.

Yet another system marks every syllable for intonation and accent with a dot above unaccented syllables, a line above accented syllables, and a curved line showing rising or falling inflection, as in,

Where are you going?   I am going home.

Phrasing: A speech phrase is a continuous utterance bounded by silent intervals. Phrasing organizes words into groups related to units of thought which help understanding. It has two components—the words linked in speech and the pauses between phrases. Which words get linked and the varying durations of pauses are left to the speaker's judgment, although there are some conventions in the language. Phrasing can help accomplish comparison, as in, "We wanted a red car | but finally bought a yellow one." It can create emphasis, as in, "We must go | now, | before it is too late!" Parenthetical comments, such as, "We must,| I think,| accomplish this tomorrow," are achieved by silent intervals. Note serial items, as in "We used the knives, | forks, | spoons, | and plates."

In addition to these meaning-related conventions, manipulation by the speaker of the number of words in a phrase and the duration of pauses can help the listener understand speech. By increasing the duration of pauses, the speaker takes into account the information absorption rate of his listener for different kinds of content and in different listening environments. The uncertain speaker, who either is not sure how to proceed or is seeking the best possible word to say, uses a pattern of short phrases and frequent long pauses.

Speech phrasing is related to breathing but does not necessarily reflect breathing rhythm. All inhalations during connected speech occur between phrases, that is, during pauses, but inhalation does not always occur with each pause. A speaker may say two, three, or more phrases on the same breath. Figure I-10 illustrates phrasing and inhalation.

With the exception of some punctuation marks, we do not use phrasing symbols in English spelling. But some conventional markings are helpful to indicate word groups, as in "Now is the time, I believe, for all of us to think about changing our attitudes on this matter." Pauses may be indicated by vertical lines using more lines for longer pauses, as in, "Now is the time, | I believe, || for all of us to think about changing our attitudes | on this matter. ||| Now,|| before it is too late."

Rate: Rate refers to the number of syllables uttered per unit of time. It is affected by both stress and phrasing patterns. Stressed syllables are typically longer in duration than unstressed ones. In phrasing, the greater the number of pauses and the greater the duration of each pause, the fewer the units of speech that will be spoken in a period of time. Individuals vary, of course, in the rate at which they talk.

Rate is usually measured by the number of words per minute and the number of syllables per second. Most adults read orally from 160 to 180 words/minute. In connected conversational speech, we average 5 to 5.5 syllables/second (average syllable duration 0.18 seconds) or about 270 words/minute.

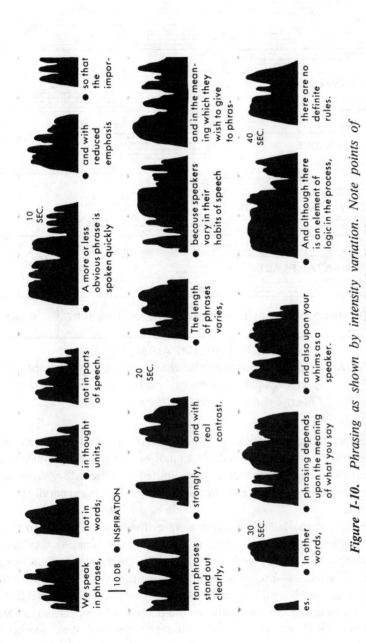

Figure 1-10. Phrasing as shown by intensity variation. Note points of inspiration marked ●. After Fairbanks (88).

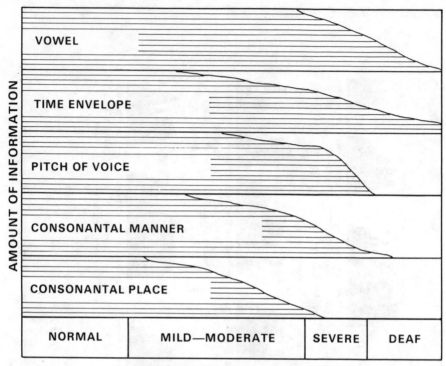

Figure I-11. *A gross composite estimate of the information features of speech related to severity of hearing loss. Courtesy James D. Miller, Central Institute for the Deaf.*

With simple repetitive articulatory movements, speakers reach maximum rates of about 8 syllables/second but cannot exceed this even with practice. Maximum speaking rate appears to be limited by articulatory movements, since reading silently, comprehending speech, and thinking generally occur at faster rates.

In English, the syllable is the unit of speech most directly related to rate. Most consonant sounds are limited in the durational variation they can undergo without losing their recognizability, while vowels—the core and longest elements of syllables—are not so limited in variations of duration. The overall rhythm of speech is an extremely complex combination of interrelated elements. Intonation occurs not only for the purpose of transmitting information about the nature of a message but also for indicating accents and emphasis, with a generally rising pitch on the stressed syllable. Emphasis is achieved not only by changes of duration and intensity, but also by phrasing, rate, and intonation changes.

Perceptual Features of Speech Rhythm

Since speech rhythm is produced through variations in intensity and frequency of *voice* and in durations of *articulation,* its sensory features will be those described previously under those two headings in this chapter. Speech rhythm, consisting as it does of repeated syllable pulses, gives rise to kinesthetic sensations, probably from the muscles of the thoracic and abdominal areas. The alternating chain of vibrations and pauses set up by syllables may also cause some repetitive tactile sensations in the resonating cavities of the speech apparatus (123). But it is apparent that these syllable pulses are monitored primarily by auditory sensations. When the auditory system is severely impaired, speech rhythm is drastically affected.

Perception of rhythm may be aided by subtle visual cues. Stressed vowels require positioning of lips and mouth opening for longer times. Movement of the larynx and tensing of laryngeal muscles are manifested in movement at the neck surface. Facial gestures, movement of the head or eyes, frowning, smiling, and facial grimacing are frequently associated with rhythmic patterns.

A gross composite estimate of the information features of speech described above as related to severity of hearing loss is given in Figure I-11.

Chapter II

Learning and Teaching Speech

Speech is learned. We have noted that speech production is not the primary function of what is commonly and collectively referred to as the speech mechanism. We learn to use parts of the body, developed for more primitive functions, to form the various sounds of speech. Capability for learning to use parts of the body to form sounds and for learning the complex phonetic-linguistic code necessary for meaningful speech is shared by all human beings and is apparently limited to humans. But we are not born "knowing" how to speak. We learn according to the speech patterns around us, growing up learning to speak Chinese, English, or Russian, depending upon where we live. In general, the entire repertory of speech sounds is learned and perfected by age 9 (67).

Learning speech is so universal and apparently so effortless that we take for granted that speech "comes naturally." But when something impedes speech development—when speech is learned poorly or not learned at all—we focus attention on learning to speak and find it to be a complex process. There are numerous requisites for learning speech, and when these are lacking or inadequate, speech will not develop "naturally." Fortunately, we can intervene to improve, revise, restructure, and augment, such as by using other sensory channels in place of or in addition to the auditory. When we do so in order to increase the probability of speech being learned, we are involved in the act of *teaching speech* (62, 90.3).

Hearing loss is a major impediment to speech development because it (1) severely restricts reception of speech and (2) reduces ability of the speaker to monitor his own speech. Because both factors are necessary for speech development, a person with severe hearing loss will not develop speech without systematic, comprehensive, and intensive intervention, that is, **teaching.** Teaching, in its broad sense, is the act of rational and deliberate intervention in the learning process for the benefit of the student. The charges for the teacher of speech are to understand the process of learning speech and to know how to intervene in order to help the hearing-impaired person learn to speak.

For our purposes, we may consider the learning and teaching of speech to involve three primary areas of concern: the **student** himself, his **environment,** and his **school program.** Within each of these areas of concern are significant influences which are important to learning speech. These influences and the overlapping nature of the areas of concern, illustrated in Figure II-1, constitute the organization of this chapter.

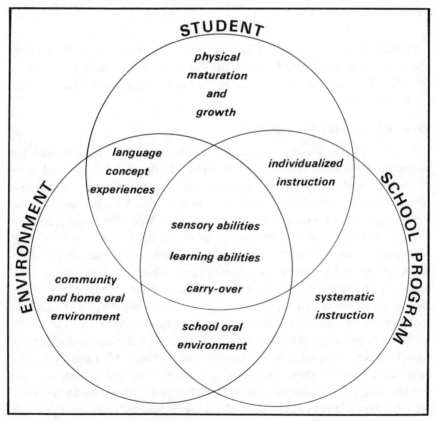

Figure II-1. *Areas of concern in learning and teaching speech.*

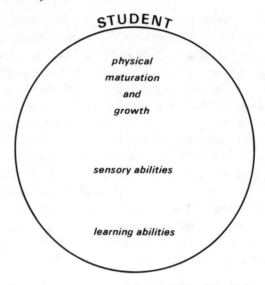

THE STUDENT

There are a number of characteristics and attributes of the student which affect the learning of speech. Prime among these are the student's physical growth and maturation, and his current and potential sensory capacities and learning abilities.

Physical Growth and Maturation

The young child grows and matures at a fairly predictable rate, with his stages of development reflected in control of his muscular strength and coordination. Schedules of growth and maturation, derived from child development studies, help the teacher know what skills of motor coordination can be reasonably expected from each child. Speech development depends on motor coordination along with sensory development. The hearing baby babbles speech sounds at random, including sounds which are not those of his language. In a few months he is imitating some babbling sounds, and by age 6 months his babbling reflects the sounds of his language. After one year he is able to form words and increases the number and complexity of words in spoken phrases during the following years until he has a vocabulary of nearly 1,000 words by age 3 years. The jaw continues to grow during the child's early school years, causing increased spaces between his teeth. After age 6 years the baby teeth begin to shed, with missing teeth making articulation of some speech sounds (particularly s) difficult. See Figure I-5 for a diagram of dental growth. The child does not perfect all his speech sounds until age 9 years. A more detailed schedule of development in early childhood is given in Table II-1.

Age (years)	Motor Milestones	Language Milestones
½	Sits using hands for support; unilateral reaching.	Cooing sounds change to babbling by introduction of consonantal sounds.
1	Stands; walks when held by one hand.	Syllabic reduplication; signs of understanding some words; applies some sounds regularly to signify persons or objects, that is, the first words.
1½	Prehension and release fully developed; gait propulsive; creeps downstairs backwards.	Repertoire of 3 to 50 words not joined in phrases; trains of sounds and intonation patterns resembling discourse; good progress in understanding.
2	Runs (with falls); walks stair with one foot forward only.	More than 50 words; two-word phrases most common; more interest in verbal communication; no more babbling.
2½	Jumps with both feet; stands on one foot for one second; builds tower of six cubes.	Every day new words; utterances of three and more words; seems to understand almost everything said to him; still many grammatical deviations.
3	Tiptoes 3 yards; walks stairs with alternating feet; jumps 1 yard.	Vocabulary of some 1,000 words; about 80% intelligibility; grammar of utterances close approximation to colloquial adult; syntactic mistakes fewer in variety, systematic, predictable.
4½	Jumps over rope; hops on one foot; walks on line.	Language well-established; grammatical anomalies restricted either to unusual constructions or to the more literate aspects of discourse.

Table II-1.   Correlation of motor and language development. After Lenneberg and Long (168.)

Control of the fine, small muscle activity of the speech mechanism increases with maturation and experience during the early years of life. It is doubtful that there is a significant correlation between the quality of control of the speech mechanism and of the large skeletal muscles of the body. The best athletes do not necessarily have the best speech. However, abnormalities in physical growth and development may interfere with speech development. Cerebral palsy, which impairs control of the muscles used in speech, and a number of other disorders occur more frequently among children with congenital hearing impairment, as is shown in Table II-2. Structural abnormali-

Additional Handicapping Conditions Age	1-5	6-10	11-15	16+
None	61.4	56.2	55.2	59.6
Brain Damage	3.6	3.5	3.5	3.2
Cerebral Palsy	1.6	2.1	2.4	4.2
Epilepsy	0.6	0.6	0.7	0.6
Heart Disorder	2.1	3.2	1.8	0.8
Mental Retardation	2.4	3.9	7.2	8.6
Orthopedic	1.2	0.6	0.7	0.7
Perceptual/Motor	1.5	3.7	3.0	1.0
Emotional/Behavioral	3.2	5.2	5.0	3.7
Severe Visual	2.9	3.9	3.4	2.7
Other	2.2	2.2	2.8	2.7
Blank/Unknown	17.3	14.5	14.1	12.3

Table II-2.   *Percent of hearing-impaired students with specified additional handicapping conditions by age group, United States: 1971-72 school year (101).*

ties may also interfere with speech development. Cleft palate and palatal insufficiency are congenital impairments which make it difficult or impossible to close off the velopharyngeal port and to direct the breath stream through the oral cavity. Such disorders should be recognized and treated as soon as feasible. Developmental abnormality of the teeth, alveolar ridge, and dental *occlusion* (the fit of the upper and lower teeth when closed) may occur with continual thumb sucking, abnormal swallowing patterns, or habitual mouth breathing. Health, energy level, and physical stamina, too, are likely to affect a child's ability to learn over sustained periods.

The teacher's responsibility for the physical growth and maturation of the student is generally *indirect* but nonetheless important. She should be alert to identify, refer, consult, and monitor whenever indicated. In this role the teacher should cooperate with professional workers from other disciplines: developmental psychologists, medical and health personnel, orthodontic and prosthodontic specialists, and speech pathologists. To fulfill her role, the teacher must be aware of their competencies and the contribution each can make to the physical growth and maturation of the learner of speech.

Sensory Abilities

The ability to detect the presence of stimuli, to discriminate differences among them, and to integrate stimuli with previous experience is basic to the learning of speech. The auditory channel is considered primary for speech learning. However, other sensory channels are or may be importantly involved. Along with **hearing**, we shall consider **vision, touch,** and **kinesthesia.** The teacher of speech should be aware of the disorders and remediation for all channels, as well as the contributions of each in learning and maintaining speech.

Hearing: As we shall deliberately emphasize throughout this book, the vigorous exploitation of residual hearing for the speech development of hearing impaired children can be of substantial benefit. Note that Chapter III is devoted exclusively to this topic with emphasis on the fundamental facts of acoustic phonetics that form the basis for teaching procedures. In recognizing the possibilities of residual hearing, the teacher will need to communicate primarily with audiologists and the student's family, but in some situations also with otologists, hearing aid dealers, manufacturers, and distributors of acoustic amplifier systems. Above all others, the teacher has the responsibility to see that there is a coordinated and consistent effort for the student to make the best use of his hearing. Her specific responsibilities include the following:

1. Maintenance of a good acoustic classroom environment with control of reverberated sounds from hard, reflective surfaces; control of external noise sources, such as ventilating ducts, hall noises, building and grounds maintenance noises; and control of extraneous classroom noises, such as scraping feet and chairs on hard floor surfaces. The teacher in an "open classroom" should be especially sensitive to the listening stress that such a situation may produce (232).

2. Ensuring constancy of hearing aid usage both at home and in school through the following: by listening to the hearing aids of every child in her class at least every morning; by having extra hearing aids, spare parts and batteries available in the school when the student's own aids are not working properly; by educating the student himself in addition to those who are in contact with him throughout the day about the use and maintenance of hearing aids; and by having periodic electroacoustic evaluations of the student's hearing aids to ensure that their gain, frequency responses, power, and distortion characteristics are appropriate.

3. Ensuring best use of hearing over time by encouraging periodic otologic and audiologic evaluation. This would include examination for possible acquisition of a conductive component in the hearing loss from cerumen (wax) or middle ear lesions. Parents should be apprised of the need for regular audiologic evaluation, at least once a year. The teacher should report to the audiologist her judgments on the effectiveness of the student's use of his hearing aids in the classroom and confer about recommendations related to the child's hearing or to the performance of his hearing aid. The teacher should be prepared to discuss and apply these recommendations as they bear on her instructional program. The results of audiological tests, particularly audiograms, need to be accessible for handy reference.

4. Provision of activities which give the student opportunity to use amplified sound in the classroom and in his daily routine.

Vision: Vision is obviously important for utilizing a teacher's speech model and for benefiting from exposure to talkers in the environment. It is also important for providing feedback to the speaker, who watches his listener's face to see whether he is being understood. Consider, for example, the importance that the skilled public speaker attaches to "eye contact." Perhaps because severe hearing impairment is such a conspicuous primary problem for the child with whom we are concerned, mild or moderate impairment of vision may be overlooked. Here is a good illustration of where the alertness of a teacher in identifying a defect may be pertinent to an instructional goal. Surveys among children considered "deaf "have shown that 50% or more have some visual deficiency which can affect their ability to learn, compared to from 20% to 30% of children with normal hearing (306). The visual disability may go undetected and learning difficulties may be attributed to other factors or to hearing impairment, or may be accepted as "natural." Routine visual examinations for all children should begin early and should be continued periodically to detect defects that may develop with growth or be acquired. The teacher can also contribute to the student's optimum use of vision by maintaining a classroom environment with adequate lighting and absence of glare. Further, she can in her routine activities stress visual awareness and discrimination of observable differences.

Touch and kinesthesia: Tactile and kinesthetic sensations of speech production may be very important for the speaker with hearing impairment (102). Experiments in oral stereognosis (the ability to recognize and differentiate the form of objects placed in the mouth) find a correlation between this ability and articulatory skill (17). Whether such tests can yield information about the tactile ability involved in speech production by deaf speakers, or can lead to training and therapeutic procedures, remains for further research. There is yet no evidence that "sense training" which involves recognition of objects by touching with the fingers has any effect on tactile perception of the oral surfaces. The common experience of local anesthesia in dental procedures numbing the tongue and thus affecting speech production demonstrates the

School dramatics
encourage speech.
A scene from
"Around the World
in Eighty Days."

PICTORIAL PRESS SERVICE

role that tactile and kinesthetic senses play in speech production. With sudden loss of hearing in adults and older children, speech production continues in an almost normal manner for some time, even though the auditory monitoring system is absent. This suggests that for the person without hearing loss a system of tactile-kinesthetic speech patterns is developed at an unconscious level, with the auditory system monitoring the output at a more conscious level. In time, without the auditory monitoring system available to determine the accuracy and correctness of speech production, speech becomes less exact and, without special training, eventually deteriorates. It is interesting that the first sound to deteriorate in cases of acquired hearing impairment is **s**. It has little if any tactile-kinesthetic feedback.

That children have learned speech without the use of hearing is evidence that conscious tactile and kinesthetic sensations can be utilized for learning and maintaining speech. Yet these systems are clearly not as efficient in monitoring as is the auditory system. Persons using primarily tactile-kinesthetic sensations for monitoring speech are not likely to be efficient predictors of the intelligibility of their own speech production (320).

Learning Abilities

Ability to learn speech depends on more general learning abilities. Pertinent for our purposes are the following learning abilities frequently associated with "information processing": *achievement effort, attention, retention, discrimination and generalization, recognition and recall, formulation,* and *monitoring.*

   Achievement effort: Central to the student's achievement effort are his physical condition and his motivation. We earlier described how physical condition affects energy level and tolerance for sustained learning effort. The teacher should recognize that when the student begins to learn speech, his motivations are unique to him, depending upon his experience with previous activities (particularly those in which he has experienced success or failure, pleasure or pain), and upon the pressures of his environment. Motivation can be influenced by the setting of realistic short-term objectives and long-term goals which give the child a chance to succeed at speech tasks, by encouraging identification of the child with peers and adults who use speech effectively, by classroom competition and cooperation, and by tangible rewards. The teacher should motivate speech not as an end in itself, but as a desirable skill relevant to the demands of everyday social experiences and as an opportunity to enrich them. Since motivation is also shaped by a reinforcing environment, the teacher should be aware of the student's proclivities, interests, and activities and offer guidance to the parents to foster motivations that are consistent and satisfying. Hilgard, a noted investigator in learning, suggests the following generalizations about motivation (125):

A motivated learner acquires what he learns more readily than one who is not motivated. The relevant motives include both general and specific ones—for example, desire to learn, need for achievement (general), desire for a reward, or to avoid a threatened punishment (specific).

Motivation that is too intense (especially pain, fear, or anxiety) may be accompanied by distracting emotional states, so excessive motivation may be less effective than moderate motivation for learning some kinds of tasks, especially those involving difficult discriminations.

Learning under intrinsic motivation is preferable to learning under extrinsic motivation.

Tolerance for failure is best taught through providing a backlog of success that compensates for experienced failure.

Individuals need practice in setting realistic goals for themselves, goals neither so low as to elicit little effort nor so high as to foreordain failure. Realistic goal-setting leads to more satisfactory improvement than unrealistic goal-setting.

The personal history of the individual—for example, his reaction to authority—may hamper or enhance his ability to learn from a given teacher.

Active participation by a learner is preferable to passive reception when learning, for example, from a lecture or a motion picture.

Meaningful materials and meaningful tasks are learned more readily than nonsense materials and more readily than tasks not understood by the learner.

There is no substitute for repetitive practice in the overlearning of skills (for instance, the performance of a concert pianist), or in the memorization of unrelated facts that have to be automatized.

Information about the nature of a good performance, knowledge of one's own mistakes, and knowledge of successful results aid learning.

Transfer to new tasks will be better if, in learning, the learner can discover relationships for himself, and if he has experience during learning of applying the principles within a variety of tasks.

Spaced or distributed recalls are advantageous in fixing material that is to be long retained.

Attention: Essential to processing information about speech is attention through looking, listening, and feeling. The child needs to develop selective or *discriminative attention,* that is, to be able to attend to pertinent (foreground) stimuli while ignoring extraneous (background) stimuli. The time period over which he attends to particular stimuli (attention span) should be progressively extended. Of course, the fundamental aim of the teacher is to develop the child's capacity and desire for self-directed attention.

Retention: The ability to store information is also important. *Short-term* retention is involved in both perception and imitation of speech sounds or units of speech, and *long-term* retention enables the talker to recall items as needed. To be truly useful, speech needs to be mastered, that is, always subject to immediate and effortless recall. Retention can be developed by relating new information to previous experience, by employing techniques of repetition and review, and by providing an environment in which there is expectancy of recall. Evidence of difficulty in retention may suggest the need for psychological evaluation.

Discrimination and generalization: Learning to talk requires ability to discriminate and to generalize. Discrimination is the determination of critical differences among stimuli; generalization is the determination of critical similarities and includes categorization and classification. Acquisition of fluent speech requires both abilities. While important differences between phonemes (**k** vs. **t,** for example) need to be discriminated, allophonic variations (as for the **k** in **koo** and the **k** in **kee**) need to be generalized as characteristic of a single phoneme.

Recognition and recall: Producing and understanding speech requires calling up bits of information which have been stored in the "memory bank" of the brain. We do this through two means—recognition and recall. To receive and to understand speech requires recognition—the matching of an element with what has been previously stored. To produce speech, other than in imitation, the appropriateness of the needed element is determined by the talker and recalled or retrieved from his memory. It is to be noted that, for production, recognition is generally easier than recall.

Formulation: In addition to recalling sounds required for an intended utterance, the talker needs to formulate or plan how these will be spoken. For example, he must formulate words that convey meaning, linguistic features such as syntactic structure, and intonation patterns that communicate particular intent. In conversation, this process seems to take place in a split second. Relatively little is yet known about formulation or how we can help to develop effective use of this ability, other than to provide practice in varied contexts. For the deaf child, who generally is deliberate in generating spoken language, this poses a formidable challenge. We need to distinguish between a child's ability to produce sounds, or combinations thereof, and his ability to formulate spoken language. The confusion of the two may lead to inappropriate teaching measures.

Monitoring: Monitoring is the process of comparing or matching one's speech to certain standards of speech correctness. For the person without hearing loss, monitoring refers primarily to listening and evaluating his own speech (320). For the person with hearing loss, it also involves in varying degrees tactile and kinesthetic monitoring. The deaf speaker's ability to judge whether he will be understood depends upon how well he can recognize whether his own speech approaches the standard patterns of his culture. He also needs to know from his experience what "errors" in his speech have the highest probability of being a cause of his not being understood and to practice strategies to guide him when a listener asks, "What did you say?" Listener responses also contribute to his monitoring.

THE ENVIRONMENT

The student's total environment is the second major area of concern in learning speech. During his early years, home and community comprise his total environment. Even after he is enrolled in "full-time" school he still spends many more waking hours in this environment than he does in school, not to mention weekends and vacations. Properly and vigorously exploited, the home and community provide valuable opportunities for substantive con-

tributions to growth and development of oral expression. These include language generating experiences, reinforcement of communication through an oral environment, and carry-over of speech behavior from the disciplined situation of the classroom to out-of-school living.

Language Concept Experiences

To speak, the student must have something to say. To have something to say he must have had experiences which lead to ideas that can and need to be expressed in language. It is incumbent upon the teacher to encourage and guide the adults and older children in the child's environment to foster and contrive situations that stimulate spoken language. She should recommend specific activities and suggest how best to take advantage of the significant aspects of experience (29). Among these are the play activities of the young child, particularly with selected toys. Also valuable are "walking tours" with adults who help discover and examine things of interest, and projects shared with adults which permit the child to participate at his own level. Other children can be a valuable source of experiences that develop concepts to be expressed in language. Properly prepared for and followed up, organized activities can make significant contributions. For the child with hearing impairment, auditory experiences suggest the useful exercise of associating sounds with sources and causes. Parents can make deliberate efforts to expose the child to interesting sounds which can be talked about: the lion at the zoo "roars," the baby "cries," the dog "barks," the door "slams."

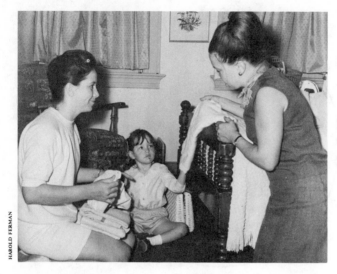

Parent is guided
to language learning
experiences.

HAROLD FERMAN

Oral Environment

Functional speech is more likely to be learned when practiced in an oral environment where its use is constant, consistent, and meaningful. Essential and salient features of an oral environment are:

1. Speech as the primary means of communication
2. Frequent need to use speech
3. Conventional patterns of speech for the student to perceive
4. Abundant opportunity to use speech
5. Encouragement to use speech.

It is interesting that the absence of even one of these features is often associated with defective speech among hearing children. Consider how indispensable they must be to ensure that the environment has been fully exploited for the speech development of the deaf child.

Carry-over

Carry-over from the classroom to the total milieu of the student implies active collaboration between school and those who are in a position to shape the child's extramural speech behavior. It is certainly more than "homework." As we have stressed previously, extramural experiences are a rich source for stimulating spoken language. Parents and others should assume the responsibility of communicating them to the school. And, of course, the school needs to do the same for classroom originated language experience. Carry-over, in essence, is best accomplished if it is conceived as a two-way channel of active and informed communication. It means not only that parents visit schools but that teachers visit homes. This sort of communication can provide an atmosphere of supportive attitudes which increase the probability that speech will be used consistently and successfully.

Our advocacy of constructive interchange recognizes the need for rational expectancies of spoken language from the student. Expectancies should neither underestimate nor discourage a child. For one child, even an attempt at speech may be all that can be expected. For another, this may be unacceptable. The layman requires help in what it is reasonable to expect and consequently to encourage. Not to be overlooked is the communication of expectancies to learning contexts in which a child is being "mainstreamed." In a sense, carry-over is the ultimate aim for what goes on in the school. Our experience suggests that the mechanisms and procedures for its accomplishment demand more serious attention than they have been given in the past.

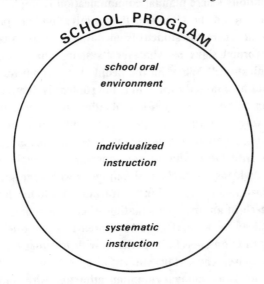

THE SCHOOL PROGRAM

We recall from Figure II-1 that a third area of concern is the school program. Wherever the hearing impaired child is educated—whether in a class for hearing children, in a special class in a school system, or in a special school—he requires instruction deliberately designed for learning speech. The design should take into account the quality of the oral environment in the school and systematic programming and organization.

School Oral Environment

No less than the home and community, the school can provide an effective environment that promotes oral communication. The classroom itself can be reinforcing when speech is used as the prominent means of communication in learning language and subject matter. It goes without saying that the lunch period, recess, and school activities of all sorts qualify admirably. From the point of view of motivation for oral expression, they may be crucial in impressing the child with the practical value of his speech skills. Someone in the school should be assigned the responsibility for stimulating awareness and developing procedures to bring this about. In a residential school where the development of speech is taken seriously, the responsibility is to see that this part of the school provides a supportive oral environment. Instructional staff should pursue oral carry-over as vigorously with the dormitory and extramural staff as they do with the parents of day pupils.

What we have said about motivation and practice has special relevance for students in situations where manual communication is emphasized. The purpose of speech may not be clear and thus motivation for speaking may be reduced or absent where the student is encouraged to use a combination of fingerspelling, formal signs of whatever "system," and speech to achieve "total communication." When all the people with whom he communicates daily understand his manual expression, the student is likely to observe that his message can be conveyed by a combination of fingerspelling and signs. *Why then use speech at all?* We believe the justification for students using speech among those who understand manual communication rests on practice for its later use with those who *do not* understand manual communication. Ability to speak widens the circle of situations in which the student can communicate, as illustrated in Figure 1 in the Introduction to this book. However, practice on speech in an artificial situation where manual communication is understood is likely to be ineffective compared to situations in which communication *depends* on speech. Experience with learning foreign languages supports this premise. The serious student of speech should experience daily people who do not know manual communication and with whom he needs to communicate. These may include teachers, counselors, resource teachers, and dormitory personnel, as well as the clerks at the neighborhood shops. Fulfilling this requirement of an oral environment is especially important in large residential schools where manual communication prevails.

Individualized Instruction

Fundamental to an effective systematic program for learning and teaching speech is the determination of the individual needs of each child. This is accomplished by a judicious combination of formal assessment of speech skills and continuing critical observation of speech behavior in all contexts. The results of assessment and observation should be the basis for decisions pertaining to placement, instructional procedures, and current and projected expectancies. The integration of an analysis of needs with a plan for action based on them should constitute the *child's individual speech program* for a conveniently designated period of time, probably an academic year. We are aware of the difficulty of achieving individualized instruction in conventional settings but our experience dictates that this is essential. Comfortable compromises on this point can negate the best of intentions to cultivate oral performance. Furthermore, in planning for individuals the teacher should not be constrained by the requirements of appealingly organized plans that address themselves to "graded" levels of speech.

Systematic Instruction

The speech program of a school should be deliberately and carefully organized, and its central focus should be the provision of systematic instruction. Of course, the development of such a program emphasizes participation by all whose competence, motivation, and responsibility are required for its successful implementation. The prominent features of an organized program include *individualized instruction, methodology,* the discriminating use of *sensory channels and aids,* and *continuity* of programming.

Methodology: There are numerous "methods" (1, 6, 43, 54, 86, 90.2, 90.6, 90.8, 90.11, 119, 318) advocated for teaching speech, as we shall see in Chapters IV and V. What merits the designation "method" is an open question. In our view a method consists of the selection of techniques consistent with a general approach to teaching speech. Fundamental to a method is a carefully determined rationale that reflects a working understanding of the array of options whose value has been demonstrated by experience. The teacher needs to know why she does what she does. Hit and miss procedures are to be avoided.

An example of generating methodology is in selecting techniques for correcting errors (90.3). Suppose a primary age student, intending to say the word *by,* has said a word that sounds like *pie,* substituting **p** for **b.** A number of techniques are at hand to "correct" the error. But which to choose? The teacher knows that speech instruction should support practice that strengthens maintenance of a skill of which the child is judged to be capable. This suggests to the teacher that she choose a strategy to reinforce long-term memory for speech production. She should give the student an opportunity to recall the correct (or his best) production, rather than identifying the error by presenting a model for imitation of the correct sound. She knows that simple imitation is not the technique of choice to develop the child's ability to decide what is required to accomplish intelligibility and then to retrieve the appropriate sound from his stored repertory (100).

With this in mind, in order to signal an error, she may begin by just telling the student she did not understand all of his last sentence. This technique gives the student maximum opportunity to appeal to his catalogue of *internalized error probabilities applicable to the particular utterance.* This may enable him to make the correct sound in the same context in which it was originally in error. If he repeats the sentence with the same error, the teacher may elect to point the student in the direction of the error, but without identifying it, by writing the word in which it is contained. Or she may give him a more explicit clue, underlining the incorrect sound. The student now has the opportunity to concentrate on what he has learned about the manner and place of production of **b** and such error as he may frequently make. If the student still does not make the **b** sound correctly in the word, the teacher may go a step further and write the letter "p" immediately above the letter "b" and then cross out the letter "p". This lets the student know the nature of his error. Now he may think through the differences in producing the **p** and **b** sounds and attempt the correct production.

Each technique the teacher has selected is consistent with her strategy of giving the student opportunity to recall what he had previously learned. She began with a technique which required considerable identification, analysis, and recall by the student, and when he was unable to correct himself, she gave him progressively more information. The next time he makes the error, he may need less help in correcting it. Sustained experience of this sort should contribute to the skill and confidence with which he responds to situations in which he is not immediately understood.

It is well here, as we consider the strategy of methodology, to remind ourselves of our statement in the Introduction of our intent to "enhance the teacher's power to analyze the task of speech instruction." A useful guide to accomplish this is to specify essential components of the act of teaching as they apply to speech. In a sense, they constitute the basis for a "lesson plan"! These components are (90.3):

1. Orientation   4. Repetition
2. Stimulation for production   5. Running evaluation.
3. Reinforcement by reward

1. Orientation is the frame of reference in which the teaching act takes place. It includes development of the child's individual speech program and sensitivity to the educational context in which speech will be taught—as a separate act, associated with other modes of communication, or concurrent with other instruction. It also involves carefully thought-out goals and procedures to stimulate a constructive motivational set for learning. Obviously, attention to the physical elements of the environment such as lighting, acoustics, esthetic decor, and arrangement of equipment is required.

2. *Stimulation for production* suggests a progression that derives from the principle that "natural" speech development is the preferred, but frequently not the sufficient, basis for speech instruction (82). Hence, the progression represents a gradient of decreasing naturalness or increasing contrivance: reinforcement of correct spontaneous production, planned stimulation without direct attempt at production by the student, awareness of error as illustrated above, deliberate elicitation of imitation of the teacher's speech pattern, demonstration of the place and/or manner of production of speech sounds, and, finally, manipulation of the student's speech mechanism.

3. *Reinforcement* by extrinsic *reward* of whatever timing, frequency, or nature (gold star, teacher praise) implies the need for the teacher to convey to the student the kind of speech behavior which elicits reward. Effective teachers do this intuitively. Yet the analysis requires attention to reinforcement and certainly to our ultimate aim that speech is its own reward. The student should come to recognize that his ability to communicate by speech expands the compass of his entire existence.

4. *Repetition* contributes importantly to the achievement of unconscious spontaneous production of speech, that is, to its mastery. This may involve a range from specifically targeted speech drills to elicited repetition in real-life situations. Whatever the item or context—whether simple consonant-vowel-consonant nonsense syllables, coarticulated clusters, or spontaneous utterances originated by the talker—the opportunity for purposeful repetition needs to be evaluated and acted upon.

The construction of speech drills needs to be based on certain essential principles. These are: (1) The drill should have a clearly stated purpose such as learning something new, or fixing or maintaining what has been learned. It should not be a useless "going through the motions." (2) When possible the child should know the reason for the drill. (3) Phonetic permutations should be adequately sampled. For example, a vowel drill should have stops and fricatives following the vowel; a consonant drill should combine with samples from all vowel classes. (4) The timing of a drill should be determined by the child's abilities at a given stage in his development. A child may be able to give a final t but may not be ready to generalize to production of final t in words ending in -ed as in *looked,* Complicated clusters should be introduced gradually. (5) The child should get reasonably frequent feedback about his performance with care taken to avoid reinforcement of inappropriate production.

5. *Running evaluation* refers to a kind of daily inventory of a child's performance that may influence speech work to be modified and adapted both immediately and cumulatively to shape longer-range strategies.

Discriminating use of sensory channels and aids: Knowledge of the sensory capabilities of a child should obviously lead to the specification of their optimum use. Optimum use requires *discriminating* use by the teacher of sensory channels and aids. How often we observe indiscriminate use! Consider the teacher as a frequent "sensory aid" who places the hand of a child on her face presumably to transmit information about a sound over the child's tactile channel. Some teachers whom we have observed usually place the hand over the same area of the face without regard to such factors as what cues she wishes to transmit (loudness, manner, or what?), the discriminability of the item over the tactile channel, the quality of the signal, irrelevant and obfuscating information in the signal (muscle tension), and facilitation or inhibition of the message when combined simultaneously with its audibility and visibility.

For example, consider the possibility of transmitting the distinction between z and zh over the tactile channel. Place the fingertips on the neck muscle (the sterno-cleido-mastoideus) just below the mastoid process of the temporal bone. Here, both sounds are sensed, but the vibro-tactile sensation for zh seems to cover a larger area than for z. If the fingertips are not directed to this area, the distinction is not communicated. Teachers should practice these possibilities on themselves. If possible, they should do it with noise in their ears to eliminate acoustic cues.

On the other hand, pragmatic use of channel and aid is indispensable to systematic instruction. The range of possibilities for generating speech or speech related signals appropriate to the child's sensory capabilities needs to

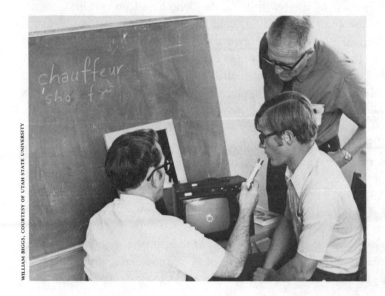

A visual
sensory aid.

WILLIAM BIGGS, COURTESY OF UTAH STATE UNIVERSITY

be carefully considered, along with the *mode* to be used over a particular channel; whether, for example, over the visual channel a signal should be lip-read, fingerspelled, written, or diagrammed. It is among these that the teacher needs to make discriminating choices for a particular purpose (26).

Implicit in these comments is the view that the **primary sensory aid is the teacher.** In the classroom she is an ever-present interacting aid, shaping her own immediate input to the child in response to his speech behavior. She decides when and whether to intervene in order to reinforce, correct, or improve speech, not to mention her important role in its development. In doing so, she has to make a choice of channel and mode to communicate to the child. Should she use his ears, his eyes, his skin, or some combination of these? Should she speak louder? Should she show the child the placement of her tongue? Should she have him feel the stream of air characteristic of a fricative consonant? Her decision will depend on the particular circumstances, based, of course, on her knowledge about the child as previously delineated in this chapter. What we are stressing here is that she exploit the possibilities inherent in her own person in communicating information about speech.

The teacher is uniquely capable of presenting to the child the kinds of isomorphic sensory cues necessary for his own monitoring. These do not require transformation of the signal. For example, an "S" Meter, on the face of which a needle is directed toward a target point when a child produces a proper **s,** requires the child to transform this visual information to properly shape his tongue to produce the **s.** This is not his natural feedback mechanism. An ideal instrument would present him with a stream of air flowing through a central aperture shaped by the tongue. A teacher can produce this stream of air herself. Along these lines, we have suggested in Chapter VI the "sensory instructional possibilities" of the various phonemes. Tables II-3 and II-4 present our estimates of the ordering of these possibilities with respect to channel. The teacher's ability to interact effectively in "real time" to exploit these possibilities is what makes her the primary sensory aid.

Nevertheless, sensory aids—considered from the conventional standpoint as supplements but not substitutes for the teacher—can be useful (21, 23, 25, 73, 131, 170, 171, 200). Some sensory aids are designed to extract and transmit features of speech that are likely to facilitate speech perception and hence speech production. Selective amplification in hearing aids (elaborated in Chapter III), visual displays of pitch dynamics such as glides, and transmission of nasal/non-nasal, voice/voiceless features to stimulators on the skin illustrate the range of possibilities that have attracted the attention of engineers and investigators. We know, too, that speech is a signal whose characteristics change rapidly in time. The rapidly changing perceptual cues of

	Visual	Tactile		Visual	Tactile
h	1	4	v₂	5	4
wh	4	5	th	4	3
p	5	5	z	1	2
t	3	4	zh	2	4
k	1	3	j	2	1
f	5	4	m	5	5
th₁	4	4	n	3	5
s	1	2	ng	1	5
sh	2	3	l	3	2
ch	2	4	r	2	2
w-	4	5	x	1	3
b	5	4	qu	4	4
d	3	4	y-	2	4
g	1				

5 = *greatest possibilities*
1 = *least possibilities*

Table II-3. *Estimated ratings of sensory instructional possibilities for consonants.*

	Visual	Tactile
oo	3	4
-oo-	2	5
aw	3	5
-o-	2	5
ee	2	4
-i-	1	4
-e-	1	4
-a-	2	5
-u-	1	5
oi	5	5
ou	4	5
u-e	5	4
a-e	3	4
i-e	3	4
oa	4	5

5 = *greatest possibilities*
1 = *least possibilities*

Table II-4. *Estimated ratings of sensory instructional possibilities for vowels.*

speech place upon the auditory system the essential requirement of making quick decisions about what has been spoken. As he listens to the flow of speech, the listener must be quick to select the cues that enable him to identify a sound as being different from all other sounds. This is difficult for the hearing-impaired person to do. Speech is simply too fast for him. The confusion in the dynamics of speech may be somewhat ameliorated by a static visual display that "freezes" a feature to be communicated and then reproduced. An example of this is a display of pitch change (frequently a line changing in horizontal and vertical dimensions) which can be contemplated by the student and serve as a target for his own production.

Sensory aids can add to the convenience, frequency, and accessibility of speech experience not easily provided by the teacher (59). By speaking louder, of course, she can amplify sound—which is what the most popular sensory aid, a hearing aid, does. But she is not likely to be able to do this over a sustained period of time. Hearing aids do not get tired and they can and should be with the user all the time. Also helpful as sensory aids are models, diagrams, and films that display pertinent aspects of the speech act. A transparent model of the head with moving parts that can be manipulated makes visible some movements and structures that are hidden, like the raising and lowering of the velum. Diagrams effectively demonstrate the arching of the tongue, and ingenious films illustrate tongue movement and laryngeal action.

Sensory aids can provide vehicles for self-instruction, particularly in their role as "error detectors." They can be imaginatively designed to appeal to children's interests and to motivate practice. Children have been observed to be intrigued by banks of bright colored lights used to signal loudness or pitch change. Here is an opportunity for enthusiastic proponents of "behavior modification" to develop suitably programmed "rewards" for appropriate speech production. Table II-5 contains a digest of the application to the primary factors influencing the intelligibility of speech of an array of sensory aids and the sensory channels to which they apply. Increasing classroom experience and ongoing research promise an augmented and progressively refined stock of aids.

A teacher's discriminating use of sensory aids—whether of her own person, common classroom devices, or elegant electronic instruments—demands of the teacher a continuing concern for their value. Does the aid deliver what is intended? Will something simpler do just as well? Does the result justify the expenditure of time, energy, and money? Will apparent initial motivation wear off? Is there evidence that it carries over to extramural speech situations? It is important to note that such "hard" evidence as exists for the value of engineered visual and tactile sensory aids is based on short-term data

Primary Factors of Speech	The Teacher	Common Classroom Devices	Sample Electronic Equipment*
VOICE			
Loudness	Intensity of acoustic signal (A)	Balloon on teacher/child face (T)	Light activated by microphone (V)
Pitch	Intensity of vibration on skin (T)	Musical instruments (A)(T)	Tactual vocoder (T)
	Frequency of vibration on skin (T)	Musical instruments (A)(T)	Pitch meter or indicator (V)
	Vertical movement of larynx (T) (V)		
Nasal / Non-Nasal	Place of vibration on skin (T)		Nasal indicator (V)
Quality	Display of muscle tension and relaxation (T) (V)		
ARTICULATION			
Manner of Production	Vibration on skin (T)		Tactual vocoder (T)
Voicing	Breath on skin (T)		
Breath	Exaggerated force (V)(T)	Feather, flame, paperstrip (V)	
Force of Articulation	Model as static display (V)		Vowel indicator (Oscilloscope) (V)
Place of Articulation	Model exaggeration (V)	Diagram, model, mirror (V)	Spectrograph (V)

Acoustic Features
  Intensity
  Frequency
  Duration
  Dynamics of Co-articulation
	Gesture (duration) (V)
	Model as slow motion (V)
	Manipulate speech mechanism (K)
		Written symbol codes (V)	"S" meter (V)
			Spectrograph (V)

RHYTHM Rate	Model (A) Gesture (V)	Written symbol codes (V) Musical instrument (A) (T)	Light activated by microphone (V) Pitch level meter (V) VU meter
Stress (accent, emphasis)	Model (A) (V) (T) Pressure on hand (T)	Written symbol codes (V) Musical instrument (A)	
Intonation	Model	Written symbol codes (V) Musical instrument rhythm (A) (T)	
Phrasing			

Table II-5. *Digest of sensory aids applied to the primary factors of speech. (A)=Auditory, (V)=Visual, (T)=Tactile, (K)=Kinesthetic Senses.*

(*The Hearing Aid, which applies to all features of speech, is treated in Chapter III.)

from laboratory contexts. *It is incumbent upon investigators to carry on evaluations in the classroom and in everyday speech situations.* Here is a splendid opportunity for teachers and investigators to collaborate effectively in pursuit of a common goal. As much as anything, the deliberations of recent conferences on speech analyzing aids, sensory training aids, and sensory capabilities of hearing impaired children point emphatically to this need (294).

Continuity of program: Continuity implies a sequence of empirically accumulated children's individual speech programs—each building on the previous one and directed to the ultimate goal of intelligible speech. While each teacher develops an annual program, supervisors should ensure that there is continuing progress in gaining speech skills over a number of years. Without school-wide coordination, the disjointed and discontinuous efforts of individual teachers—some of whom may be transient members of a staff—can contribute to confusion, insecurity, and negativism toward speech. Illustrative of what frequently characterizes discontinuity is variation in systems of orthography, in appeal to devices such as color codes and particular sensory aids, and in convictions of the teacher as expressed in the recognition of the features of an oral environment previously listed.

Checking a hearing aid.

KEN NICOLAI

CHAPTER III

Using Hearing for Speech

This chapter is concerned with the use of hearing as an extremely powerful and important tool, but not necessarily an exclusive one, for teaching speech to deaf children. Modern, wearable, electronic acoustic amplifiers—hearing aids—can now bring some of the sounds of speech within the range of most deaf children. Furthermore, space-age technology promises increasing exploitation of limited hearing in the future.

To ignore the benefits of hearing through electro-acoustic amplification today, is to deprive deaf children of a precious resource that may enrich their entire lives. *But the effective use of hearing for speech is not easy!* Use of hearing through amplification requires application of knowledge about audiology, phonetics, and hearing aids, as well as careful monitoring of hearing and amplification, and the use of training techniques that focus on the relation of hearing to speech production. This effort can be most productive if classroom teachers, special speech teachers, audiologists, hearing aid technicians, parents, and in some situations speech/language pathologists, work together in a cooperative and demanding role as "teachers of speech." Requirements of basic preparation for this role comprise the content and organization of this chapter.

SPEECH ACQUISITION AND HEARING

Hearing is the primary sensory channel through which children acquire speech and language. The acoustic products of speech match the auditory characteristics of the normal ear, especially its range of sensitivity for intensity and frequency. The ear provides more rapid temporal resolution than the eye of the flowing sequences of sounds in connected speech, separating them into component units so that the speech code can be rapidly deciphered. Unlike the eye, the ear is always open so that speech may be heard whenever it is present. The ears are largely non-directional. The listener is not required to face the speaker in order to receive a message, so that much of what we learn is "overheard," behind us or "out of the corner of our ear."

We use our hearing to receive numerous examples of units of speech from others, giving us repeated patterns to imitate. We also use our hearing to monitor our own speech, listening to what we say. Then we can compare *directly* our own production to the model of others through the same sensory channel—hearing—and revise our production again and again until it matches the sound of the target model. Through a simultaneous dynamic process, using our hearing, we also acquire language—learning its semantic, syntactic and pragmatic features. Our accuracy and fluency in formulating spoken language contributes considerably to the intelligibility of our speech.

It is not surprising that the learning of speech and language will be imperfect when hearing is significantly impaired at birth (*congenital hearing impairment*). The greater the degree of congenital hearing impairment, the less adequately will speech be learned. Furthermore, *all* aspects of speech production will be influenced because each depends upon hearing for its acquisition. Articulation of speech sounds, coarticulation of their combinations, nuances of speech rhythm, modulation of loudness of voice, and the complexities of spoken language will not be learned adequately if hearing impairment is severe.

Not only is the learning of speech deficient when hearing is significantly impaired at birth, but the capability of *maintaining* speech after it has been learned is not likely to be equal to the task. This is because the speaker's impaired hearing also impairs his ability to monitor the production of his own speech. Even if he learns by some means to produce an s sound, for example, he is not likely to produce it satisfactorily every time, because his own production is not fed back to him through his ear. We commonly observe that as adults lose their hearing in later life (*adventitious hearing impairment*), their speech deteriorates because their auditory monitoring is impaired (346). Some observations on the influences of adventitious and congenital hearing impairment on speech are delineated in Table III-1.

Even when hearing is severely impaired, it may still be utilized in acquiring and teaching speech. The auditory channel may be the most effective channel for teaching many aspects of speech, however much it may be limited, because as we have seen, it is the *natural* channel for learning speech. For some

Postlingual Adventitious Loss	Prelingual Congenital Impairment
1. As a person born with normal hearing loses his hearing, his speech deteriorates.	1. A child born with severe hearing impairment does not acquire speech naturally or adequately.
2. The greater the hearing loss becomes, the greater the deterioration of speech.	2. The better the child's hearing level, the better his speech and the easier to acquire or develop.
3. As hearing loss progresses in severity, deviations in speech occur first in articulation, and then in voice quality and rhythm.	3. The child with mild to moderate hearing impairment has speech deviations primarily of articulation.
4. The longer a person has a serious hearing impairment, the greater his speech deterioration.	4. A child with severe hearing impairment has serious deviations in articulation and voice quality, and may have abnormal speech rhythm.
5. With sudden severe-to-profound hearing loss, speech does not deteriorate immediately, but deteriorates gradually.	5. The child with severe-to-profound hearing impairment can be taught to speak but his speech may deviate considerably from that of a child with normal hearing.

Table III-1. *Common observations relating speech production to hearing impairment, both adventitious hearing loss after language has been learned (postlingual) and congenital hearing impairment before language has been learned (prelingual).*

hearing-impaired children it may be the **primary** sensory channel for speech development, improvement and maintenance. The exploitation of impaired hearing to teach speech is feasible because of the following conditions:

(1) Hearing impairment is seldom total. Complete deafness is rare and most hearing-impaired children have a useful remnant or residuum of hearing. Audiometric tests describe the variety of hearing levels and auditory capabilities found among deaf children.

(2) Not all of the speech signal must be heard for it to be useful. Distinctive features of speech are transmitted by different acoustic information

received from the speech of others or fed back from the speaker himself. Some important features are communicated simply by the presence or absence of sound energy, or by the low-frequency energy that is usually available to deaf children.

(3) Amplification of sound through electro-acoustic hearing aids can make up for some of the impairment to sensitivity of the ear, particularly by rendering audible some of the important features of speech. Great progress has been made in designing powerful, wearable hearing aids, and there is promise of continued progress.

(4) A program of audiologic and otologic surveillance, along with careful monitoring of the use of acoustic amplification, can help provide an environment of constant availability of the speech examples of others and auditory feedback from the child's own speech.

(5) Instructional procedures can be tailored to emphasize the use of hearing for developing, for improving, and for maintaining the speech production of hearing-impaired children.

The above points lead to the organization of this chapter into the following sections:

DESCRIBING THE HEARING OF DEAF CHILDREN

THE ACOUSTIC FEATURES OF SPEECH

ELECTRO-ACOUSTIC AMPLIFICATION FOR SPEECH

MONITORING HEARING AND AMPLIFICATION FOR SPEECH

USING HEARING TO TEACH SPEECH

Each section has been the subject of articles and books, some of which we have listed as the end of this book. Each section might well be the subject of separate courses for the preparation of teachers or audiologists. The outline of sections suggests a curriculum for a course of study by those seriously interested in using hearing to teach speech. In this chapter we present the essential components, relevant to our purpose, of each area of study in a sequence that relates them to each other.

DESCRIBING THE HEARING OF DEAF CHILDREN

Pure-Tone Threshold Levels

Measurement of hearing is a first important step toward utilizing a deaf child's auditory channel for his speech development. The *audiometer* is an electronic device used to measure the level of hearing. The pure-tone audiometer delivers to either ear tones of known frequency and intensity to which the listener is expected to respond. When the softest intensity level of a tone is reached at which the listener can just detect the tone and respond (usually to 50 percent of presented tones), that level is called the listener's *hearing-threshold level* for that tone. Sometimes it is called simply the "hearing level" or "threshold level."

Threshold level responses for the different frequencies are commonly plotted on a chart called a *pure-tone audiogram.* People with "normal hearing" do not hear tones of different frequencies equally well. The audiometer and the audiogram adjust for this normal variation in sensitivity for the different frequencies and designate the average threshold level for normal listeners as a **0** (zero) level for each of the tested frequencies. To indicate the range of threshold-level responses among normal listeners at each frequency, the audiometer and audiogram usually include **-10** dB for levels softer than the average threshold level.

The remainder of the audiogram relates the responses of an individual to "normal hearing," based on the responses of a statistically appropriate sampling of people who have no complaint of hearing disability and no history of ear pathology. The pure-tone audiogram form in Figure III-1 serves as a referent for this section.

The vertical dimension of the form designates differences in *intensity* that correlate roughly with the differences in *loudness* we might hear. As the numbers from top to bottom grow larger, the intensity in *decibels* (commonly abreviated **dB)** increases, and the perceived loudness of the tones is greater. Note that the audiogram form in Figure III-1 includes levels of 120 decibels and greater. These levels would be extremely loud to a person with normal hearing, about like standing near a jet airplane engine, but it might be merely a threshold level for some profoundly deaf listeners.

The horizontal dimension of the form designates tones of different *frequency* that reflect the range of *pitch* we hear. As the numbers from left to right grow larger, the frequency in *Hertz* (commonly abbreviated **Hz)** increases in successive doubling steps and the perceived pitch of the tones is higher. An audiometer usually includes tones from 125 Hz, to 8000 Hz. Hertz refers to the number (or frequency) of sound pressure cycles in one second. A tone of 125 Hz has a low frequency and we would hear it as low pitched, about like a male bass voice. An 8000 Hz tone has a high frequency we would hear as very high pitched, like a thin whistle. Normal ears can hear frequencies up to 20000 Hz, but these are seldom of concern for deaf listeners.

When a listener's threshold level is reached, the *audiometrist* marks the audiogram form at the intersection of vertical and horizontal lines that corre-

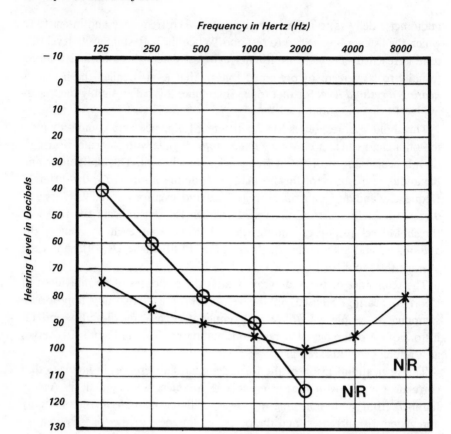

Figure III-1.   *A pure-tone audiogram form with hearing-threshold levels and audiometric curves for the right ear (O) and left ear (X) of a person with severe-to-profound hearing level. NR indicates that no response was given to a tone at maximum intensity output of the audiometer.*

spond to the frequency and intensity of the tone, that is, the hearing-threshold level for that particular person for that tone. As threshold levels are marked for each of the tones tested on one ear, they are connected by a line that displays the ***audiometric curve*** or configuration. In Figure III-1, audiometric curves for the right and the left ears of a child are shown, using the symbol **O** for the right ear and the symbol **X** for the left ear. Speech and other sounds plotted on the audiogram form above the audiometric curve are inaudible (below the listener's threshold), and those plotted below it are audible (above the listener's threshold).

It is customary to refer to these complex configurations for each ear as being at a single decibel level. This is usually the average level of 500 Hz, 1000 Hz and 2000 Hz, commonly called the *speech frequencies*. This generalization may obscure important information and differences between the ears. Note that in Figure III-1 the average of the speech frequencies would be the same, 95 dB, for either ear. However, the audiometric configurations of the ears are very different and the ears have different characteristics for use with amplification.

An additional generalization is to refer to the overall hearing level of a deaf child by the average threshold level of 500 Hz, 1000 Hz, and 2000 Hz in the *better ear.* For this purpose, "better ear" refers only to the average of the three frequencies and not the audiometric configuration. The hearing levels reviewed in Table III-2 refer to this better-ear generalization, and relate hearing-threshold levels to expected deviations of speech and language.

Large-scale demographic studies also use this better-ear average in reporting hearing-threshold levels among large numbers of hearing-impaired children. For example, a recent report of hearing level among United States children who were enrolled in special schools and classes for hearing-impaired children showed the following proportions of children at these hearing level categories:

Under 40 dB	10%
41 to 55 dB	9%
56 to 70 dB	13%
71 to 90 dB	25%
91 dB and above	43%

Tolerance and the Dynamic Range of Hearing

Much important information is contained in analysis of a child's hearing at sensation levels above his threshold. After all, we listen to speech well above a mere detection level, and it is *supra-threshold* hearing in which we are especially interested for speech development.

When sound is raised above hearing threshold, it eventually reaches a level so intense that it cannot be tolerated. This is as true for deaf children as it is for persons with normal hearing. This *tolerance* level can be measured, and it should be plotted with a bold line on an audiogram form for each ear, along with the hearing-threshold level. When sound exceeds this level it can cause the sensation of discomfort, tickle, and even pain as the intensity is increased. Continuous exposure at those levels may further impair the child's residual

Hearing-Threshold Levels	Speech and Language Expectations
− 10 to 20 decibels (normal hearing)	No related speech or language deviations.
20 to 35 decibels (mild hearing impairment)	No related speech deviations. Language may be slower in developing.
35 to 55 decibels (mild-to-moderate hearing impairment)	Some defects of articulation. Speech and language may be slower in developing.
55 to 70 decibels (moderate hearing impairment)	Abnormalities of articulation and voice. Vocabulary may be deficient
70 to 90 decibels (severe hearing impairment)	Articulation and voice quality likely to be abnormal. Syntax and other aspects of language may be deficient. Will need to be taught to speak.
90 decibels or poorer (severe-to-profound hearing impairment)	Speech rhythm, voice and articulation likely to be abnormal. Speech and language must be developed with careful and extensive training. Supplements to the auditory channel will be helpful.
100 decibels or poorer (profound hearing impairment)	The auditory channel is often helpful, but will need use of non-auditory channels for speech development.

Table III-2.   *Hearing-threshold levels (better ear average) related to speech and language learning by children, and expected deviations in speech and language.*

hearing in that ear. In Figure III-2, both the threshold level and tolerance level are plotted for one ear, reflecting the range of intensity for each tone from "just detectable" to "too loud." This range is the *dynamic range* of hearing for that ear. Since the tolerance of a normal ear and an impaired ear can be at about the same level, the dynamic range of hearing for an impaired ear will be very restricted compared to that for a normal ear. In Figure III-2, for example, the dynamic range of hearing at 1000 Hz (95 dB to 120 dB) is limited to only 25 dB, compared to a dynamic range for a normal ear of 120 dB or more. This limitation has great significance for applying acoustic amplification at that frequency. The amplified sound must be sufficiently above the listener's threshold to be heard easily and yet not so far above the threshold that it becomes uncomfortable.

Resolution of Frequency, Intensity and Duration

Perception of speech requires that the ear resolve the subtle differences in frequency, intensity and duration that characterize the different sounds of speech. The speech sounds we produce match the ability of the normal ear to

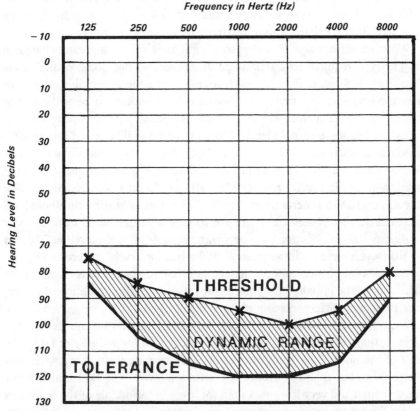

Figure III-2. *A pure-tone audiogram form with hearing-threshold levels and audiometric curve for the left ear (X) of a person with severe-to-profound hearing level, the tolerance level for each frequency measured for the left ear, and the resulting dynamic range of hearing in that ear.*

discriminate. When an ear has sensorineural impairment, as is generally the case among deaf children, the perception of these important acoustic differences may be very limited (110, 239). Even though speech may be made loud enough to be audible, the hearing-impaired person's ability to resolve differences may remain limited. Therefore, speech may be "heard" but not always "understood."

Discrimination of differences among sounds is described in terms of *difference limens,* or differential thresholds. When a tone of a given frequency is changed in *frequency* so that the listener just notices the difference, that difference is called the *difference limen for frequency* or **DLF.** The DLF of the normal ear is somewhat different for each of the frequencies included on the audiogram, growing larger as the frequency is increased. It requires a greater difference in frequency to discriminate differences from a high-frequency tone like 4000 Hz than from a low-frequency tone like 250 Hz.

When an ear has significant sensorineural impairment, a greater change in frequency is required to discriminate differences so that some of the subtle frequency differences among speech sounds may be imperceptible, even with acoustic amplification that renders sounds loud enough to be audible. For lower frequencies such as 125 Hz and 250 Hz, sensorineural impairment that leads to a hearing-threshold level of 20 dB to 35 dB (mild hearing impairment) produces a nearly ten-fold increase in the DLF compared to normal listeners. At 500 Hz and above, such an increase in the DLF is not produced until the hearing-threshold level reaches 55 dB to 65 dB (moderate hearing impairment). As a general trend, the DLF increases as hearing-threshold level increases at all frequencies. There are considerable individual differences in frequency resolution among listeners with hearing-threshold levels at 70 dB to 90 dB (severe hearing impairment). When hearing levels are profound, frequency resolution becomes no better than that for tactile sensations on the skin, so that the impaired ear contributes little to the discrimination of important frequency differences among speech sounds.

When a tone is changed in *intensity* so that the listener just notices the difference, that difference is called the *difference limen for intensity* or **DLI.** The DLI of the normal ear is approximately 1 dB varying from about 4 dB near threshold to less than 0.5 dB at high sensation levels. The DLI is also larger for very high and very low tones than for tones in the middle of the frequency range. Severe hearing impairment seems to have less influence on the difference limen for intensity than on the difference limen for frequency.

Judgments about differences in duration also appear to be less influenced by severe hearing impairment than are judgments about frequency. Children with severe or profound impairment vary in their ability to make discriminations among acoustic events in time (126, 127).

Speech Audiometry and Informal Tests

The quality of the speech that hearing-impaired children produce is strongly influenced by their ability to perceive their own speech and the speech of others (22, 209, 270, 278, 296, 328). Most of the standard audiologic tests of speech perception are inappropriate for deaf children. They may require greater auditory or linguistic competence than many young deaf children possess. In fact, the inability to understand speech is sometimes used to define "deaf," as in this description: "A *deaf* person is one whose hearing disability precludes successful processing of linguistic information through audition, with or without a hearing aid." Nevertheless, some speech stimuli may be useful in describing hearing capacity, yielding information in addition to the pure-tone testing described above (172). Table III-3 presents an auditory skills matrix that relates various levels of speech stimuli to increasingly difficult perception and response tasks. This matrix may be used by the teacher or audiologist to suggest informal tests that help describe a child's ability to respond to speech stimuli. It may also be used to help establish goals for auditory training.

A speech audiometer delivers to either ear a high-fidelity speech signal that can be adjusted to receive sounds from very soft speech to intensities of sound that reach ears with profound hearing impairment. When the listener just detects the presence of speech, the level is called the *speech detection threshold* or **SDT**. When the intensity is increased so that the listener can just recognize about half of a set of familiar two-syllable words, the level is called the *speech reception threshold* or **SRT**. Speech audiometers are calibrated so that the average speech reception threshold level for normal listeners is set at a **0** (Zero) dB level in order to correspond to the **0** dB level for pure tones. Since it requires less intensity to *detect* speech than to begin to *recognize* it, the audiometer's speech detection threshold occurs at a less intense level than either the speech reception threshold or the pure-tone threshold. For a deaf child, the speech detection threshold should occur at a slightly less intense level than his best pure-tone threshold, usually at 125 Hz or 250 Hz.

One speech test that describes differences in the capacity of deaf children to perceive speech involves a word-recognition task. Familiar two-syllable words, with almost equal stress on each syllable (*airplane, baseball, cowboy*), are presented at comfortable listening levels above the child's speech detection threshold. As a list of 25 words is presented orally and out of sight, the child

Perceptual Task	Speech Stimuli	RUNNING CONNECTED SPEECH	PHRASES AND SENTENCES	WORDS	SYLLABLES	INDIVIDUAL PHONEMES	SPEECH FEATURES
COMPREHENSION understanding the meaning of words or larger units of speech					▓	▓	▓
RECOGNITION identifying familiar units or features of speech							
DISCRIMINATION comparing and determining that stimuli are the same or different							
DETECTION being aware that speech is present or absent							

Table III-3.   Auditory skills matrix for perception of speech that relates difficulty of the perceptual task to complexity of the speech stimuli. (After Erber and Hirsh, 1978) (83).

writes the word he thinks he recognizes from among a familiar small set. Since each word has the same number of syllables, its identification requires some hearing for frequency differences. Hearing-impaired children tend to divide into two groups on this test. Those with average pure-tone hearing levels (speech frequency range) of less than 85 dB score from 70 to 100 percent correct, while those with average pure-tone hearing levels of more than 100 dB score from 0 to 30 percent. However, the group with pure-tone hearing levels, between 85 dB and 100 dB, is variable. For this group, a word-recognition task may test something more than pure tones do, something that can differentiate children with similar pure-tone audiograms, or may even point up a difference between the hearing level of a child's two ears.

Another simple but clever test seeks to determine whether a young child "hears" or "feels" speech, that is, whether he can perceive the frequency components of speech or only the gross intensity and time information. This Auditory Numbers Test (**ANT**) does not require a special speech audiometer, and can be delivered by live voice through a high-fidelity amplifying system that can present speech at least 20 dB above the listener's speech detection threshold. The young child is asked to discriminate among and recognize the numbers *one, two, three, four* and *five,* each consisting of a single syllable when spoken. Five cards are placed before the child; each depicts groups of one to five ants with corresponding numerals. The examiner points to each card and counts aloud the number of ants. When the test begins, the examiner covers his or her mouth and says a single number, such as *five,* and observes the child's pointing response. A child who discriminates frequency spectrum information (one who "hears") will point to the #5 card, while a child who detects only the presence of a single syllable pulse (one who only "feels") will point to the #1 card. The examiner then alternates presenting a single number and counting numbers, noting how the child responds to each single number. Each ear is tested separately (81).

The capacity to recognize the pattern of syllables in words, even if words are not understood, should contribute to the child's perception of speech and to monitoring the syllable patterns of his own speech production. While giving the Auditory Numbers Test, the examiner may note the young child's accuracy in identifying the number of syllable pulses as the examiner counts *one, one-two, one-two-three,* etc.

A more difficult test of perception of syllable patterns combines words of one syllable, words of two syllables with equal syllable stress, and two-syllable words with primary stress on the first syllable. This test requires not only recognition of the number of syllable pulses detected, but discrimination between a long-short (or strong-weak) pattern and a long-long (or strong-strong) pattern when the child hears a two-syllable word. Children with pure-tone threshold levels of less than 95 dB have little difficulty perceiving these syllable stress patterns, while those with pure-tone threshold levels greater than 95 dB vary widely in their accuracy, suggesting a capacity for determining stress patterns not predicted by pure-tone testing. The child's experience or training with perception of syllable stress patterns may be reflected in these variations (345).

In this section we have cited only a few examples of ways to measure the hearing capacity of deaf children. The growing body of literature on the audiology of deafness is relevant for the teacher of speech. The auditory skills matrix of Table III-3 may suggest further tests or procedures that can be developed for perceptual tasks at several levels of speech stimuli in order to determine the difference between ears and/or a child's overall ability to detect, discriminate, recognize and comprehend speech. A useful battery of speech-feature tests may be developed by considering each of the acoustic features of speech described in the next section.

THE ACOUSTIC FEATURES OF SPEECH

The Speech Spectrum

Speech is very complex in *frequency* compared to a pure tone, containing combinations of frequencies ranging from as low as 100 hz to as high as 10000 Hz (24, 60, 61, 253, 284). The speech we produce matches the characteristics of the normal ear, so that most speech information is carried in a range of frequencies where the ear is most sensitive, between 400 Hz and 3000 Hz. Therefore, 500 Hz, 1000 Hz and 2000 Hz on the audiogram are called the "speech frequencies." In order to understand speech easily, the range of frequencies (frequency bandwidth) from 500 Hz to 2000 Hz should be audible. Most telephones, accordingly, have a frequency bandwidth from 300 Hz to 3000 Hz.

The *intensity* characteristics of speech are also complex. When one person talks to another at a distance of about 1 meter or 1 yard, speech is received at an average level of about 50 dB above the normal threshold for hearing. In ordinary conversational speech, there is an intensity range of about 30 dB from the softest to the loudest speech sound. In order to understand speech easily, this 30 dB range of intensity through the speech frequencies should be audible to the listener.

Speech also varies in overall intensity from moment to moment, and at any given moment varies in intensity among areas of frequency. The relative intensity among different frequency areas of speech is called the **speech spectrum.** The average spectrum of conversational speech of several talkers recorded over a long period of time, and taking into account the sensitivity of the ear for different frequencies, would be heard by a normal ear at levels shown on the audiogram form of Figure III-3. The intensity range of 30 dB for conversational speech is about − 18 dB and + 12 dB around each of the average hearing levels for the different frequencies included in Table III-4.

The threshold audiogram at the bottom of Figure III-3 illustrates that conversational speech would be completely inaudible to a person with the indicated hearing level. Even if speakers shouted they might only reach an average level of 75 dB and still be inaudible to a person with the threshold-hearing level of the left ear. The need for amplifying the speech spectrum is obvious if speech is to be audible.

Voice

The *fundamental frequency* of voice is determined by the rate of opening and closing of the vocal folds as described in Chapter I. The listener perceives the fundamental frequency, which is the lowest frequency component of

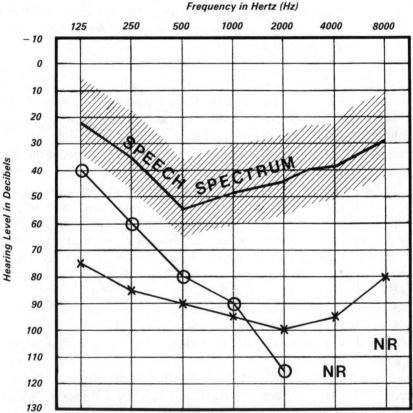

Figure III-3. *A pure-tone audiogram form showing the long-term average speech spectrum at a normal conversational level. Since the speech spectrum is at a level much greater than 0 dB (normal hearing-threshold level), the entire spectrum is heard by a normal ear. The hearing-threshold levels and audiometric configurations shown for the left ear (X) and right ear (O) of a person with severe-to-profound hearing level indicate that none of the unamplified speech spectrum is audible to either ear.*

Frequency in Hertz	125	250	500	750	1000	1500	2000	3000	4000	6000	8000
Earphones	22	36	55	52	49	48	46	40	39	33	29
Field	20	41	55	52	49	50	54	52	52	40	32

Table III-4. *Average hearing level in dB of the spectrum of conversational speech under earphones (ANSI 1969) and in sound field. The typical range of intensity of the speech spectrum is − 18 dB and + 12 dB around these averages. (Courtesy David Pascoe, Central institute for the Deaf)*

speech, as the pitch of the speaker's voice. As indicated in Chapter I, typical fundamental frequencies are about 100 Hz to 150 Hz for men, about 225 Hz for women, and 265 Hz for preadolescent children. Normal listeners distinguish a male from a female speaker primarily by the great difference in voice pitch, but they may also use the typically greater loudness of the male voice for a cue as well.

The fundamental frequency of voice is an intense component of the speech spectrum (72). Fortunately, the normal ear is less sensitive for these low-frequency sounds or otherwise they might "mask" out softer sounds of higher frequencies where most speech information is contained. The speech spectrum of Figure III-3 was averaged from a mixture of male and female voices, but a male speaker's spectrum would include slightly more audible energy at 125 Hz.

Most persons with severe-to-profound hearing levels have better hearing sensitivity at lower frequencies than at higher frequencies, exemplified by the threshold audiogram for the right ear in Figure III-3. Usually their hearing-threshold levels at 125 Hz and 250 Hz, near the fundamental frequencies of voice, are better than at the frequencies where most of the information necessary for understanding speech is carried, 400 Hz through 3000 Hz. Therefore, if the speech spectrum of Figure III-3 was merely made somewhat louder overall, it might be possible for the deaf person to "hear" speech, that is, to detect the fundamental frequency or sound, but not to "understand" speech, since he would not hear the important speech frequencies.

Voice quality refes to the combination of fundamental frequency and the harmonics that are commonly emphasized by resonance in a speaker's vocal tract. The harmonics are of higher frequencies than the fundamental frequency and decrease in intensity as frequency increases (see Chapter I). A deaf person with better hearing sensitivity in the lower frequencies might hear the fundamental frequency of voice but hear little or none of the higher harmonics. Therefore, a deaf person is less likely to perceive the quality of voice that distinguishes one speaker from another with the same fundamental frequency. Some deaf persons may not even be able to distinguish human voice from other kinds of noise. It may be possible, however, for a deaf person to recognize whether a voice he hears is that of a male or a female, using cues of differences in fundamental frequency and loudness.

Even though a deaf person may not hear enough of the higher frequencies necessary to comprehend speech, or hear the harmonics of voice quality in order to recognize speakers, it is important that his own voice be made loud enough to be audible so that he can monitor it. It is also important that the voice of others be made audible because the fundamental frequency carries useful information about the articulatory and rhythmic features of speech.

Speech Rhythm

The rhythm of conversational speech, described in Chapter I, differs markedly from either musical rhythms or the highly repetitive rhythms of poetry. When we produce speech with its usual and conventional rhythm, we contribute both to the naturalness of its sound, and to the understanding of words. Because speech rhythm involves units larger than the segments of phonemes and syllables, its features are sometimes referred to as the "suprasegmental" aspects of speech.

Many features of speech rhythm are carried by the acoustic information that is usually readily available through hearing aids to deaf listeners. Even if a listener cannot understand individual words, he may be able to receive important aspects of speech rhythm through the ear, helping both his perception and production of speech.

If a listener can detect whether sound is present or absent, and can determine when a sound is continued and when it is terminated, he can perceive the *phrasing* of speech (see Chapter I). A speech phrase is a continuous utterance bounded by silent intervals or pauses. Each phrase usually consists of several words produced in concatenation and within a given period of time. This grouping or chunking of speech presents the listener with the continuous sound of words that are related in meaning in order to help in his perception of rapid speech. It also forces the speaker to link words by coarticulating the sounds that occur at the ending and beginning of words. If any part of the speech spectrum can be heard, a deaf person may perceive the phrasing of normal speech, attempt to imitate it, and monitor his own production.

The process of deliberately formulating accurate syntax and careful articulation tends to slow the rate of speech of deaf children, often causing them to produce speech in disjointed, word-by-word segments. This abnormal phrasing interferes with intelligibility and causes their speech to sound unnatural. Since speech phrasing may be available through hearing aids even to very deaf children, and since it conveys information about timing as well as the grouping of words, it is apparent that phrasing is one important aspect of speech that should be made available through the auditory channel.

Accent is the stress placed on a syllable within a word compared to other syllables in that word (see Chapter I). It is characteristic of English that each word of more than one syllable has a syllable stressed above the others, and that stressed syllables are audibly different from those of lesser stress. *Emphasis* refers to the stressing of a word or words within a phrase or sentence. Both accent and emphasis are produced by a speaker placing greater physiological force on the production of the stressed unit, resulting in an increase in the acoustic *frequency, intensity* and *duration* of the stressed unit.

Any one of these acoustic features may be significant by itself for the perception of stress. While listeners with normal hearing may use all three features to determine stress, it may be possible for a deaf person to recognize stress just by the increased loudness, or by the increase in duration of a continued sound, or by a combination of the two features. It is the *relative* loudness and duration of the sound that must be perceived rather than an *absolute* level. The task of the listener is to determine whether there was a sudden increase in loudness or an unusual extension of the duration of a syllable or word above the ordinary pattern of timing. Since both duration and loudness perception are less likely to be affected by deafness than pitch perception, these two features of accent and emphasis may be available, with amplification, through the auditory channel.

As described in Chapter I, *intonation* involves changes in the fundamental pitch of voice over an entire speech phrase, in addition to whatever pitch changes might occur for accent and emphasis. It adds meaning to phrases, telling the listener whether the speaker has finished, whether the utterance was a statement, an exclamation or a question, and it can also indicate a mood of excitement or enthusiasm. Intonation patterns, like accent and emphasis, involve *relative* differences in pitch, rising or falling in relation to the previous pitch level, rather than absolute pitch levels. The task of the listener is to determine whether there was a change in pitch, whether it was rising or falling, and how rapidly it was changing.

Since pitch discrimination is very likely to be affected by severe hearing loss, perception of intonation through pitch changes may not be available to all deaf children, even with amplification. Tests for determining this ability in individual children would be appropriate. Changes in pitch might be perceived as changes in overall loudness by some deaf children, since they usually hear sounds of different frequencies at different loudness levels. A rising *pitch* might thus be heard by a typical deaf child as a sound of decreasing *loudness*. However, if the production of intonation patterns is to be learned by deaf children, even though much of the pitch information may not be accurately perceived, experience suggests that in order to learn production of these patterns at an early age it will have to be learned through the auditory channel.

Articulation

Articulation is the shaping of the breath stream, whether voiced or voiceless, to form the phoneme segments of speech, as described in Chapters I and VI. The task for the speaker is to produce the phonemes in varied combinations so that they can be recognized by a listener in order for their combinations to be associated with words of the language. Recognition of the phonemes depends upon the listener receiving and discriminating a complex pattern of frequency, intensity, and durational relations. Since phonemes occur in different phonetic contexts, and since they are produced by speakers with different fundamental frequency of voice and different sizes of the resonating cavities, the acoustic cues for each phoneme are not always invariant. Consider, for example, the influence of phonetic context on the differences among the sounds of the phoneme *t* in the word *too* (where it is released with an audible explosion of breath), in the phrase *can't do* (where it is essentially a moment of silence between two other sounds), and in the word *better* (where it is almost a **d** sound).

The phonemes are produced, however, with **redundant** information: that is, their acoustic features are more than is absolutely necessary for their recognition, so that a listener may recognize a phoneme without necessarily receiving all of its acoustic information. The process by which we recognize phonemes in order to understand speech is not fully understood, but it is clear that a mutually understood code of essential acoustic information must pass from the speaker to the listener.

Vowels

Vowel phonemes are characterized by predictable bands of frequency with peaks in which intensity is especially high. These acoustic peaks, formed by the resonating cavities above the glottis, are called *formants,* and are written F_1, F_2, F_3, etc., to designate the first formant (peak at the lowest frequency), the second formant (peak at the next highest frequency), and the third formant, respectively. Although there may be several formants associated with a particular resonant sound, the first two or three are most important to be heard and discriminated by a listener, and vowels can usually be recognized when only the first two formants are audible. Both the frequency position and the separation in frequency of formants appear to be important acoustic cues for vowel recognition.

In Figure III-4, the first (F_1), second (F_2), and third (F_3) formants of the vowel **oo,** averaged for conversational speech, are plotted on an audiogram form at the frequency areas and intensity levels at which they might be heard by a listener with normal hearing. Like the rest of the speech spectrum, these formants of the vowel **oo** will not be audible to the ears whose hearing threshold levels are represented on the audiogram of Figure III-4 unless the speech signal is amplified. However, if the speech spectrum were to be amplified 30 dB to 40 dB *equally* across the speech frequencies, only the first formant would be audible to the right ear and the listener would not recognize the vowel sound as **oo.** *Selective frequency amplification* would be required to make at least the F_1 and F_2 of **oo** audible to this deaf listener.

In order to estimate potential audibility of the formants of **oo** and other vowels for other deaf listeners using amplification, the formants of each of the vowels may be similarly plotted on an individual's audiogram form, using the values for center frequencies and relative intensities of averaged vowels spoken by women, shown in Table III-5. Formant frequencies for men are typically lower and for children somewhat higher. Greater lip rounding tends to lower the frequencies of all formants. Differences and similarities among vowels may be noted in Table III-5. For example, if only the first formants of vowels were audible, **ee** and **oo** (310 Hz and 370 Hz) would sound nearly the same, while if their second formants (2790 Hz and 950 Hz) were audible, they would sound very different. Similarly, **-a-** and **-o-** have nearly identical first formants (860 Hz and 850 Hz) while their second formants (2050 Hz and 1220 Hz) are very different. Note, also, that **ur** does not differ greatly from **-u-** in either its first or second formants, but that adding their third formants (1960 Hz and 2780 Hz) would make them sound different.

When vowels are stressed, either in accented syllables or in emphasized words, the greater vocal effort makes the overall vowel sound louder with proportionally greater intensity in the second and third formants. Vowels are among the loudest speech sounds, requiring very little vocal effort to increase their loudness. The vowels **aw, -o-, -u-,** and **-a-,** for which the mouth is open widest, tend to be the loudest.

Vowels also vary in duration, but the acoustic information from durational differences may not be so important for identifying the vowel sound as in telling about the consonant sounds that follow the vowel. For example, most vowels are shortened when followed by a voiceless stop consonant (**p, t,** or **k**), as in *beet* and *back,* and most vowels are lengthened when followed by a nasal consonant, as in *bean* and *bank.* Vowels are also lengthened when given stress for syllable accent or word emphasis. Since any part of the vowel that is audible may carry cues about duration, this kind of information is likely to be available to the deaf listener through amplification.

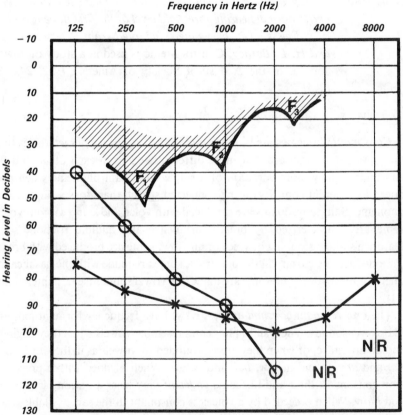

Figure III-4. *Averaged center frequencies and sensation levels above normal hearing-threshold level of the first three formants of the vowel oo (/u/) spoken by women. See Table III-5 for other vowel formant values.*

Vowel Formants		ee /i/	-i- /ɪ/	-e- /ɛ/	-a- / æ /	oo /u/	-oo- /ʊ/	aw / ɔ /	-o- / ɑ/	-u- / ʌ /	ur / ɝ /
F_1	Hz	310	430	610	860	370	470	590	850	760	500
	dB	49	54	56	58	52	57	58	58	57	52
F_2	Hz	2790	2480	2330	2050	950	1160	920	1220	1400	1640
	dB	41	41	47	50	40	48	52	55	50	46
F_3	Hz	3310	3070	2990	2850	2670	2680	2710	2810	2780	1960
	dB	38	38	41	43	22	31	31	37	38	42

Table III-5.   *Averaged center frequencies and approximate sensation levels above normal hearing-threshold level of the first three formants of vowels spoken by women. (adapted from Peterson, G. E. and H. L. Barney,* Control Methods used in a study of vowels. Journal of the Acoustical Society of America *1952, 24, 182) (245).*

Consonants

Consonant phonemes are more diverse in their acoustic characteristics than the vowels. Not only are they more differentiated from each other, but the consonants show more variation of a single consonant phoneme when produced in different contexts during connected speech than does a single vowel phoneme. Some consonants are produced with voice and some without voice, some are characterized by breath turbulence and audible friction, some feature a sudden stopping of voice or air flow, some are produced with breath exploded from a closure in the oral tract, some are made with the nasal cavity open for resonation, and some are made like vowel sounds (see Chapters I and VI).

The *oral resonant consonants* (r, l, w, y) have frequency formant patterns like vowel sounds. The r and l phonemes resemble vowels when they begin or end an utterance, or when they are surrounded by vowels as in the words *row, bar* and *arrow,* and in *low, ball* and *below.* When blended with a preceding stop consonant, the r and l become *glides* of very brief duration, as in *green* and *blow.* When preceded by a voiceless consonant in the same syllable, the r and l are made essentially as voiceless sounds as in *try* and *play.* The resonant consonants w and y also have frequency formant patterns resembling the oo and ee, respectively. The w has slightly lower formants than oo, and the y has slightly higher formants then ee. The w and y are always glides of very brief duration, and are always followed by a vowel sound. The rapid transitional movement from the **r, l, w** and **y** formant positions, as they change to the formant positions of the following vowel sounds, appear to be the critical acoustic cues for recognition of these brief resonant consonants. Hearing the formant *transitions* of the first two formants of **w** and **y** is sufficient for their recognition, while the **r** and **l** usually require hearing the formant transitions of the first three formants.

The *nasal resonant consonants* (**m, n, ng**) have formant bands, too, but with an additional band of energy centered around 250 Hz (99). Their higher formants are weaker than formants for vowels, and the normal listener's overall impression is that the nasal resonant consonant is softer than the vowels around it. The band of energy around 250 Hz, usually available to a deaf listener through amplification, may be sufficient for recognizing a sound as being a nasal resonant when the higher formants cannot be heard. Discriminating which of the three nasal resonant consonants was heard seems to depend upon the transition of the formants (particularly the second formant) between the nasal consonant and the following vowel. The *place* of closure for the nasal resonant consonants influences this transition of formants so that the **m**, which has its closure at the lips and is lowest in frequency, deflects the beginning of the second formant of the following vowel toward the lower **m** frequency. The **n**, which is closed by the tongue tip against the alveolar ridge and is higher in frequency, inclines the beginning of the second formant of the following vowel toward the higher **n** frequency. The **ng**, which is closed by the back of the tongue against the front of the velum and is still higher in frequency than the **n**, inclines the beginning of the second formant of the following vowel still more sharply toward the higher frequencies.

The *stop consonants,* like the nasal resonant consonants, are characterized by rapid closure in the oral tract—at the lips for the **p** and **b**, at the tongue tip and alveolar ridge for the **t** and **d**, and at the back of the tongue and front of the velum for **k** and **g**. The stops are very brief sounds, and the **p, t,** and **k** are made without voice so that they are not easily audible. Acoustic information about the place of closure in the oral tract (distinguishing **p** and **b**, from **t** and **d**, from **k** and **g**) seems to depend greatly upon the deflection toward a higher or lower frequency of the second formant of the vowel that either precedes or follows the stop consonant, rather than upon hearing the rather weak stop consonant itself. The stop consonant itself consists of either an attenuation of sound (**b, d, g**) or a short period of silence (**p, t, k**), sometimes followed by a burst of exploded voice or breath. The attenuating-stopping period is shorter for the voiced stop consonants (**b, d, g**) than for the voiceless stop consonants (**p, t, k**). In order to recognize the **t** in *into,* the listener would need to hear the short period of silence (indicating a voiceless stop consonant) and the deflection of the second formant of the vowel **oo** toward a higher frequency (signaling closure by the tongue tip at the alveolar ridge) as the vowel begins.

The *fricative consonants* are among the least intense speech sounds (**th** being the weakest of all) and are high pitched compared to the vowels and resonant consonants (68). As a result, they are the least likely to be available to a deaf person through the auditory system. The voiced fricatives, **v, th, z,** and **zh,** include the low-frequency sound from vibration of the vocal folds. Voicing in fricatives is also signaled by the relative duration of a vowel and the following fricative. The vowel before a voiced fricative (*leave*) is longer than the same vowel before a voiceless fricative (*leaf*), and the voiceless fricative is shorter than its voiced counterpart (long vowel + short fricative = voiced fricative; short vowel + long fricative = voiceless fricative). The frequency spectrum of the fricatives, other than the voicing component below 500 Hz, is very broad and the formants are not as clearly defined as are vowels. The **s** has very little energy below 3000 Hz, and has its energy peak at about 4000 Hz. The **sh** is the strongest fricative and has its lowest energy peak at about 2200 Hz, with its main energy peak at 3000 Hz. The **th** has its major peak at about 2200 Hz, but it is relatively weak and its other frequency peaks are above 4000 Hz. The **f** has a broad spectrum with little apparent peaking and is also relatively weak. The **h,** being influenced by the vowels that precede and follow it, has no predictable formant structure of its own.

The acoustic features of speech described above suggest to the audiologist some speech-feature tests that might yield important information about the hearing ability of deaf children (12, 13, 162, 239). In addition to hearing sensitivity at threshold and at tolerance levels, supra-threshold abilities necessary for perceiving speech include discriminating frequency differences, intensity differences, and temporal differences among sounds. The importance of the transitions between phonemes in understanding speech suggest that judgments about the direction and the rate of change in frequency and intensity may also be essential to perceive.

We have suggested some references at the end of this book on the increasingly useful body of knowledge about acoustical phonetics and speech perception. This area of study is as relevant to the teacher as to the audiologist concerned with using hearing to teach speech (18). One example of the classroom or clinical application of phonetics is in choosing material for auditory training. Since we know that acoustic information necessary for recognizing the products of articulation includes the transitions and the influences that phonemes have on each other when produced in connected speech, auditory training exercises for helping a child develop and maintain speech should include units of speech that are at least a syllable in length, so that these important acoustic coarticulation effects will be available.

The features of speech described in the literature and summarized in this section also suggest the task of electro-acoustic amplification for speech—to reproduce those essential acoustic features of speech, and to make them audible to the ears of varied hearing levels described in the first section of this chapter (243).

ELECTRO-ACOUSTIC AMPLIFICATION FOR SPEECH

There are two concepts in the title of this section that should be clarified at the outset. *First:* it is acoustic energy or sound that is to be amplified, not the auditory system or the ear. Amplified acoustic energy is applied to the ear and drives the auditory system, but a hearing aid only amplifies sound. It does not make the ear or hearing more normal. *Second:* there is a difference between amplification *of* speech and amplification *for* speech. When used to help someone produce his own speech, acoustic amplification requires some special considerations. Of course the speech that one hears from others contributes significantly to speech development, but hearing one's own speech is very important for monitoring what is produced and is essential for comparing it to the speech of others.

The Nature of Acoustic Amplification

The intensity of the speech spectrum matches the sensitivity of the ear so that people can talk easily a few meters away from each other. Speech becomes inaudible when the speaker is either too far away or does not speak with enough effort, or when the listener has impaired hearing sensitivity. The simplest form of speech amplification is to "speak up" or move closer to the listener. Long before electronic hearing aids, very young hearing-impaired children were taught on a teacher's lap as she spoke in a strong voice directly into their ears. Mechanical hearing aids used the principle of the funnel, altering the original sound by receiving and collecting sound energy over a large area and presenting it to the ear concentrated in a smaller area. "Ear trumpets" sometimes had a long tube that reached out to be closer to the speaker. These devices often raised the intensity of the original sound enough to give real help to a hard of hearing person, and even the cupped hand at the ear raises the sound by about 10 decibels. The mechanical aid or cupped hand probably helps most by signalling the speaker to raise his voice, perhaps adding another 10 dB or "human-effort amplification."

Electronic or electro-acoustic amplification involves the principle of substituting a strong new source of sound for the original weaker sound source, and using the original source to tailor the pattern of the new sound. The sound of speech consists physically of sound waves—pulses of compression and rarefaction of air pressure produced at the larynx and in the mouth. Similar sound waves can also be produced by electronic equipment, using a battery or electrical current from a wall socket to push the diaphragm of a loud speaker or earphone so that it sets up audible pulses of compressions and rarefactions of air pressure. The electronically produced sound can be much stronger than is possible for the sound produced by the human speech mechanism, depending upon the strength of the amplifier's power source.

Figure III-5 illustrates the nature of electro-acoustic amplification. The original sound of speech from the mouth is diffused from its source, decreasing rapidly in intensity as its distance from the source increases, so that it is much lower in intensity by the time it enters the ear of the distant listener. Because of the listener's hearing impairment, the sound may be inaudible or not loud enough to be understood. The sound waves from the original speech source are intercepted by a microphone, converted (transduced) into a pattern of electrical energy flowing along a wire, and directed toward a transistor. A power source (the battery of a hearing aid) generates a strong electrical current that flows along another wire toward the diaphragm of a loudspeaker (the receiver or earphone of a hearing aid). The transistor is interposed along the wire to act as a valve that can control the flow of electrical current. If the transistor is not activated, the strong current is steady and the diaphragm is stationary. As the pattern of electrical energy from the original speech source reaches the transistor, it activates the transistor's valving action so that the very strong and steady electrical current flowing from the power source is alternately increased and decreased, responding to and reflecting the pattern from the microphone. The strong electrical current flowing from the power source now pushes and pulls against the diaphragm of the earphone, causing it to create sound waves in the air that mirror the original sound waves from the human speaker, but at a much more intense level. These strong sound waves arrive at the ear of the hearing-impaired listener at a level that may now be audible.

Basic electro-acoustic amplification systems consist of the following components:

(1) *A microphone* to receive the pattern of sound waves of the speech signal and convert or transduce it to a pattern of electrical current.

(2) *A source of electrical power* that can produce a strong steady flow of electrical current.

(3) *An amplifying circuit* that brings together the pattern of electrical current from the microphone and the strong steady flow of electrical current from the power source in a transistor-valving action that tailors the pattern of the strong current from the power source.

(4) *An earphone* (sometimes called a "receiver") that receives the strong pattern of electrical current and converts or transduces it into a pattern of sound waves that forms a strong speech signal.

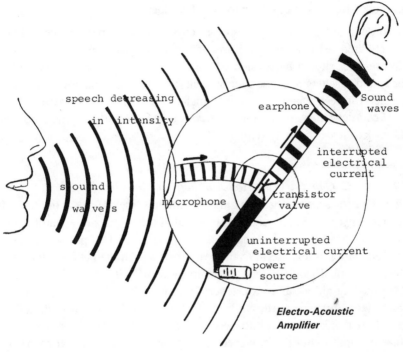

Figure III-5.   *Diagram to illustrate the principle of electro-acoustic amplification. Speech sound waves from the mouth, too weak to be audible to the distant or impaired ear, are received by a microphone of the electro-acoustic amplifier. Here they are converted to electrical energy and transmitted to transistors in an amplifying circuit. A power source drives a strong, steady electrical current to the transistor where the current is interrupted by the energy pattern from the microphone. The strong electrical current, mirroring the pattern of energy from the microphone, pushes against the diaphragm of a loudspeaker or earphone, creating a strong pattern of sound waves that is received by the ear.*

(5) *Controls* that usually include an "on-off" switch to prohibit or permit the flow of current from the power source, and a volume dial to reduce or increase the flow of current from the power source.

Other controls can be added to these components, and electro-acoustic amplifying systems can be packaged in a variety of ways, ranging from a tiny all-in-the-ear hearing aid to a large public-address system (16). The type of package depends upon the characteristics of the system considered desirable.

Desirable Characteristics of Amplifiers For Speech

In order to design the best possible electro-acoustic amplifiers that will help deaf children learn to produce and maintain speech, their most desirable characteristics should be considered (38, 57). Compromises may have to be made, and teachers and audiologists will have to assign priorities. Here we consider fourteen charactristics that include *acoustic characteristics, directional characteristics,* portability or *wearing characteristics* of the amplifier, and *maintenance* of the system.

Acoustic Characteristics

1. Functional Gain Sufficient for Audibility of Speech

The *acoustic gain* of a hearing aid is traditionally the difference (increase) in decibels between the input signal, measured at the microphone, and the output signal, measured at the loudspeaker or earphone. This physical measure of amplification is less useful to the teacher of speech than is *functional gain* (243). Functional gain describes the improvement in the intensity of speech that a hearing aid yields to a listener. It is the difference in decibels of the speech signal, arriving at the eardrum without a hearing aid and with a hearing aid. It therefore takes into account not only the characteristics of the acoustic amplifier but the influence of the body and head, the ear canal, and the ear mold. Functional gain is measured using audiometric procedures with the listener wearing the hearing aid, and the results can be plotted on an audiogram form.

The gain of a hearing aid should be sufficient to raise the level of speech comfortably above the listener's hearing threshold. *But how far above his threshold?* Since the speech signal at which normal listeners easily understand speech is approximately 50 dB above their thresholds (see Figure III-3, page 79), it would seem desirable to have gain from a hearing aid that would present the speech signal to deaf persons at a level 50 dB above their thresholds. With the hearing-threshold levels of a deaf person presented in Figure III-3, a 95 dB average for the speech frequencies in either ear, it would first appear appropriate, therefore, to present speech at a 145 dB (95 dB + 50 dB) hearing level in each ear in order to recreate for this deaf person the sensation of listening to speech at the comfortable supra-threshold level that a normal listener experiences. However, this would present speech at a level well above the listener's tolerance level, as was illustrated in Figure III-2, page 73, so that speech would not just be uncomfortable to hear, it would be painful as well (285). To avoid discomfort, speech can be presented only 15 dB to 20 dB above this deaf listener's hearing-threshold level. With speech presented at such soft levels, discrimination and understanding of speech is greatly reduced, and children may ignore the difficult-to-hear signal altogether.

In order to amplify speech for the ear whose hearing-threshold levels and tolerance levels are presented in Figure III-2, we will have to make compromises. The gain of the hearing aid will have to be such that speech is presented above the threshold level but not at or above the tolerance level. In the example of Figure III-2, speech cannot be presented more than 25 dB above the threshold level of the left ear at any frequency without exceeding the listener's tolerance level.

In addition, the natural 30 dB intensity range of the speech spectrum cannot be presented to this deaf listener since the dynamic range for that ear is only 25 dB at 500 Hz, 25 dB at 1000 Hz, and 20 dB at 2000 Hz. The closer the gain of the hearing aid brings the average of the speech spectrum to the tolerance level, the more restricted the intensity range of the speech signal will necessarily be.

2. Amplification of the Acoustic Spectrum of Speech

In order for the important frequencies of the speech spectrum to be audible to the listener, it would be desirable for the acoustic amplifier to reproduce acoustic energy in a frequency bandwidth at least from 400 Hz through 3000 Hz, and preferably from 200 Hz through 8000 Hz (105, 243). The frequency response of the microphone, the amplifying circuit, and the loudspeaker or earphone should combine with the characteristics of the earmold to provide the listener with this broad bandwidth of speech energy. Any reduction in this spectrum bandwidth causes distortion of the speech signal that is known to make understanding speech more difficult for listeners with normal hearing. Not all hearing aids provide such a broad frequency response.

3. Fidelity of Reproduction of the Speech Spectrum

Not only should the frequency bandwidth of the speech spectrum be reproduced, but it should be reproduced so that the spectrum through the speech frequencies is presented to each ear appropriately above hearing-threshold levels. "High-fidelity" that reproduces the amplified speech spectrum with equal gain throughout the spectrum bandwidth is not enough for the person with hearing impairment. The configuration of the threshold audiogram must be taken into account so that the **amplified speech spectrum is reproduced relative to the listener's hearing-threshold levels** at each of the important speech frequencies (243). The relative perceived loudness of the different frequencies amplified at supra-threshold levels may also need to be tested in order to maintain the relative loudness level of the original speech spectrum.

In Figure III-6, amplification of the speech spectrum has been tailored as nearly as possible to the hearing-threshold configuration of the left ear of a listener. However, note the compromises that have been made compared to ideal amplification. *First:* we cannot present speech at 50 dB above the

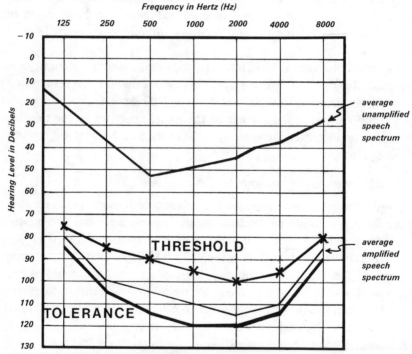

Figure III-6. *Amplification of the average speech spectrum above the hearing-threshold level of the listener's left ear but below the tolerance level. The amplified speech spectrum is reproduced relative to the listener's hearing level and tolerance level at each of the frequencies on the audiogram. Note that the listener's restricted dynamic range of hearing limits the intensity range around the average amplified speech spectrum.*

listener's threshold because this would exceed his tolerance. At best he will receive speech only 15 dB or 20 dB above the level at which he just begins to hear speech. The teacher may want to listen to speech presented at 15 dB to 20 dB above her own hearing-threshold level in order to experience the effort that a deaf child must expend in order to attend to amplified speech. *Second:* the natural 30 dB intensity range of speech sounds will not be possible because the listener's dynamic range of hearing is no greater than 25 dB at 500 Hz and 1000 Hz, and only 20 dB at 250 Hz and 2000 Hz. In order to permit some range of intensity above the average, the average level of amplified speech cannot be presented close to the tolerance level. Otherwise, loud speech sounds would cause discomfort or pain. *Third:* the relative sensation level of different frequencies of the amplified speech spectrum cannot be maintained to resemble exactly how a normal listener hears the different parts of the unamplified speech spectrum. Compare the relation of normal-hearing threshold and the average unamplified speech spectrum to the impaired listener's threshold and the average amplified speech spectrum. By presenting amplified speech with sufficient gain to be audible at each frequency and yet not exceed tolerance, we will have to vary the relative intensities of some parts of the spectrum. In order to present amplified speech to this ear, we have already introduced three kinds of distortion of the original speech signal.

4. Controlled Power Output

As the input of the speech spectrum varies in intensity with its natural 30 dB range, and as some speakers talk louder or move nearer, the left ear of the deaf listener in Figure III-6 would experience discomfort and perhaps pain with amplification as the sound exceeded the tolerance levels at different frequencies. Even when tolerance levels cannot be easily and accurately measured, as with very young children, it is unwise and even dangerous to permit unlimited output from a hearing aid. To avoid this, the electro-acoustic amplifier should have controls to regulate its *maximum power output (MPO)* at or just below (less than) the tolerance level (measured or estimated) for each of the frequencies for that ear. Two methods of controlling the power output of a hearing aid are "peak clipping," a process by which the speech signal is constantly limited to a fixed maximum, and "compression," in which the gain is automatically reduced as the input increases. Both methods introduce additional distortion in the speech spectrum since each reduces the intensity of the loudest components in relation to the softest.

> In order to illustrate the desirable acoustic characteristics of amplification for speech, and also to point out the difficulty in achieving the ideal, we have used the especially difficult case of an audiogram which represents the hearing-

threshold level of a profoundly deaf person. This is to emphasize our earlier observation about the limitations of an impaired auditory system for teaching speech, and to remind the teacher and audiologist that hearing cannot be made "nearly normal" by the use of a powerful hearing aid.

As a further reminder of the realities of acoustic amplification, we recommend that the amplified speech spectrum be displayed between the threshold level and the tolerance level on the audiogram form, for each ear of each child. This is in preference to displaying the "amplified threshold" or "aided audiogram" for hearing tones. The amplified threshold, that plots the listener's response to tones closer to normal hearing-threshold levels while wearing his hearing aid, suggests an improvement in hearing and may mislead those who teach deaf children about their auditory capabilities.

Awareness of the limitations of using the auditory channel for teaching speech, however, should not deter the teacher from attempting to use hearing to the fullest. Though limited, it may still be a very useful tool in learning speech, even for profoundly deaf children. For the child with greater dynamic range than our example, accommodating the amplified speech spectrum will be less difficult and the benefits for speech are likely to be greater. Demographic data suggest that more than half of the children in schools and classes for hearing-impaired children will have better hearing than our profoundly deaf example. This underlines the necessity of constructive interaction between the *teacher* and the *audiologist* in any school program that takes seriously the use of hearing to teach speech.

Here are two questions, related to acoustic characteristics of the amplifying system, that need to be mutually addressed by the speech teacher and audiologist.

Which amplified acoustic characteristics are best for each of a given child's ears for speech perception?

Which amplifying system (hearing aid components and ear mold) best meets these requirements?

Directional Characteristics

5. Speaker Feedback

For the purpose of aiding a deaf child to produce speech, it is essential that the microphone that picks up the speech signal be placed so that the speaker can hear his own speech output. Otherwise he will not be able to monitor his speech. In a wearable hearing aid, the microphone should be close enough to the child's mouth to receive his speech easily. In some group amplifiers, a single microphone may be placed close to the teacher's mouth in order for her speech signal to predominate over the background noise of the classroom. Such a system deprives the child of acoustic feedback for his own speech. To avoid this, a teacher may move the group-amplifier microphone back and forth between herself and each of the children as they speak, but this places constraints on ease of communication and on mobility of teacher and class. Another solution is to have a microphone at each student's desk or on his amplifier, in addition to the microphone near the teacher's mouth. The arrangement that permits each child feedback of his own speech and yet controls the input of unwanted background noise in the classroom is not easy to accomplish. Here the teacher and audiologist may have some additional questions to consider.

How do we know that a child can hear components of his own speech with an amplifier?

How well does a particular amplifying system feed a child's speech production back to him?

How can we compare different amplifying systems for the quality of speech feedback?

6. Speech Model Reception

For the purpose of aiding a deaf child in producing speech, it is important that the microphone permit hearing the speech of other persons in order to receive speech examples that can be compared with the child's own speech production. In the classroom, his teacher's speech and that of his fellow students should be available to each child. On the playground, too, and in other situations throughout the day, the speech patterns of those who come into contact with the child should be available to him. It is obvious that the microphone of the amplifying system should be portable enough so that the child can carry it with him to places where he talks to people, and that people should not always have to move very close to the microphone in order for the child to hear them talk. For speech model reception, the teacher and audiologist have another question to consider.

With a particular amplifying system, how close must other persons be to the microphone in order for the child to receive their speech pattern?

If the child uses a wearable hearing aid, he and his teacher should be aware of this critical distance for the aid to provide speech amplification.

7. Location of the Source of Speech

Facility with conversation contributes to development of a child's speech. Conversation usually involves eye contact, or at least a speaker and listener facing each other. In a group of people, it is important for a listener to know who is speaking in order to attend to that person and address him in response. For the deaf child, "attending" to the speaker may include speechreading that contributes significantly to speech perception and comprehension. Microphone placement of the amplifier should, therefore, help the listener identify the speaker by permitting him to localize the source of speech.

Here, we consider how the normal listener localizes the source of speech. When speech comes from the right-front of a person, it is received a split second later and sound is slightly softer in the left ear compared to the right. As the listener turns toward the right, he experiences a balance in time and loudness of the speech signal for the two ears, and confirms his judgment by seeing the moving mouth of the speaker. Even if the source of the sound is not visible, a listener can judge its location by moving in the direction in which the sound becomes louder.

When an amplifying system has a single microphone that feeds the speech signal to equally impaired ears, the listener will always perceive the speech as coming from directly in front of him. If one ear has a greater loss than the other, he will hear speech coming from the direction of the better ear. However, he will not be able to localize the source of sound except by moving in the direction in which the sound becomes steadily louder. If amplified speech is delivered to only one ear when both are severely impaired, speech will always seem to come from the ear with amplification.

It is obvious that having individual, balanced amplifying systems for each ear is the best condition for locating the source of speech. Of course, microphones should be set far enough apart to permit a difference in the arrival time and loudness of speech. However, if one amplifier should be adjusted so that it delivers speech at a higher sensation level than the other amplifier, speech will always seem to come from that direction. If the gain characteristics of a hearing aid change or if a child's hearing level changes because of an ear infection on a given day, the child will have difficulty locating speakers throughout that day. This suggests *daily surveillance,* both of the output of hearing aids and of the child's hearing level, in order to maintain the hearing-impaired child's ability to localize sources of speech and other sounds. In their work together to help the child with speech, the teacher may now discuss these questions with the audiologist.

How can we tell when a child is localizing the source of sounds to the best of his ability?

What is the best distance for separation of the microphones of amplifiers for the two ears?

How should two hearing aids be set each day to achieve a balance of loudness for the two ears of each child?

8. High Speech Signal-to-Noise Ratio of Amplified Sound

The acoustic amplifier does not just amplify speech. It amplifies all sound, including all unwanted noise within its frequency and intensity range. If microphones of an amplifying system are placed in such a way that they amplify the speech signal and background noise of the classroom so they are presented to the ear at equal sensation levels, we would have a 1/1 signal-to-noise ratio. Persons with normal hearing would have difficulty understanding speech under these conditions. For hearing-impaired children, it is desirable to have the speech signal well above the noise of the background as it reaches the ear (232). Having the speech signal at least 30 decibels above the level of background noise is a desirable target.

In addition to reducing background noise, a favorable speech signal-to-noise ratio can be achieved by positioning the microphone as close to the speech-signal source as possible. A microphone on the child's chest is less desirable than one at the ear or just to one side of the speaker's mouth. A single microphone hanging from the ceiling or on a table in the classroom invites background noise, while reducing the speech signal when children and teacher are far from it. The greater the distance a speaker is from a child's wearable hearing aid, the poorer the signal-to-noise ratio is likely to be. The teacher and audiologist may raise these queastions.

What are the signal-to-noise ratios for a child's amplified sound under various conditions throughout the regular teaching day?

How can signal-to-noise ratio be improved by positioning the microphones of an amplification system?

Wearing Characteristics

9. Comfort

The system should be comfortable enough so that a child can use or wear it all day. The ear inserts should fit comfortably, or if muffs are used with earphones they should not be too tight against a child's head or too heavy for daily wearing. The weight of a wearable unit should not be a burden, particularly to a young child. Attachment straps of body-worn hearing aids should not be tight on the child.

10. Freedom of Movement

The amplifying unit should permit maximum movement within and outside a classroom throughout the day. Some wired systems require that the child stay at his desk where the group amplifier terminal is positioned, or require that he take off his amplifier while working at the chalkboard or reciting before the class. Some systems may require that the children stay close to the teacher or stay in one classroom throughout the day. Particularly for young children, freedom of movement seems to be an important condition for learning language.

11. Simplicity of Operation

Operation of the amplification system should be within the ability of the child to manage, if at all possible, and not so complex that difficulties of its management by the teacher deters its habitual usage. If its operation and adjustments are not well understood by the classroom teacher, or require a great deal of care and adjustment, he or she is not likely to use it at maximum efficiency on a regular basis.

12. Consistency Throughout the Day

The amplifying unit should not have to be taken off for recess or other activities. If more than one acoustic amplification system is used during the day, the characteristics of the different systems should be very similar. Otherwise, the child may receive different information from the speech signal through the two systems and not experience a consistent pattern to match to his own production.

Maintenance Characteristics

13. Ruggedness

The amplification system should be sufficiently sturdy to avoid frequent breakdowns that may result from the normal activities of infants and children. Hearing aids that are designed with the careful adult in mind are seldom rugged enough to survive the usual activities of little children. If parents or teachers fear that hearing aids will be damaged during daily activities, they may be inclined to have them taken off and thus may deprive children of opportunities to use them in real-life communication situations. Young parents of infants may be especially concerned that their curious and active baby will damage the expensive hearing aid. Children should be able to engage in most physical education activities, except swimming of course, without having to remove their hearing aids.

14. Repairability

The amplification system should be easily repairable, especially its vulnerable parts, without frequent recourse to return of the unit to a distant factory or laboratory. Repair services should be accessible without undue delays for "down time" when the child may be without amplification, and thus be without either feedback from his speech or the reception of speech models from others.

Systems of Electro-Acoustic Amplification

The speech teacher should keep in mind the desirable characteristics of amplifiers for speech as she considers the array of electro-acoustic devices that are now available and will become available in the future (15, 16, 94). The perfect system, offering all the desirable characteristics described above, is not yet available. Selection entails important compromises.

The "hard-wire" group amplification system is among the oldest in use. It consists of one or more microphones wired to a large amplifying circuit that delivers sound by wires to several sets of earphones. It can have numerous controls and adjustments, and its primary advantages are its wide frequency bandwidth and powerful gain. It limits mobility of the child and is not available outside the classroom. Hence, consistency of amplified sound is not possible. A smaller version of the hard-wire group system is the more portable "desk model." This can be moved from place to place, and can be adjusted for characteristics relevant to each student, but it is not a wearable device that can go everywhere and it usually has only one microphone for receiving speech.

The wearable hearing aid is probably the most common amplification system in use among hearing-impaired children, primarily because of its portability. It is available either as a bodyworn amplifier and microphone case with a cord leading to an earphone, or worn over and behind the ear. The wearable aid enables the greatest mobility and the possibility of a consistent amplified signal throughout the day. Since the microphone is on the child's own body, it can provide good feedback from his own speech, but its distance from other speakers admits unwanted noise resulting in a poor speech-signal-to-noise ratio. Separated microphones of two aids also offer an opportunity for sound source localization, especially when hearing aids are worn on the head to facilitate "searching."

Loop induction systems use magnetic radiation from a microphone and transmitter, utilizing wires looped on the floor, often under a carpet. The child's wearable receiver picks up sound through magnetic radiation rather than from the air, amplifies it and sends it to the ear. When the microphone is close to the teacher's mouth,the child can receive the sound of her speech across the room without the interfering background noises of the classroom that would have been received through the air. The child's reception of sound amplified in this fashion is limited to the classroom equipped with the loop of magnetic wire.

Air broadcasting systems provide the teacher with a microphone connected to a portable amplifier and transmitter, much like a miniature radio station. The child wears a receiver, like a small radio, tuned to the frequency of the teacher's transmitter. When the microphone is close to the teacher's mouth, the child can receive the sound across the room without the interference of background noise from the classroom that would have been received through a microphone located on the child. Such RF (Radio Frequency) or FM (Frequency Modulation) systems often include controls for using a microphone on the child's unit so that he can receive his own speech feedback.

Space-age technology suggests promising advances in providing amplification for deaf children over infra-red rays and perhaps laser beams. Repositioning of micropohones and loud speakers, and increasingly compact circuitry hold promise for increasing gain without feedback squeal in small hearing aids. The future looks promising for improved systems of electro-acoustic amplification for deaf children.

MONITORING HEARING AND AMPLIFICATION FOR SPEECH

We emphasize that a basic principle underlying the use of hearing for developing, improving, and maintaining speech is that the amplified speech signal must be *constantly available* so that the child can rely on its use. This principle is important both for receiving the speech patterns of others and for receiving one's own speech feedback patterns. It is especially important that the child maintain auditory feedback as a significant part of his speech feedback pattern, along with tactile and kinesthetic feedback. When an "auditory only" approach to speech teaching is intended, the constant availability of amplified speech is essential. To assure constancy of amplified speech, a program of careful monitoring is needed (273).

A program of monitoring amplification for speech goes well beyond seeing that the child "has on his hearing aid" every morning. The speech teacher will need the frequent assistance of a hearing aid technician and an audiologist, *preferably on the school campus.* Guidelines for audiology services in schools have been developed by teachers and audiologists (271, 272). One audiologist and one hearing-aid technician have been suggested for each 75 to 80 children in a school, or in closely connected classes. This provides for some regular surveillance of each child's use of amplification. It also provides the possibility of immediate correction at times when a child's hearing aids may not be working properly. Essential elements of a beneficial monitoring program are described below.

Regular and Periodic Hearing Evaluation

A complete hearing evaluation of each child should be performed by an audiologist at the beginning of each school year. Middle-ear impedance tests, as well as those measures that describe the deaf child's hearing capabilities and are necessary for hearing aid selection and fitting, should be conducted at this time. Evaluation of the child's use of amplification should also be made, especially for feedback of the child's own speech. In order to establish this *beginning-of-the-year hearing baseline* for a large group of children within the first few weeks of school, it may be necessary to begin audiologic evaluations for some children before the starting day of school, to add additional audiology staff, or to utilize two or more audiological facilities, since each evaluation may take two hours or more. A hearing-screening evaluation should be performed after the children return from their midwinter recess. In cold climates where ear infections may be more prevalent, this *mid-year evaluation* should be started earlier. The results of the mid-year evaluation and other evaluations during the year should be compared with those of the initial baseline evaluation.

Regular and Periodic Hearing Aid Evaluation

An electro-acoustic examination of each hearing aid should be conducted *at the beginning of each school year,* and then no less than *once a month throughout the school year.* Records of the gain, maximum power output, frequency response, and distortion characteristics should be kept for each hearing aid or classroom amplifier, and placed in a card file or computer so that changes that occur in the response of each hearing aid can be observed. Significant changes in an amplifier are indications for preventive maintenance or replacement (14).

Each morning, a parent, teacher, dormitory counselor, or some other person appointed for this purpose should check the hearing aid by a listening test through an ear insert or other device, check the level of the battery, and check the cord connections for intermittency. This daily test should be carried out as carefully on weekends as on school days. The teacher who first works with the child each day, and the parents on weekends, should also observe the child's responses to amplification by using some simple behavioral tests. As early as possible, the child should be taught to conduct his own tests of his hearing aid batteries, and to listen carefully in order to judge whether his hearing aid is working satisfactorily.

Regular and Periodic Examination of Outer Ear, Ear Canal and Earmold

At least weekly, a special effort should be made by the school nurse, audiologist, or other person appointed for this purpose, to examine each child's ear canals for accumulation of wax and for irritation, and the concha portion of his pinna for signs of irritation from the ear mold. Each ear mold should be cleaned and examined at that time, including a check of its seal with the receiver or tubing. Abnormal feedback squeal should be reported and the cause determined. New ear-molds should be made as needed.

Emergency Hearing and Amplification Services

The times when a child is without his regular amplification or when he is not responding well to sound should be treated as *educational emergencies* when hearing is depended upon for teaching speech. Accordingly, a number of emergency services should be readily available near the location where children are taught, *preferably on the school campus.* These should include immediate electro-acoustic examination of the amplifier or hearing aid when it is not functioning well or when the child is not responding to amplified sound in his customary manner. If the amplifier is not working properly, the school should arrange to have the aid repaired by a technician *on the premises,* or should arrange to have available a similar instrument that can be lent while the child's own aid is being repaired. A reasonable target is to not have the child deprived of his customary amplification *longer than one hour* during any day.

When a child is found not to be responding to sound as well as he usually does and the hearing aid is in good operating condition, an immediate hearing evaluation should be conducted. This should include tests for middle-ear function and inspection of the ear canal, considering the possibility of infection or of something impeding the transmission of sound through the middle ear. Medical referral should be made as needed.

Efficient Medical Referral Services

Middle-ear infections seem to be frequent among hearing-impaired children, particularly children under the age of 8, and closure of the ear canal by inserts or muffs reduces ventilation of the skin of the ear. With chronic ear infections or draining ears, "down time" for amplification may be considerable. A slight increase in hearing level caused by temporary middle-ear impairment may raise the child's hearing threshold beyond the regularly set gain of his hearing aid. Arrangements should be made in advance with the family and the child's physicians, or with a school physician, to have an efficient medical referral system so that a hearing-impaired child wearing amplification can receive *priority treatment.* The importance of avoiding extended periods when the child is not receiving appropriate amplified speech will need to be made clear.

USING HEARING TO TEACH SPEECH

Procedures for teaching speech may be planned especially to emphasize the use of hearing as an important tool in *developing,* in *improving,* and in *maintaining* speech production. For some children, hearing may be the preferred channel for stimulating and supporting speech production. Chapter IV includes a description of the "Auditory Global Approach," the general approach that places emphasis on the use of hearing. Some speech programs adopt an "auditory-only" philosophy, using hearing as the nearly exclusive channel for teaching speech, regardless of the degree of hearing impairment of their students (179, 288, 334). Whatever the emphasis placed on hearing to teach speech, auditory training provides an important foundation for its utilization (42, 80, 81, 83, 112, 137, 150, 161, 315, 327, 330, 337).

Auditory Training for Speech

The notion of influencing the sense of hearing of deaf persons through auditory training goes back many centuries, with systematic investigation of such training beginning in the 19th century by Itard, Gallaudet, Urbantschitsch, Bezold and others (112, 313). The development of wearable, powerful, electro-acoustic hearing aids in the twentieth century has stimulated renewed interest in the potential of amplification and training. Auditory training assumes that there are specific exercises or experiences that will help a hearing-impaired person use his hearing better than he would with constant amplification alone without such training (66, 77, 137, 150, 161, 330, 337). The training is presumed to improve the person's *use* of hearing, rather than to improve hearing itself, although the influence of amplification and training on the anatomy and physiology of the auditory system is a continuing controversy (117, 315).

Interest in auditory training for deaf children has focused primarily upon helping them perceive a variety of sounds and understand speech (65), although some teachers have undertaken auditory training for the purpose of improving the child's speech production. It is reasonable to assume that auditory training which helps children perceive speech will also help them produce speech, since they may profit from having available an acoustic example to imitate and to compare to their own production (122). The considerable body of literature on auditory training in general, both historical and recent, is therefore relevant for the teacher of speech but outside the scope of this book. Some references are included at the end of this book.

The following conditions are prerequisites for auditory training of speech production:

(1) Selection and use of an amplification system that responds to a comprehensive description of the hearing in each of a child's ears and amplifies the important acoustic features of speech.

(2) Selection and use of an amplification system that provides feedback of the child's own speech production as well as models from the speech of others.

(3) Monitoring and maintenance of the child's hearing and of his amplification system so that acoustic amplification is consistent and constantly available.

(4) Availability of an oral environment as described in Chapter II, pages 50-54.

Whatever procedures are adopted for auditory training should take into account those things we know about achievement effort and motivation that were discussed in Chapter II. They should also be procedures that fit into the *systematic instruction* program of the child's school, recognizing the need for sometimes individualizing instruction, and for coordinating it with other methodology of the academic program.

Developing Speech Through Audition

Here we consider two aspects of *systematic instruction* that were introduced in Chapter II: the principle of *stimulating production of speech by the most natural approach possible* before resorting to less natural avenues or techniques, and: the principle of *making discriminating use of sensory channel and aids*. While it has been commonly observed that babies with normal hearing often look closely at the mouths of their mothers as they develop speech, a great deal of their speech acquisition depends upon using the auditory system exclusively without supplemental visual information. Furthermore, since visual information is not available to the child as part of the natural feedback from his speech production, we consider a third important guiding principle: that *techniques used in developing speech should include those that help maintain speech production* when the child is away from the mother or teacher. Observance of these principles suggest the strategy of using auditory stimulation for speech development without accompanying visual information, whenever possible.

The teacher will need to use careful judgment in determining which children can benefit from auditory stimulation without accompanying visual information for developing speech. The pure-tone threshold audiogram may offer some guidance (see Table III-2), but it is likely that "trial and error" through investigative instruction will be most useful. The teacher will need to determine whether the perceptual task required of the child is appropriate for his age and experience, whether the speech stimuli are appropriate for his language level, and whether the child is cooperative and giving his best effort. The teacher may also find it possible for the child to "work up" to the intended speech stimulation task through a series of steps with simpler, smaller units of speech. When a child does not respond initially to the auditory-only mode, providing him for a short time with associated visual or tactile stimuli may give him sufficient experience with the overall stimuli for its auditory perception (74).

Some teachers advocate that all speech training sessions be conducted so that the child cannot see the teacher's mouth. This is commonly accomplished by the teacher talking either beside or behind the child, or by the teacher shielding her mouth with her hand or a paper card. When the latter technique is used, the teacher should be careful not to distort her speech signal by letting the shield interfere with her natural mouth movement or by causing reflection off the mouth-concealing card. The teacher may also ask the children to close or "hide their eyes." The intention of hiding the movement of the lips is to avoid the *distraction* of the visual speech signal and to make the hearing-impaired child *dependent* upon the acoustic speech signal. Lacking the visual lip-reading signal and learning to depend upon the acoustic signal is thought to increase the child's attention to the acoustic signal, and thus to improve his use of hearing for speech.

Observation of the acquisition of speech and spoken language by children with normal hearing suggests a sequence of phases that is relevant for teaching speech to hearing-impaired children through audition. These four stages or phases of development are included in Table III-6.

In the *first phase* the baby with normal hearing is "bathed" in the spoken language and vocal noises of the adults around him. The adult does not expect the child to respond, but persists in talking to the child. The child listens, remembers and begins to make some rudimentary language associations between the acoustic vocal-sound code and meaning. Good *child-directed speech* features heightened syllable accent, word emphasis, and phrase intonation patterns that focus and hold the child's attention to the speech model, and that apparently facilitate his memory for speech units.

In the *second phase* the baby attempts to produce some of the vocal noises he has heard. He may imitate the pattern just produced by the adult, particularly when the adult pauses expectantly after a speech utterance. The adult who is an effective speech model may tailor the stimulus by repeating it several times, simplifying it to short words or syllables that he or she believes will be easy for the child to produce, or by using vocal utterances that he or she has heard the child produce earlier. The child's attempt at imitating the adult speech pattern may not be highly accurate, but only an approximation of the adult pattern, or it may consist of a syllable that is babbled.

As the hearing baby grasps the understanding of spoken language as a pragmatic interchange of meaning, rather than just vocal play, he may be beginning the *third phase*. Now he responds to the spoken language of the adult with what might be considered an answer, or a response that is not a mere imitation of the adult's pattern. This is the stimulus-response level of language, a level at which there is an association between the stimulating model and the responding pattern that comprises rudimentary conversation. The skillful parent interprets and anticipates the child's interests—"Do you want a cookie?" inviting the child's attempt at "Yes." The child's early response pat-

Phase 1. Input of sounds and spoken language are directed to the child by adults without observable responses, particularly vocal responses, being expected of the child.
Phase 2. The child begins to imitate the spoken language of the adults who talk to him, repeating as best he can the sequence of speech sounds and speech rhythm he hears.
Phase 3. The child responds to the spoken language of the adults who talk to him, not merely imitating what they say, but by answering with a different vocal response.
Phase 4. The child initiates speech sounds or spoken language without the immediate, associated stimulus of an adult speech model, talking to himself or initiating conversation with the adult.

Table III-6.　Four phases of the acquisition of speech and spoken language by children with normal hearing in a sequence relevant for teaching speech to hearing-impaired children.

terns may not be clearly articulated speech but they are distinctly different from the stimulating model or question of the adult.

In the *fourth phase* the child initiates spoken language to begin a conversation. He may comment on something, demand something, or ask a question that suggests a specific response by the adult.

These four phases are not entirely exclusive nor perfectly sequential for children with normal hearing. Some babies try to imitate utterances very early. A baby may at one moment be content to listen and absorb without response. A baby may sometimes respond to the adult stimulus with an answering response and sometimes be content just to imitate the adult pattern. In a quiet time with no adult around, the baby may initiate some sounds of his own for the pleasure of listening to himself, and then perhaps try to imitate his own surprising and pleasing utterances. Some children apparently spend a very short time in the imitating phase or the answering phase, initiating conversation early and answering whenever appropriate. However, the identity and sequence of the four phases becomes most apparent when a child with normal hearing fails to progress through them. For example, some children persist in a period of imitating called "echolalia" in which they repeat the adult pattern even if it is a question. Other children may persevere at the stimulus-response level but not initiate conversation on their own. Still other children are observed to have a problem in imitating speech. Such problems are often referred to a speech/language pathologist for remediation.

For the speech development of a hearing-impaired child, these four phases may comprise the outline of a curriculum for stimulating and teaching speech production through audition. That is, the natural sequence observed as babies with normal hearing *acquire* speech suggests a sequence for the activities involved in *teaching* the hearing-impaired child. The teacher may expect to spend some time providing the hearing-impaired child with directed acoustic stimulation, predominantly spoken language, before expecting the child to imitate the teacher's utterances. For many deaf children, the teacher will have to elicit imitation of her speech directly through selected activities. The teacher may expect the child to have to gain some skill in imitating speech units from the teacher's model before expecting him to produce an answering response to the teacher's question or eliciting stimuli. For some deaf children the teacher will have to instigate answering responses directly by using selected situations. Also, the teacher might expect the child to have experience in listening, imitating and answering speech before expecting him to formulate speech and initiate conversation.

The four phases of Table III-6 also provide an outline for observation that is diagnostic or prognostic for the speech development of hearing-impaired children. When a child does not seem able to move from one of these phases to the next, it may signal that other teaching procedures or other sensory avenues of stimulation may be necessary. When the child does not begin to imitate after considerable carefully applied acoustic speech stimulation and instruction, it may suggest that he will need the lipreading signal in order to begin imitating. Some children seem able to imitate but do not advance easily to the stimulus-response or question-answer level, suggesting that a change in teaching techniques is needed for developing understanding of the "interchange" nature of spoken language. Some hearing-impaired children learn to imitate and to respond appropriately when the response is elicited, but do not seem to advance easily to the level of formulating their own language and initiating conversation. It is not always appropriate to consider those children who persist at one level and not advance to the next as having a "language learning disorder," a "specific language disability," or to be multiply handicapped. Rather, it may suggest considering a change in the teaching techniques, intensifying instruction, or adopting other avenues of sensory stimulation.

Correcting or Improving Speech Through Audition

Some aspects of speech may be especially well presented to children through the auditory-only mode at times when they produce an error. The teacher should keep in mind the principle, described in the *Methodology* section of Chapter II, pages 55-57, that *speech instruction should provide practice that strengthens maintenance of a skill* of which the child is judged to be capable. Accordingly, she should not be too quick to provide the child with an acoustic, visual or tactile speech pattern for simple imitation when he makes an error. Merely *signaling* the presence of an error, in order to permit the child to correct himself by recalling his internalized catalogue of error probabilities, is preferable for maintenance of a speech skill. Even the levels of intervention that point out the *place* of an error or the *nature* of an error is preferable to the teacher immediately telling or showing the child the correct production, in order to promote memory for self-correction. Long-lasting improvement in speech seldom takes place without some practice that requires long-term retention. But when a teacher determines that the appropriate level of intervention to correct a speech error or to improve a poor production is to present the correct model, she should consider doing so first through the auditory-only mode.

An example of the kind of correction of articulation that lends itself well to acoustic illustration is that of vowel duration. Tactile-kinesthetic feedback of vowel production is enhanced by holding the tongue and lip position long enough to "get a feel" for the formation, tending to make deaf children elongate both the vowel itself and its transitions with the consonants that occur before and after. Since vowel duration errors are prevalent among deaf children and significantly influence intelligibility, correction of these errors so that they can be avoided by the child through his auditory speech maintenance feedback system is highly desirable. In a word like *beet* where the **ee** should be very brief, a deaf child is likely to say **beeeeeut**, inadvertently producing an **-u-** sound as he slowly moves the tongue from the extended **ee** position toward the **t** position. Good representation of the brevity of the **ee** is not well presented by visual lip-tongue movements, since the child cannot see where the **ee** stopped and the **t** began. In Chapter VI we have presented some other ways, like using written symbols, to indicate brevity. But acoustic stimulation is likely to present this information most clearly, even to profoundly deaf children.

An exercise that may be helpful here, is first to identify the poorly produced word, taking it out of its connected speech context perhaps by writing it on a chalkboard or paper, and then to ask the child to listen to the teacher's auditory-only model production. The child should then be asked to repeat the word, imitating the teacher's production as closely as possible. The teacher may need to repeat the model until the child can move his speech mechanism through the articulatory sequence both rapidly and accurately. When the poorly produced word is of several syllables, the teacher and child may have to try several examples and imitations before a satisfactory production is accomplished.

In order to emphasize the nature of the child's error, the teacher may now wish to present the child with an auditory-only production of the word as she produces it with the vowel-elongation error present. Exaggeration of the elongation, in order to emphasize the error further and point up the difference, may also be helpful. Then the child should be asked to produce the word with the elongated vowel and with the preferred shortened vowel, imitating alternate productions by the teacher.

When the preferred vowel duration has been mastered in the word, the teacher should recall the general principle of *returning any corrected unit of speech to connected speech context in order to determine whether it can be produced appropriately*. She might first ask the child to produce the entire sentence by writing it on the chalkboard. If the child reverts to the elongated vowel duration on the key word in the sentence context, the teacher may present an auditory-only model of the entire sentence, or of a phrase of several words until the child can produce the vowel satisfactorily in the full sentence.

A number of other aspects of articulation, particularly the manner of consonant production, can also be presented through the auditory-only mode.

Several aspects of speech rhythm, such as accent and emphasis, phrasing, and phrase duration lend themselves easily to effective speech correction through the auditory-only mode. Intonation, that requires changes in fundamental voice pitch, is more difficult for profoundly deaf children to perceive, but children with severe hearing impairment may imitate intonation remarkably well when models are presented for practice with exaggerated changes in pitch.

The teacher should be careful, however, not to misinterpret the basis for a child's judgments, unless the child can *imitate* what he hears. For example, some speech teachers recommend correcting production of the s sound through the ear. Wearable hearing aids seldom reproduce high-frequency energy with sufficient amplification for the s to reach the threshold of a deaf child. Profoundly deaf children, severely deaf children, and even many of those considered moderately impaired with poor hearing in the higher frequencies, will receive little if any acoustic information about this relatively weak and high-frequency sound. Yet one can demonstrate convincingly that a deaf child can discriminate an s from a more powerful sh sound with its wider frequency spectrum. By writing an "s" and an "sh" on a chalkboard, and with the teacher saying each sound as she points to it, even a profoundly deaf child can differentiate the two sounds in the auditory-only mode—but probably on the basis of the absence (for s) and the presence (for sh) of sound, and not on recognition or identification of the s or the sh sounds.

Maintaining Speech Through Auditory Feedback

Maintaining the quality of one's own speech production over a period of time requires both: *(1) the availability of adequate and constant sensory feedback;* and, *(2) the opportunity for comparing that feedback directly with standard models of speech.* The combined tactile and kinesthetic senses provide constant feedback of one's speech production, but that feedback is neither adequate for all speech sounds (s for example), nor does it offer the possibility for a direct comparison with standard models. We cannot tell how it feels when another person produces speech. The lip movements of another speaker with normal hearing and good speech provide a visible standard model of speech, but it is not entirely adequate for displaying all speech sounds (k for example), nor does it offer the possibility for a constant direct comparison with one's own production. We cannot tell how we look when we produce speech, unless we have a mirror constantly available. The hearing-impaired person who relies on tactile-kinesthetic sensation for feedback of his own speech production, and on the visual sensation of lipreading for a standard model of speech, will have neither the availability of adequate sensory feedback nor the opportunity for comparing that feedback directly with standard models of speech. He will need the assistance of a person who has normal hearing from time to time to help him judge and monitor his speech production, as we shall discuss further in Chapter V.

Only hearing can offer a direct comparison through the same sensory channel (an "iso-morphic" comparison) of one's own speech with the speech of others. Of course, devices that convert the acoustic speech signal to a visual display or to tactile sensations can provide a direct sensory comparison, but they are typically not wearable and thus not constantly available to the speaker in real communication situations. Neither do they always provide adequate sensory information about speech. Even though it may be severely impaired, *hearing* offers the best sensory channel for the individual to make comparisons that maintain the quality of his speech production, with the help of appropriate acoustic amplification.

We have previously mentioned the necessity of monitoring hearing and amplification in order to provide constant acoustic speech information. It is also important for the hearing-impaired child to receive training that will help him learn to listen consciously for the comparison of standard models with his feedback. A simple word-identification task in the auditory-only mode is an example of training for this aspect of maintaining speech. The teacher might, for example, place pictures of several familiar objects before the child, conceal her mouth, and ask the child to identify the word she says. Without the availability of lip movement or written words, the child will have to "think auditorily." That is: he will have to recall what each word sounds like, and then match the teacher's acoustic signal to his sound memory pattern for each of the words in order to recognize them.

In accordance with what we know about motivation for learning discussed in Chapter II, pages 48-49, it is important for a child to meet success with this task in order to gain confidence in his auditory word-identification ability. The above exercise is liable to fail on the first trial unless the teacher takes into account the hearing ability of each of her children and the acoustic features of the speech signal of each of the words. This suggests that she should have in mind a *gradient of acoustic word differences* that ranges from great-differences (easy-to-discriminate) to slight-differences (hard-to-discriminate). The number of options, or the "set" of words among which to choose, will also influence the difficulty of the task, as will the background noise present in the room. Differences in hearing ability among children suggest that the teacher may have to conduct these exercises with each child individually, or with carefully chosen groups of children who are at a similar level of hearing ability.

An initial exercise might consist of asking a child to identify the spoken word *dog* when the two pictures presented are of a *dog* and an *airplane.* The teacher may begin by reminding the child of the different sound of these two words, asking him to listen as she points to each word and says it with her mouth concealed. Then when the teacher says the word *dog,* the child has the simple choice of a one-syllable or a two-syllable word. The value of this exercise for speech production maintenance may be enhanced if the child is requested to say the word aloud each time as well as point to the appropriate picture. Even the most profoundly deaf child is likely to be able to succeed at this simple word-recognition task. Repeating the word himself before pointing to the picture will give him direct practice in comparing the feedback of his own acoustic signal to the signal he receives from the teacher.

This simple two-word exercise may also be used for an auditory word-discrimination task that provides further comparison of the child's speech production with the model of others. In this version of the task, the child chooses one of the two words and says it aloud. The teacher conceals her mouth and says either of the words aloud, asking the child whether her word was the same as or different from his. The child may again be asked to repeat the teacher's word before making his "same"-or-"different" decision.

As the child succeeds at these simple speech identification and speech discrimination tasks, the exercises can be gradually increased in difficulty by increasing the number of words in the set, by increasing the similarity of the words in the set, and by using written phrases or sentences rather than pictures for words.

From the important foundations established in these first three chapters on Speech and Its Production, Learning and Teaching Speech, and Using Hearing for Speech, we move on to applying this background for Developing Speech in Hearing-Impaired Children.

Chapter IV

Developing Speech

In this chapter we are concerned with deaf children who when first encountered have acquired little or no speech, and with the teacher's role in developing their speech. The actual chronological *entry age* of these children varies, depending upon how early they were identified and how quickly they were directed to a school or clinic. Given the encouraging trend toward early identification and intervention, efforts to develop speech may begin as early as the first year of life in parent-child programs and clinics, and in schools by the third or fourth year (71). Some congenitally deaf children, for whatever reason, may not begin their first experience with speech instruction until their sixth year or later. This diversity in entry age requires programs for developing speech to have the flexibility to tailor initial instruction to each child's level of physical maturation and growth, as well as to fit the other concerns of learning speech illustrated in Figure II-1: the child's *learning abilities,* his *sensory abilities,* and his *language experience.* Age and maturation should influence selection among instructional techniques, such as those presented in Chapter VI, taking into account assumptions about "optimal periods" and "readiness levels" for learning.

APPROACHES TO DEVELOPING SPEECH

In this section we delineate what we consider to be three prominent alternate approaches to developing speech suggested by successful experience. Of course there are overlapping or common elements in these approaches, but as a general proposition they are discrete and distinctive enough to merit separate treatment. They differ primarily in: (1) the *sensory channels* used to transmit information about speech, (2) the *size of the unit of speech* for stimulation and practice, (3) the *area of teacher control* and direction in eliciting speech production, and (4) the relative *emphasis they place on each of the four phases of speech acquisition and development,* (as outlined in Chapter III, Table III-6, page 108). We recall these phases below:

Phase 1. The child is stimulated by presentation of speech patterns.

Phase 2. The child imitates the speech patterns.

Phase 3. The child responds to spoken language by answering non-imitatively.

Phase 4. The child initiates speech sounds or spoken language without requiring any form of stimulation.

We have puzzled over how to label these approaches in descriptive terms. For convenience of communication, we shall label them the *Auditory Global,* the *Multisensory Syllable-Unit* and the *Association Phoneme Unit* approaches. What is important is not the labels, but the exposition of the approaches which in turn gives significance to the labels.

Auditory Global Approach

This approach varies in its systematic choice among instructional techniques that are usually considered methods (10, 85, 179, 288). Terms used to label these methods include: "Auditory-Oral," "Aural-Oral," "Acoupedic," "Unisensory-Auditory," "Auditory-Verbal," and the "Acoustic" method. However, these variations generally derive from important features that are common to these methods. The principal features of the Auditory Global approach are: (1) that *the primary, although not always the exclusive, channel for speech development is auditory,* (2) that *the predominant input is fluent, connected speech,* (3) that *the influence of the speech teacher is comprehensive, extending well beyond the classroom,* particularly as (4) *the emphasis of this approach is placed on the first phase of speech development* (Table III-6), stimulating the child by presentation of speech patterns.

Maximum Emphasis on the Use of Hearing

The underlying premise of the Auditory Global approach is that the most satisfactory way to achieve intelligible speech is by placing maximium if not always exclusive emphasis on the use of hearing. Some who practice methods subsumed under this approach limit the eligibility of hearing-impaired children to exclude those with severe-to-profound hearing levels. Others would employ this approach with deaf children, however much hearing sensitivity and clarity are reduced. In developing speech, the use of hearing is intended for the following purposes:

(1) To direct systematically the input of spoken language that will equip the child with a reserve pool of models of speech patterns to be imitated, and with a basis for language-learning generalization that will prepare him to formulate and produce spoken language.

(2) To channel the acoustic speech stimulus for eliciting specific units of speech from the child, and to shape his productions in order to correct or improve them.

(3) To serve as the primary sensory channel upon which the child is dependent for monitoring his speech production.

The Auditory Global approach rests on a foundation for the use of hearing elaborated in Chapter III. Prerequisite to beginning direct instructional procedures is the careful measurement of each child's hearing capabilities, followed by selection of an electro-acoustic amplification system that will present to the child the important acoustic features of his own speech and the speech of others. Essential, also, is establishment of a system for monitoring the child's hearing and of his amplification system to insure constant exposure to the sounds of speech as spoken language is directed to the child.

A. Directing Spoken Language to the Child: Directing the acoustic information of spoken language to the child's hearing is the essential, and usually the initial, instructional procedure of the Auditory Global approach. At its extreme, proponents may endeavor to facilitate the child's speech acquisition merely by insuring that he receives sufficient acoustic stimulation to progress without further intervention by teachers or therapists. Given a program of appropriately enriched acoustic stimulation, the child is expected to proceed through the four phases of acquisition of spoken language described in Table III-6, and to reach the language milestones listed in Table II-1, page 43. The earlier the child begins a program of enriched acoustic stimulation, the more likely he is to achieve language landmarks at a chronological age approximating that of children with normal hearing. Some advocates suggest designating a "hearing age" for children, when they have been fitted with appropriate amplification and the program of enriched acoustic stimulation is underway. Phases of speech acquisition and language progress might then be based on this hearing age rather than on chronological age.

Two variables are thought to influence the success of this "facilitate-only" strategy—the child's *entry age* and his *hearing level.* Intervention should start at the earliest possible time, as soon as the hearing loss is identified. Immediate institution of a program as outlined in Chapter III is required. Early initiation of this facilitating program is urged to insure that the child will develop an *auditory* basis for language acquisition, rather than a primarily *visual* one, whether by lipreading, by some means of gestures or "body language," (or by a formal system of manual communication). Some teachers believe there is a critical period or time for developing this auditory basis for language acquisition, and if the child has not had sufficient experience to develop an auditory basis by that time, he will never do so. The controversy on this point centers around questions of limitations of the critical period: (1) definition of the "natural" language of deaf people, (2) whether oral communication can ever be learned well as a "second language" by a deaf person, and, (3) whether deaf children can develop simultaneously both auditory and visual bases for language. Research may yield some answers to these questions beyond popular conjecture.

Hearing level is the second variable that influences the outcome. Here opinion ranges from the belief that any child, regardless of hearing level, can achieve an auditory basis for acquiring speech if started on an intensive stimulation program early enough, to the conviction, on the other hand, that only a very few exceptional deaf children can receive enough of the important features of speech through the ear ever to develop an auditory basis for spoken language. Between these extremes, teachers and audiologists endeavor to predict success from pure-tone threshold audiograms, or from trial periods of stimulation and teaching. Procedures for describing the supra-threshold as well as threshold hearing capabilities of deaf children, (such as have been suggested in Chapter III), need to be correlated with controlled programs of facilitation and instruction in order to develop better predictors of the probability of success in helping deaf children develop speech and oral language through hearing.

In addressing spoken language to the child's hearing, the teacher and audiologist should first make sure that the amplification system meets the important criteria described in Chapter III, pages 92-101. Then the teacher directs her speech signal toward the child at a distance and at a voice volume that she knows will permit her signal to reach his microphone and be amplified so that it will be audible, comfortably above his threshold level if possible (84). She must also insure that background noise in the immediate area is not sufficient to mask out her speech signal. Especially for early work, speech stimulation needs to be conducted in very quiet, ideal surroundings (232).

Next, the teacher must be sure that the child is attending to her speech signal. This can be achieved by the teacher's body positioning, by establishing eye contact with the child, or by permitting the child to see her mouth move during speech. Once the child has associated the teacher's acoustic speech signal with her visible mouth movements, she may present some speech with the mouth hidden, as described in Chapter III, page 107. Of course to maintain attention, periods of speech stimulation should not exceed the child's attention span and interest level.

The teacher's speech signal should be presented with disciplined precision of enunciation so that phonemes are clear, and yet not so exaggerated that her speech sounds unnatural. Radio and TV announcers and actors practice and use this level of unobtrusive clarity. Phrasing should be appropriate for the age of the child, using fairly short phrases for very young children, with delineating pauses between phrases. Particularly for very young children, the patterns of speech rhythm should be clearly distinctive. That is, syllable accent and word emphasis may be given slightly more force of articulation than one would use with another adult, and the amount of pitch change for intonation may be greater than for adult conversation. These marked features of speech rhythm are what seem to mark good "child-directed" speech, even for children with normal hearing. They also seem to help maintain the child's attention. Some teachers accompany speech with complementary facial expressions, gestures or bodily movements to given greater animation and hold attention.

The teacher may tailor the phonetic content of her speech signal on different days to emphasize difference units of speech. For example, she may emphasize one of the vowels or consonants in a speech stimulus session, placing it frequently in initial, medial and final positions of words or phrases. Or she may purposely vary pitch levels or intensity levels in an exaggerated manner to direct the child's attention to these changes. If the child should begin his own speech production during this stimulation phase, his productions may guide the teacher to select speech sounds or rhythm features in which the child seems especially interested. Otherwise, in different stimulation sessions she may wish to emphasize each of the speech sounds and rhythm features, from an inventory of those described in Chapter I.

Except when a child's hearing level is moderate and of a primarily conductive nature, most teachers agree that developing the child's use of hearing for speech requires instructional procedures beyond acoustic stimulation with connected speech. Most likely the teacher will notice that the child's speech production will be missing some connecting words, that some speech sounds do not emerge despite considerable stimulation with those sounds in connected speech, or that the production of some sounds is inadequate or incorrect. This suggests that she may need to channel the acoustic speech stimulus in order to elicit specific units of speech from the child, and to shape his productions to correct or improve them.

B. Eliciting Specific Units of Speech: Hearing may be useful for eliciting units of speech that have not emerged with enriched connected speech stimulation, and for shaping the child's productions to correct errors or improve poorly produced speech units. To elicit a specific unit of speech, such as a phoneme like **m** or **oa**, the teacher may choose first to have the child imitate an auditory-only stimulus. This may be achieved by directing the child's attention to the teacher's mouth, covering her mouth with a card or her hand, and then producing the speech unit. The next critical step is to indicate to the child that he is to *imitate* the teacher. If the child's first attempt is not satisfactory, the teacher may repeat the speech unit several times, giving the child experience with matching the sound of his own production to the sound of the teacher's example.

If the child does not attempt imitation, the teacher chooses among several steps, and does not abandon imitation of the acoustic stimulus. She may judge that a young child does not sufficiently comprehend the idea of imitating her. Then she could proceed through a series of steps, having the child imitate several other actions not connected with speech—stacking blocks, putting toys in a box, walking on a line, jumping over a block, hand and finger positions, head positions, mouth or eye movements, striking an object that makes a sound—before returning to the speech imitation task. She may need to use combined mouth movements and speech sounds to get the child to imitate what he both sees and hears, before requiring imitation of only what he hears.

The teacher may also alter the size of the unit of speech to elicit specific imitation, especially when improvement of a particular unit is intended. In this case the child should be stimulated to imitate target units in the context of the largest possible unit of speech, and running speech if possible, but the size of the speech unit should be reduced as necessary. She may give the target unit special emphasis in a phrase. Then she may use the unit in a word or a syllable if it is not imitated. If imitation is still not forthcoming or the unit is not well produced, it may be presented in isolated form. Once the target unit has been imitated in a small segment of speech, it should be restored to larger connected segments. In so doing, its coarticulation features can be appreciated.

In the case of the older child when correction or improvement of a target unit is intended, it may be useful to present both correct or good production along with the incorrect or poor production, contrasting the two and having the child imitate both. This gives him a feeling of control over the target unit, and an opportunity to discriminate between acceptable and unacceptable productions. It also encourages the child to depend on hearing for feedback and monitoring of his speech production.

C. Using Hearing for Monitoring Speech: The sensations accompanying speech production are fed back to the normal-hearing speaker through the tactile, the kinesthetic, and the auditory senses, as discussed in Chapter I. This sensory feedback is used to monitor the individual's speech production, both by checking the accuracy of production and by continually reinforcing memory for how it was produced. Auditory feedback of a person with normal hearing is comprised of sound delivered to the cochlea in two ways: *internally* from the larynx and oral structures by conduction through the bones of the skull, and *externally* out the mouth through the air to the tympanic membrane and to the middle ear. We note the difference in how our own voice sounds when listening to a recording that does not include our internal bone conduction. Deaf people do not hear the internal component, nor do they hear the external component, unless it is amplified.

Impairment in the transmission of information over any of the three sensory systems can disrupt the normal production of speech. Dental local anesthesia that temporarily reduces sensations from the tongue, for example, can make speech sound slurred. The normal listener hears this slurring and attempts to move the tongue more accurately, depending primarily upon his auditory feedback to judge the success of his efforts. In the absence of auditory feedback, as is the case with profound deafness, the tactile and kinesthetic sensations become the primary sensory feedback of speech production. Normal listeners experience this problem temporarily when they speak in a situation where noise is so loud that they cannot hear their speech. The teacher may wish to experience this situation herself and see what happens to her speech by talking while wearing earphones connected to a noise source. As was noted in Chapter III (Table III-1, page 67), with a sudden major loss of hearing, as from a viral disease, speech production gradually deteriorates from its normal pattern, demonstrating that feedback through the tactile and kinesthetic sensory channels alone is *not* sufficient to maintain speech that meets our expectations of sounding natural. However, the tactile and kinesthetic systems *can* support the maintenance of speech production that may be intelligible and fluent, but not entirely natural, if the loss of hearing occurs well after the individual's speech production patterns have already been mastered through monitoring by an intact auditory system. The speech of profoundly deaf persons who have lost their hearing after 9 years of age attests to this.

Maintaining speech with only tactile and kinesthetic feedback, once it has already been successfully acquired and frequently used, and *developing* speech by attempting unfamiliar productions dependent upon tactile and kinesthetic feedback, seem to require different capabilities. Experience with deaf persons suggests that developing speech is less successful than maintaining speech, partly because the learning process seems to require auditory input of speech models in order to establish natural speech patterns. Learning speech without auditory input of speech models forces the hearing-impaired child to reply on visual models—the speech gestures of the lips, tongue, and lower jaw. Not all movements necessary for producing the range of speech sounds in our language are visible, nor can the eye resolve all the rapid movements involved in connected discourse.

The deaf child who does not have the benefit of acoustic amplification, therefore, must attempt to produce speech as he feels it looks. This situation provides him neither a complete speech input model nor a direct sensory (isomorphic) comparison for monitoring his productions. The teacher's "normal" ear must judge the acceptability of the child's speech, while the child attempts to remember how an occasional, acceptable speech production felt. His acceptable productions may not occur frequently enough to establish and maintain long-term tactile and kinesthetic memory that insures repeated satisfactory production whenever needed. This sensory mismatch contributes to the difficulty that deaf children experience in developing speech.

Surveys show that the speech intelligibility of prelingually deaf children seems to be substantially correlated with their level of hearing and use of amplification, suggesting that when residual hearing is used, it contributes significantly to the quality of speech production. The intention of the Auditory Global approach is not only to establish the auditory channel as primary for receiving speech models, but as the primary channel for the child's own feedback to facilitate monitoring his speech. If this dual function is achieved, it should contribute both to developing good speech production patterns and, once learned, to maintaining them.

Essential for monitoring speech production through hearing is experience with comparison of auditory speech input with auditory speech feedback. In Chapter III we have suggested the type of exercise that can accomplish comparison for auditory discrimination. Avoiding the *distraction* of lipreading, and the possible *dependence* on that source of speech input, is also important. See Chapter III for useful techniques to avoid visual distraction.

Emphasis on Connected Speech

Another prominent feature of the Auditory Global approach is the emphasis on connected speech, whether initiated by the teacher or in response to a child's utterances. Large, global units of spoken language that carry important speech rhythm features and linguistic information are preferred to shorter, insular phrases taken out of context, for stimulating the child to speak (9). The best possible program for the maximum use of hearing may be ineffective unless the following are taken into account:

(1) The amount of connected speech directed to the child.

(2) The content or nature of the connected speech.

(3) The way in which connected speech is directed to the child.

A. Amount of Connected Speech: The overall amount of connected speech input should be increased over that which would normally be directed to a child without impaired hearing. The child with normal hearing effortlessly "listens in" on distant conversations that are not directed to him, hearing most of the speech patterns he receives in infancy "out of the corner of his ear," so to speak. Only a small part of the speech he hears is actually *directed* to him. To compensate for this deprivation of a good deal of incidental speech input, a concerted effort needs to be made to increase substantially the amount purposely directed to the child.

If equipped with an effective amplification system, television offers a valuable source of interesting and meaningful speech input. Television and radio comprise a great deal of the speech input of normal-hearing children. Although lipreading is not easy from the typical television production and not at all available on cartoons, environmental sounds and speech associated with action are constantly available. TV is a supplement to live speech input, but cannot replace it.

It is helpful for the hearing-impaired child to have language and speech input from children with normal hearing of his own age. Such children provide speech models from vocal tracts of the same size. Vowel formant positions, described in Chapter III, will thus be easier to imitate than those of adults.

Much of the increased speech input will have to come from a special effort in the home and at school. Using connected language, parents and teachers can learn to describe and explain what they and the child are seeing or doing. They can narrate stories and they can recapitulate experiences. Situations should be arranged to stimulate the child to associate spoken language with observation and action.

B. Nature of Connected Speech: We caution on two popular oversimplifications about stimulation with connected speech. One is that the parents, teachers, and all people in the child's environment should treat the child exactly as they would a child without hearing loss, talking to him as though he were hearing and understanding all that is said. Another is that these people should "talk, talk, talk" to the child. While such advice stresses the importance of increasing the amount of speech in the child's environment, it frequently neglects the need for tailoring the nature of the connected speech or directing it to the child to compensate for his hearing loss.

The Auditory Global approach exploits the strong possibility of attainment by the child of natural *speech rhythm* and *language* competence that contribute invaluably to speech intelligibility. Connected spoken language which is characterized by natural rhythm gives the child the opportunity to hear a model of the important patterns of speech and to imitate them. It is not out of order to conjecture here that the naturally patterned speech of the teacher is likely to be adversely affected, as will the intelligibility of the child's speech, if it must accommodate to the temporal features of simultaneously presented manual signals, especially for very young children. The naturally recurring patterns associated with declarative sentences, questions, and exclamations may be slightly exaggerated in the speech of the teacher to create a flow which the child may imitate in his own speech, even if, as we have seen in Chapter III, his residual hearing is concentrated only in the low frequencies.

By hearing repeated examples of connected speech, the child with normal hearing not only imitates what he hears but formulates inductively what he believes are the rules of spoken language. However, the restricted auditory sensitivity of the hearing-impaired child reduces the redundancy and linguistic cues of the language available to him. Nevertheless, there may still be sufficient phonologic, syntactic, and semantic cues to facilitate inductive acquisition of the rules of speech and language. Of course, the connected speech of the teacher should take into account the state of the child's language development as suggested by Simmons-Martin in Figure IV-1.

When the child has begun to use connected words meaningfully, the parents and teacher can employ the strategy of *expansion* (29). In expanding what the child has said, the adult imitates the child's words, usually retaining the same word order, but adds something to them to form a complete and grammatically correct sentence. For example, if the child has said, "Dog bark," the adult might expand his utterance by saying, "Yes, the dog is barking." This kind of expansion provides the child with a corrective model which informs him that the adult has understood him and is interested. The adult may expect the hearing-impaired child to imitate the expanded model at a level appropriate to his stage of development.

After the child has learned to use a number of meaningful words and phrases, the parents and teacher can also use the strategy of *modeling* (40). To model speech and language is to comment relevantly on what the child has

```
                              SKILLS
                         Reading, writing,
                         spelling and composing
                      MATURE LANGUAGE
                         Involved syntax and reflection
                         vocabulary of 5000+
                    CONNECTED LANGUAGE
                         Simple structure — requests and
                                             questions
                  LARGER EXPRESSIVE UNITS
                    Prepositional phrase
                    Participial phrase
                LIMITED EXPRESSIVE LANGUAGE
                    Naming — Adjectives
                         Few verbs
              IMITATIONS
                  Actions including mouthing
                  Sounds including speech
          FREE COMPREHENSION
              Concepts
              Connected language
        SITUATIONAL COMPREHENSION
            Concrete items
            Visible actions
      AWARENESS
        Concepts
        Vocabulary
EXPOSURE
```

Figure IV-1 *Some steps of language development. Courtesy of A. A. Simmons-Martin, Central Institute for the Deaf.*

said, rather than to improve on it by expansion. If the child has said, "Dog bark," the modeler might say, "Yes, there is a cat in the tree." This not only serves to reward the child but may also enrich his vocabulary and elaborate his syntax.

When the child is very young, the teacher does not attempt deliberately to correct speech sounds, nor does she call specific attention to an error or to poor production of a pattern. Perceived error should guide the classroom activities to help the child move closer to the desired production by increasing in the teacher's own speech the frequency of the indicated model.

C. Directing connected speech to the child: The Auditory Global approach stresses the auditory signal as primary speech information supplemented by visual, "real" speech information. Throughout we have repeated the importance of proper use of sound amplification. For example, proper microphone technique is important. To avoid "pattern distortion" the microphone should be held a little to the side of the teacher's mouth so that her direct breath stream will not cause plosives and fricatives to be heard as extra syllables. However, holding the microphone too far from hers or the child's mouth may cause the speech signal to fall below classroom noise levels, and moving a microphone too quickly or not quickly enough may cause failure of parts of the signal to be transmitted over the acoustic amplifier. In addition, we believe speech development can be aided by watching the speaker's face while listening, but that watching all the time is neither necessary nor desirable. Some advocates of versions of the Auditory Global approach take pains to see that the child does not receive visual speech information while listening. This persistent "unisensory" emphasis rests on the view that the child should learn to depend on the auditory signal alone in order to develop the fullest use of his hearing. Whether this technique is essential for the development of speech through hearing is still an open question.

Comprehensive Intervention for Speech

Although systematic and coordinated auditory stimulation is the central focus of the Auditory Global approach, it achieves its full potential only if the intervention is timely, broad, comprehensive, and generally individualized. For this approach—appreciably more than for other approaches—the "classroom" is the child's total environment. He is "in school" all of his waking hours. On the gradient of instructional requirements, teacher control and direction stress at all times the opportunities for acquisition of speech by abundant auditory experience. This is particularly true in the case of the very young child. This is not to say that other methods exclude this need, but rather that in the Auditory Global approach it places a greater demand on the teacher's time and energy and occupies a more prominent place in her planning.

At the core of comprehensive intervention is the development and maintenance of a milieu positively responsive to the child's speech output. Even though a child may get some enjoyment from the feedback of his own voice,

Experiences build language.

PETER FERMAN

he is likely to cease talking if he is not encouraged. Responsiveness is especially important to the child with hearing impairment because reduced or absent feedback limits the appreciation of his own voice. Responses may include "primitive" rewards, fulfillment of the purpose of the speech utterance, and related spoken language. Utterances by the very young child should elicit immediate personal-human rewards of smiling, approving words, or affectionate patting. A parent may also invent his own system of auditory-visual rewards such as clapping the hands in response to speech or speech-like sounds. As the child grows older, more tangible rewards such as special privileges or items of appealing value may be effective. Such rewards are extrinsic to speech itself and should not be emphasized or continued for long periods. The quality of the utterance and the stage of development of the child's speech should influence reward-giving. This is a matter of judgment. The ultimate reward, of course, should be the satisfaction of having communicated by spoken language. Another kind of rewarding response is directly related to the utterance and should teach a child that speech is generally pragmatic. When he says, "want cookie," and receives a cookie, he learns that speech is not only reward-giving but also accomplishes a specific purpose.

A third kind of especially valuable response is the spoken language of the person to whom the child's speech is directed. For the very young child this may be the simple repetition of the speech-like sounds of his babbling and other vocalization. Parents will naturally select for repetition the speech sounds of their native language, thus reinforcing the sounds appropriate to the desired speech pattern. When utterances of the baby resemble words of the language, parents can repeat the words as they usually pronounce them, or perhaps emphasize some aspect of the words—such as accent—so that the child might focus on what he previously may not have perceived. In order that the child begin to use these utterances to communicate, it is important for the parent to indicate the meaning of words to the child by pointing, gesturing, or other means.

To this point our exposition of the Auditory Global approach has focused on very young children. This has been intentional since, as we shall see later in this chapter, we shall recommend it for all children as the initial approach of choice. However, as the child grows older and we have had sufficient opportunity to observe his progress, specific needs will be revealed that require deliberate attention. The child's performance may indicate a change to the Multisensory Syllable-Unit approach or the Association Phoneme-Unit approach to be described later, or to a continuation within the framework of what can still properly be labeled the Auditory Global approach. Later in this chapter we shall suggest criteria for choice of continuation or switch of approach, but here we shall consider important aspects of the continuation of the Auditory Global approach. In discussions with teachers of whatever methodological persuasions, we have found some difference of opinion regarding the most suitable procedures for speech development of the child at this stage.

Experience with the Auditory Global approach has generally been confined to its use with children of preschool age and younger. As children have "graduated" from it, the choice for their continued speech development (and improvement, correction, and maintenance) has been some form of "integration" with minimal attention to speech, or a "traditional" method of the Multisensory Syllable-Unit approach. The difficulty seems to stem primarily from the assumption that these are the only choices and secondarily from the question of when and how to make these choices. Although there has not been extensive experience with the Auditory Global approach at the primary and elementary levels, we believe the Auditory Global approach is a distinctively viable option beyond the preschool.

It may be properly argued that what we propose as being distinctive about the Auditory Global approach beyond preschool should be subsumed under improvement, correction, and maintenance, as discussed in Chapter V, rather than development. Nevertheless, we believe that some development would still

Responding to connected speech input.

be in process and that no useful, practical purpose is served in trying to establish a fine, indisputable line of demarcation. Our experience leads to a number of pragmatic points about the Auditory Global approach as it is continued.

Although the age at which structured and targeted *auditory training* should commence is variable, its usefulness for individual children should be kept in mind. Firm documentation is lacking for the value of particular exercises. However, there are some specific bases for training which we repeat here: discrimination between presence or absence of sound and between loud-quiet, high-low, long-short, sudden-gradual, simple-complex, and steady-changing; ability to use information given by rhythm, stress, intonation, number and rate of syllables; capacity to code, retain, and recall the sequential order of phonemes, words, and sentences spoken; and ability to supply information relative to inaudible items in a sequence on the basis of a knowledge of language that is acquired through previous adaptive experience.

We have noted that *precision of articulation* is the chief need of children whose evaluation suggests continuation by the Auditory Global approach. These children are likely to have developed satisfactory patterning and voice quality by the maximum use of hearing, comprehensive intervention, and the emphasis on connected speech. As we shall see when we deal with choices among approaches, development of these features of speech is a crucial criterion. Of course, previous procedures need to be continued, but articulation—without sacrifice of achieved fluency—demands more concentrated attention.

At this stage *selective reinforcement* of speech is important. Until now the child has been rewarded for *any* and *all* speech utterances. Unintelligible expression, generally characterized by poor articulation, should not be accepted if it is known that the child has the skill to be intelligible. Helpful here is agreement by parents and teachers on the child's speech capabilities that will influence their expectancies and demands. Practice of selective reinforcement, based on intelligibility, needs to take into account that a child's speech is undoubtedly more intelligible to his teacher and parents than to others. He has given them auditory training. Therefore, what is demanded may require judgment of the probability of whether an utterance would have been understood by listeners not too familiar with the child's speech. This is a subtle judgment that depends on the teacher's confidence in prediction and on the child's skills and attitudes. The teacher will need to seize and, if necessary, contrive opportunities to observe the child speaking to others. This experience should enhance her competence to predict. Where there is no oral atmosphere, these opportunities are unfortunately limited or absent. We simply call attention to this point. It needs to be addressed regardless of the method that is being employed.

Mastery of articulation is abetted by equipping the child with a suitable *orthographic system* of the kind described in Chapter I. We recall that we recommend that General American symbols with gradual progression to diacritical markings used in standard dictionaries. The child now learns to sound out words. Written symbols are generally associated with sounds in words rather than in isolation. Nevertheless, situations may call for attention to a sound in isolation, but a child should not be considered to "have" a sound until it is given correctly in the variety of phonetic and linguistic contexts in which it occurs in spoken language. This provides the child with the power of attack on the pronunciation of new words and gives the teacher a visual code of communication about speech that is used by his culture. The language of other aspects of speech production can now be introduced to facilitate communication about it. Important among these are structure and function of the speech mechanism and their related vocabulary having to do with manner and place of production—such as breath, voiceless, voice, plosive, fricative, palate, velum—and descriptive adjectives such as soft, loud, high and low. Diagrams, mirror demonstrations, and films are helpful.

Multisensory Syllable-Unit Approach

The Multisensory Syllable Unit Approach is popularly considered to be the "traditional" approach to teaching speech to the hearing impaired. We hasten

Explaining speech terms.

to point out that we do not use the term "traditional" in any pejorative sense. On the contrary, its value has been historically demonstrated by the substantial number of those who have achieved impressive functional speech. Of course, the Multisensory Syllable-Unit approach has much in common with the Auditory Global approach, but its more distinctive characteristics are: (1) *multisensory stimulation for speech production*, (2) *the syllable as the basic unit for speech instruction*, (3) *the teacher applies direct efforts at school toward the development of speech units* through (4) *emphasis on the second and third phases of speech development* (Table III-6), prompting the child to imitate and to respond with speech.

Multisensory Stimulation For Speech

An underlying premise of the multisensory approach is that the impaired auditory system of many deaf children is inadequate for speech development. Other sensory channels must also be brought into play. The auditory, visual, tactile, and kinesthetic senses are used selectively and discriminatingly for speech instruction. The teacher is guided in her choice both by the information-bearing properties available in varying units of speech and, of course, by the sensory capabilities of the children (1, 2, 3, 59, 72, 74, 76, 78, 79).

As we have seen in Chapter I and Chapter III, phonemes and speech rhythms vary in their potential for transmission, perception, and feedback over the different sensory systems. Considering the "sensory products" of the unit under instruction (36), the teacher may emphasize one sensory channel or the other, or may take advantage of combinations of channels that generate a strong sensory impression for the child. As we have recommended for those childen who have a great deal of usable hearing, the auditory channel should be the primary one for most speech instruction, supplemented by the other sensory channels. For children with less usable hearing, the auditory channel may be supplementary, generally reserved for teaching such speech features as phrasing, accent and emphasis, syllable duration, and the presence or absence of voicing. In some cases, combinations of sensory channels may be used initially to develop awareness of differences, resulting in some possible auditory discriminations.

The Multisensory Approach requires the teacher to select sensory channels carefully and rationally. For example, in the case of the bilabial consonants **p, b,** and **m,** visual information through lipreading and mirror observation can help the child develop each of them by clearly viewing the place of articulation. A mirror permits direct same-sense feedback of the child's production and comparison with the teacher's model. Yet these phonemes cannot be discriminated from each other by vision alone since they are *homophenous*— that is, they look the same on the lips. The difference in manner of production of the three sounds may or may not be discernable through the auditory system, depending on the child's hearing level. If they cannot be discriminated through the child's hearing, the alert teacher exploits sensitive tactile differences by having the child feel the puff of air on the back of his hand from the **p,** comparing the voiceless **p** to the vibration of voice on **b,** and placing his fingertips on the nose for **m.** Although feedback is accomplished for each of these sounds by the tactile sensation of the lips touching, the teacher may, through demonstration, emphasize the special kinesthetic feedback of **p** caused by relatively greater bilabial muscle tension necessary for this voiceless plosive, and the intense vibrotactile feedback of **m.**

The Syllable as the Basic Unit for Speech Instruction

This approach assumes that extensive use of units smaller than the longer sequences of connected speech is fundamental to instruction. The syllable, as described in Chapter I, is sufficient to demonstrate coarticulation of phonemes and yet is small enough to allow for accuracy of articulation since it does not demand much motor memory. Furthermore, it is the irreducible unit of speech necessary for demonstration of voice quality, inflection, and stress. The familiar instruction that the "accent is on the __ syllable" illustrates the point.

If the patterns of connected speech are well developed, these are, of course, conserved and improved. But where patterns are arhythmic or nonexistent, articulation may be well under way before serious attention is given to the acquisition of prosody. Patterning proceeds from the simple to the complex and is approached deductively from general rules applied to specifically targeted practice. At the outset the child may learn that "mother" is accented on the first syllable. Then he learns, for example, the contrast in duration and inflection of the word "Bill" in the sentences, "My name is Bill," and "My name is Bill Brown." The approach requires drill on frequently occurring linguistic patterns such as this.

Even in the initial stages the child is required to imitate babbled syllables such as *bubububu-* and *mumumumu-*. As the child progresses, drills typically include the combinations of the vowels and consonants that occur in English. This does not rule out particular attention to single sounds in isolation, but such sounds are not to be considered "learned" until they are produced in conventional syllables. Drills should generally proceed from simple patterns to more complex ones as the child gains in skills. Syllable drills may be systematized and greatly elaborated to form the substance of sequential speech instruction that is part of a speech-teaching curriculum (91, 118). *It is misleading, however, to suggest that syllable drills, no matter how organized, are sufficient for speech instruction.* As we have pointed out in Chapter II, repetition of syllables, no matter how skillfully or automatically performed, does not necessarily prepare the child for formulating and initiating useful and intelligible connected speech.

A useful approach to syllable drills is to prepare an inventory of the vowels and consonants in the positions in which they commonly occur. For example, if the target phoneme is **t**, it should be practiced with accompanying vowels (V) when **t** is in the initial position (**t**V), in the final position (V**t**) and in the medial position (V**t**V). Drills for **t** with the **ee** vowel, for example, should include *tee, eet,* and *eetee.* Vowels selected for practice in the **t** syllables should be those with which **t** commonly occurs in speech. The final **t** should be practiced both released with some explosion of breath, and unreleased (see Chapter VI). Then the **t** might be practiced in some of the common dual-consonant contexts within syllables such as the following:

st$V$ as in *steam*	Vsht as in *washed*
tr$V$ as in *tree*	Vst as in *west*
twh$V$ as in *twin*	Vnt as in *want*
Vts as in *waits*	Vlt as in *salt*
Vkt as in *act*	Vft as in *laughed*
Vcht as in *touched*	Vrt as in *art*
Vpt as in *dropped*	

Later the teacher may consider practicing some of the more complex consonant clusters with **t,** such as:

str*V* as in *stream*
*V*kts as in *acts*
*V*sts as in *guests*
*V*fts as in *gifts*
*V*lts as in *wilts*
*V*nts as in *wants*
*V*rts as in *starts*

The child's developing skill with these combinations can also serve as assessment of articulatory skills. Rockey (267), in her phonetic lexicon, has provided an excellent source of monosyllabic and some disyllabic words arranged
according to their phonetic structure, and Calvert (36) gives lists of words with
phonemes in various contexts. Other sources for drill are also available (88,
316). Ling presents a record for an inventory of phonemes in isolation and in
syllables (183, 184).

Another elaboration of syllable drills is to have the child produce *repetitive*
or *alternated* syllables. Practice on repetitive syllables reflects the observation
of children with normal hearing who babble, repeating syllables for sheer
enjoyment (55). It has been employed to begin connected vocalization in deaf
children before the days of electro-acoustic hearing aids. Avondino's classic
work on the Babbling Method dates from 1918 (6). At the simplest level, the
child is asked to imitate a continuous series of consonant-vowel (CV)
syllables, using different consonants and different vowels in each series, such
as *bubububububububu.* An exercise that requires more skill is to have the child
imitate a given number of syllables, such as *bububu* or *bubu-* and then stop.
There appears to be a difference in the skill required to produce a continuous
series compared to a finite series of two, three or four syllables and then stop.
These repetitive syllables may also begin with the vowel sound, such as
-ubububub and close with the unreleased *b.* Work toward improving the rate
of repetitive syllables may be carried on until the child approaches the maximum diadochokinetic rate of the speech mechanism for his age: 3.5
syllables/second at age 6, 4.5 syllables/second at age 12, and 5.5 syllables/sec-
ond at age 18. Inability to approach this rate of syllable repetition may be
prognostic for eventual attainment of fluent speech.

Production of alternated syllables adds further complexity to these drills
that strive to make articulation "automatic." A series such as *bubee-
bubeebubee* apparently requires more skill and conscious control than does

repetition of the same syllable. The teacher can create numerous variations using the same consonant with two different vowels, and then two different consonants with the same vowel, as in ***butubutubutu-***. To add further complexity, the syllable drill might involve several repetitions of three different vowels, or three different consonants.

Practice on multiple syllables also provides opportunity to practice variations of speech rhythm. Repetitive syllables might be practiced with stress on every other syllable to simulate the requirements of accent on words as in ***bubúbubúbubú-***, or ***bububúbubúbú-***. Intonation that requires changes in pitch can also be practiced with repetitive syllables, for example, with a rising fundamental pitch on the final syllable of ***bubububububu,*** similar to the intonation pattern for a question requiring a "yes" or "no" answer.

Some warnings about syllable drills are in order to reinforce what we have said about *repetition* in Chapter II. First, in considering how to increase the complexity of tasks utilizing these syllable drills, the teacher should observe the common-sense strategy of adding only one new task to each drill the child has mastered, rather than requiring him to take on two or three new tasks at a time. The drills can be prompted either by direct imitation (auditory, visual, tactile, or using a combination of sensory channels), or by prompting with written symbols, such as the General American speech and phonic symbols. Second, practice in producing syllables with phonemes in positions where they do not occur in speech is to be avoided. For example, final **h** or **wh** sounds do not occur in English. We do not ordinarily terminate a syllable with the vowels **-a-, -e-, -oo-,** or **-u-,** and practicing them as terminating sounds is likely to exaggerate their usually short duration. When practiced in syllables, they should be terminated with a consonant. In English, the **ng** and **oo** sounds do not initiate an utterance and should not be practiced in that position. The **w-** and **y-** sounds are always released into vowel sounds and should be so presented in syllable drills.

Direct Development of Speech Units

The Multisensory Syllable Unit approach assumes that speech will *not* develop just from the child's hearing and seeing connected speech in the conventional course of conversation, nor will it develop completely with a special program of speech stimulation, however natural or planned. Accurate articulation of speech sounds and their combinations will need to be learned by focused instruction.

When by chance a child does produce an acceptable speech sound during stimulation or even at play, the teacher takes advantage of his unprompted production, has the child repeat it, rewards him, and then associates the sound with the appropriate written orthographic symbol. Here the symbols of the General American system, described in Chapter I, are useful. Later the teacher may write the symbol on a chalkboard in order to prompt the child to recall and produce the associated speech sound.

However, the development of phonemes is not left to chance. Unlike the Auditory Global approach in which all speech sounds are in some discernible state of development, speech sounds are introduced a few at a time and in a pre-determined order. A limited number of new sounds may be introduced while other sounds are still emerging in the process of development and still others have already been mastered. The rate and sequence with which new sounds are introduced are governed by the child's progress toward mastery of the sound in syllable combinations.

The order in which speech sounds are developed is important for building on previous experience. Some teachers recommend the same order of development for hearing-impaired children that occurs when children with normal hearing acquire speech, but others suggest that the limitations of impaired hearing contraindicate this sequence. For them, a useful guide has been to order development based on the ease with which children have been observed to learn the production of sounds. Those sounds which are easiest to learn would be taught first, progressing to sounds of increasing difficulty. The child thus has maximum opportunity for successful experience with speech development. Table IV-1 shows a consensus of judgments of a sample of teachers experienced in the Multisensory Syllable-Unit approach about the relative difficulty of developing phonemes. Certainly there are individual differences in judgment. It is interesting, nevertheless, that our *ad hoc* sampling and the

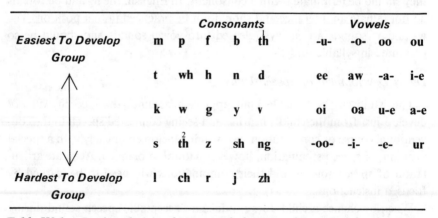

	Consonants					Vowels			
Easiest To Develop Group	m	p	f	b	th	-u-	-o-	oo	ou
	t	wh	h	n	d	ee	aw	-a-	i-e
	k	w	g	y	v	oi	oa	u-e	a-e
	s	th̃	z	sh	ng	-oo-	-i-	-e-	ur
Hardest To Develop Group	l	ch	r	j	zh				

Table IV-1. Rank ordering of groups of phonemes by ease of development, made by teachers of deaf children.

data on difficulty of development reported by Hudgins and Numbers agree impressively well (139). Of course, spontaneously produced speech sounds should be reinforced regardless of the order in which they occur. If a child has special difficulty with one sound, the teacher should move on to another rather than persisting.

It is interesting to note here, as we do in our discussion of errors of articulation in Chapter V, that inadequate coordination of voicing and articulation results in **p** being heard as **b,** **t** as **d,** and **k** as **g** when combined with a vowel. Yet these confusions seldom if ever occur in the production of the isolated consonant. The voice onset time, defined as the interval between the release of the stop closure and the onset of the following vowel, is different for **p** and **b.** It is much shorter for **b,** and if voice onset time is not long enough for **p** it will be heard as **b.** This observation suggests that order of development could take into account classes of combinations that have common features. For example, voiced stops joining vowels (**bu-, du-, gu-**) might be first, then voiceless stops plus vowels (**pu-, tu-, ku-**). Since no particular order of development has been convincingly validated, it is essential to be alert to all possibilities and to depend on what seems to "work."

Given the Multisensory Syllable-Unit approach as the general approach of choice (as determined by criteria discussed later in this chapter), it is implicit that a period of the day will be set aside for speech work. This period will be devoted to work on development, with introduction at the outset of an orthographic system, as well as to the child's specific needs. The child for whom the Multisensory Syllable-Unit approach is indicated is likely to require a good deal of repetitive practice and directed drill. It goes without saying that the teacher will be alert to promote transfer of skills acquired in the special period to use in all other situations. As the crucial monitor of the child's speech, she will probably practice more frequent spontaneous correction. Of course, she will exercise discriminating judgment as to what is accepted without correction. Her understanding of a child's capability and motivations will necessarily guide her reinforcing behavior.

The teacher might maintain in the classroom a visible inventory of each child's development of speech sounds, sometimes reflecting accomplishments of a class of children with charts or written General American or Northampton symbols, or she may create individual workbooks in which she writes symbols for the sounds each child has mastered. Children take great pride in accomplishments that are concrete, and an orthographic symbol on a chart or in a book can be shown to their parents or others as evidence and reminder of what they have accomplished. The potential motivational value of such speech books or charts should not be overlooked.

The teacher's own inventory should be more sophisticated, recognizing the child's stages of accomplishment for each phoneme in various contexts, and suggesting what is yet to be accomplished. We recommend that the teacher keep an inventory record of phonemes and other speech units similar to that developed by Moog and Kozak (219) for language structures. Table IV-2 (consonants) and Table IV-3 (vowels) suggest forms for such an inventory of phonemes. These tables consider phoneme development in three ways: PRO-DUCTION, whether and how well the phoneme *can* be produced; PRAC-TICE, whether the phoneme *does* or *does not* occur when prompted in exercises for speech practice; PURPOSE, whether the phoneme *is used* when the child's spoken language is intended for purposeful communication.

For each manifestation of phoneme development noted at the top of the inventory of Tables IV-2 and IV-3, the teacher may observe 3 levels of achievement as follows:

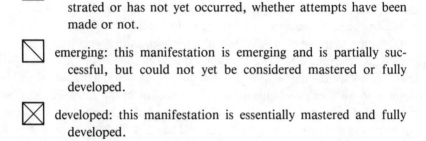

absent: this manifestation of development has not been demonstrated or has not yet occurred, whether attempts have been made or not.

emerging: this manifestation is emerging and is partially successful, but could not yet be considered mastered or fully developed.

developed: this manifestation is essentially mastered and fully developed.

The inventory forms may also be used as a record of speech development objectives, using dashed lines to indicate that a level, not yet achieved, is the goal or teaching objective for the immediate future or for a given period of time. Such a record documents the ***child's individual speech program*** that was suggested in Chapter II. This helps support planning for speech in each child's Individualized Educational Program (IEP).

For each of the three areas considered in phoneme development (PRO-DUCTION, PRACTICE, PURPOSE), there are three manifestations or situations for the teacher to assess. With 3 levels of achievement (absent, emerging, developed) for each of the 9 manifestations, the teacher has 27 possible judgments for describing the development of each phoneme. The tables provide quick-scan visual profiles of a child's overall phoneme development that point up difficulties with certain classes of phonemes (stops, fricatives, affricates, etc.), and show progress in moving from simple produc-

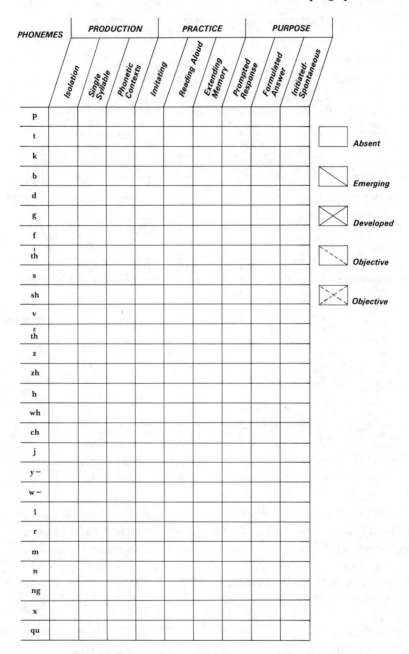

PHONEMES	PRODUCTION				PRACTICE			PURPOSE	
	Isolation	Single Syllable	Phonetic Contexts	Imitating	Reading Aloud	Extending Memory	Prompted Response	Formulated Answer	Initiated-Spontaneous
p									
t									
k									
b									
d									
g									
f									
¹th									
s									
sh									
v									
²th									
z									
zh									
h									
wh									
ch									
j									
y –									
w –									
l									
r									
m									
n									
ng									
x									
qu									

□ Absent

◺ Emerging

☒ Developed

⬎ Objective

⧄ Objective

Table IV-2.   Consonant phoneme inventory of development and record of teaching objectives.

| | PRODUCTION | | | PRACTICE | | | PURPOSE | | |
	Isolation	Single Syllable	Phonetic Contexts	Imitating	Reading Aloud	Extending Memory	Prompted Response	Formulated Answer	Initiated-Spontaneous
ee									
−i−									
−e−									
−a−									
oo									
−oo−									
aw									
−o−									
−u−									
ur									
u−e									
a−e									
oa									
oi									
i−e									
ou									

Legend:
- Absent
- Emerging
- Developed
- Objective
- Objective

Table IV-3.   *Vowel and diphthong phoneme inventory of development and record of teaching objectives.*

tion to drill practice or from practice to purposeful use, and that suggest the relation between the quality of a phoneme's production and its usage.

The nine manifestations provide a broad range of situations for describing the status of each phoneme. Their definition and description follows:

The first three manifestations of PRODUCTION concern whether a child can produce the target phoneme.

Isolation

Some children do not readily imitate a speech sound from the teacher's example, but make an attempt that resembles the model phoneme in some important way. They may produce correctly either the *manner* (stop, fricative, affricate, nasal resonant, oral resonant) or the *place* (bilabial, labio-dental, lingua-dental, lingua-velar, lingua-alveolar, lingua-palatal) of articulation (see Figure I-8), but not produce both correctly. Or, the place and manner of articulation may be satisfactory but *voicing* is inappropriate. Vowel sounds may be produced with adequate voicing but the tongue height may be just one position higher or lower (see the vowel diagram, Figure I-7) than it should be. The voicing and vowel position may be correct but the lips are inappropriately rounded or unrounded, or there is hyper-nasality in the voicing (see Chapter I). The child may be able to produce accurately either component of an affricate (the stop or the fricative) but not both in a single impulse. These approximations that the teacher judges to be progress in the right direction, but not yet satisfactory for production of the phoneme in isolation, may be marked with the "emerging" diagonal line.

Some children will imitate some phonemes adequately the first time or two they are prompted to do so, skipping over the approximation stage. The teacher may then mark the "developed" **X** if the phoneme's production is satisfactory and seems to be mastered.

Single Syllable

Some children, skipping over the isolation stage, imitate some phonemes in a syllable the first time or two they are prompted to do so. For this manifestation of development, the teacher will mark for adequacy of production, and whether the sound can be produced in the different positions of a syllable. When the phoneme is produced only in the initial position of a syllable, the diagonal "emerging" line should be made. The teacher may mark the "developed" **X** if the phoneme can be produced in medial and final positions of syllables, as well.

Phonetic Contexts

Phonemes occur in a variety of phonetic contexts in addition to the typical consonant-vowel (CV) combinations. This was previously illustrated for the **t** sound in the section on systematizing syllable drills, where the **t** occurred in such clusters within a syllable as **st, tr, ts, sht, kts, sts, rts,** etc. In addition, consonants that end one syllable adjoin other consonants that begin the next for combinations that do not occur within a single syllable. For example, the **t** may occur in the following combinations:

td as in *hotdog*	**tn** as in *last night*
tb as in *batboy*	**tl** as in *out late*
tg as in *it goes*	**tr** as in *it runs*
tp as in *that pie*	**tf** as in *outfit*
tk as in *what kite*	**tth** as in *that thing*

Exercises with syllables that build skill in these combinations and others with **t** should be included in considering a child's progress on producing this phoneme in *phonetic contexts.* When a child can produce all the appropriate blends, clusters and combinations for **t**, the "developed" **X** should be marked. When he can produce about half of those that the teacher includes in her inventory for that sound, the "emerging" diagonal mark should be given.

*The next three manifestations concern whether a child **does** produce the target phoneme in **practice** exercises.*

Imitating

Once a phoneme can be produced successfully in isolation or in a syllable, it is usually practiced in various exercises or drills. Such practice need not wait until the phoneme can be produced in all of its possible phonetic contexts. Exercises requiring the least amount or shortest term of memory for speech are those prompted for immediate imitation, whether they be elicited from an auditory example, a visual (lipreading) example, a tactile example, or any combination of these.

Practice for very young children may begin with imitation of the phoneme in isolation or in single syllables, but commonly the emphasis is on producing the phoneme in consecutive multiple syllables at a rate that approaches the rate of syllables produced in connected speech. One simple exercise requires the child to repeat the same syllable a number of times in succession. The teacher may prompt the child just to produce the syllables repetitively, or to produce the exact number of syllables prompted by her example, and to produce them at a rate of about three syllables/second (par for age 6 years). Another syllable exercise requires the child to produce alternated syllables, such as *beebobeebobeebo-,* with the two syllables differing in only one phoneme. Ability to repeat the same syllable usually precedes this skill. For this alternate syllable exercise, there are a great many combinations possible, considering the number of consonants, vowels and diphthongs available, and also considering that a vowel or consonant may begin in the middle, or terminate the syllable.

The imitated unit may also be a segment of meaningful language. The teacher may ask the child to imitate a word, phrase, or sentence. As the teacher observes the child's ability to imitate nonsense syllables or units of spoken language, she may judge that the target phoneme is "absent" from most attempts at imitation, is "emerging" (diagonal line) and occurs some of the time, at least in short segments, or that it occurs almost all of the time and may be considered "developed" (*X* mark).

Reading Aloud

Another context for practicing speech production is oral reading. This may include producing isolated phonemes prompted by the associated General American symbols, or by reading syllables, words, sentences and paragraphs aloud. When reading aloud, most deaf children are more likely to produce a phoneme, such as **s**, when they see it written than they are to produce it when prompted by a picture or object, or when using it spontaneously. The written symbol "s" reminds them to include this sound, which is difficult for deaf children to monitor. Sometimes when a child omits the **s** in a word like *boats* during spontaneous or object-prompted speech, the teacher may remind him of the absent sound simply by writing the word *boats* on the board so that the child corrects himself. When a child is just beginning to include the phonemes in oral reading, or when he is just beginning to correct himself from the written prompt, the "emerging" diagonal marks should be used, while the "developed" *X* should be used only after the child has mastered this symbol-sound correspondence and produces the sound whenever it is written.

Extending Memory

Exercises that require extending memory for production of speech units are commonly used to bridge the gap between simple imitation and purposeful usage by the child. Simple imitation of a few coarticulated phonemes, syllables or words requires only a kind of "echoic" short-term memory in which the child may produce the speech unit without necessarily storing the pattern for later reproduction (48, 49, 50). Since the object of learning speech is to be able to produce the appropriate speech unit at an appropriate time in the future, retention of the pattern of producing the speech unit, so that it can be recalled and reproduced, is a basic goal.

Exercises that extend speech memory take a number of forms and are used for teaching both speech and language (189). A teacher may say a word or phrase and then ask the child to "turn around" and say the unit to another person or to the class of children, requiring delayed imitation. Or, the teacher may ask the child to read a phrase, either aloud or silently, and then to say the phrase from memory. Commonly, the teacher will help the child with producing parts of a long phrase, and then ask the child to say the entire phrase with the appropriate sequence of words. In these exercises, the child is not required to formulate or recode spoken language, since the speech unit he is asked to produce is the same as the example presented to him.

In exercises for extending speech memory, some phonemes are less likely to occur than when the child simply imitates speech. The teacher may observe and note which phonemes are "absent" or occur rarely, which occur occasionally and are "emerging," and which occur most of the time and may be considered "developed."

*The next three manifestations concern whether the target phoneme **is used** or not when the child's spoken language is intended for **purposeful** communication.*

Prompted Response

Much of the speech that occurs in a classroom is prompted or elicited by the teacher. At the prompted response level, the child is required to call upon his memory for the appropriate response to an eliciting stimulus, sometimes having to shape or formulate his response to fit the stimulus. This is the beginning level for using speech purposefully.

A rudimentary exercise involves showing the child single objects or pictures and asking him to say the name of each object. A more complex exercise is to show the child pictures of objects with descriptive modifiers and to elicit a speech response that requires some formulation of language such as "three balls," "a red car," or "a big house." Toys may be moved through actions suggesting increasingly more complex language structures so that the child may be asked to describe that "the dog jumped on the bed," for example. The teacher may also elicit a specific grammatical structure by her verbal prompting, for example, by showing a dog with a bone and saying, "The dog has a bone," then removing the bone to elicit from the child "The dog does *not* have a bone."

Most of these exercises seem to be directed toward developing the use of vocabulary and grammatical structures in spoken language. They also contribute to the child's experience in *using* phonemes while he is formulating spoken language, particularly those phonemes that he has previously learned to produce and has practiced in imitative and memory-extending exercises. In the controlled conditions of the classroom, some deaf children use phonemes regularly that might be frequently omitted during their spontaneous speech. Many teachers have noted, for example, that "his speech is pretty good in the classroom, but it gets sloppy when he is talking to friends."

During such prompted response in the classroom, the teacher may judge that a particular phoneme is almost always included in his response and mark the "developed" X, she may judge that the phoneme is used frequently, but is absent many times and merits an "emerging" diagonal mark, or she may note that when a child formulates spoken language, certain phonemes are almost never used unless the child is reminded about them.

Formulated Answer

The most common way of eliciting spoken language is to ask a question. The answer, as a manifestation of spoken language, requires that the child formulate language—determine vocabulary, decide on appropriate grammatical structures and word order, and consider the phonemes to be produced (see Chapter VII). Because of the complexity of formulation, the child is more likely to omit phonemes or to produce them very poorly.

Questions vary in the degree of formulation required for response. A question that suggests a simple "yes" or "no" answer requires very limited formulation. When the child understands that his teacher already knows the answer, he is aware that it is the *form* (speech and language production) of his answer that is important, rather than the *content*. Some questions, because of their similar vocabulary and language structures, suggest the form of the answer so that only a little original formulation is required of the child. Still others are open-ended and require a great deal of original formulation.

In observing children's responses to this range of questions, the teacher may judge that a particular phoneme is almost always included at the level of the child's best ability and mark the "developed" *X*. When the phoneme is occasionally omitted or poorly produced, she marks the "emerging" diagonal line or notes that the phoneme is omitted most of the time.

Initiated-Spontaneous

This context for the use of speech occurs when the child wants to communicate information on his own that the receiver does not already know. The *content* of his spoken language is important to him, rather than its *form*. Under these conditions, many deaf children make errors of articulation or omit phonemes that they might otherwise include in more controlled situations. It is a test of how automatic and habitual a child's articulation of phonemes has become. The teacher needs to plan to sample the child's spontaneous speech in several situations. The receiver may be a classmate, an adult, a visitor, or any of the individuals in recurring communication situations illustrated in Figure 1 of the *Introduction* to this book. The "developed" *X* mark should be reserved for phonemes that are used in spontaneous speech in nearly every situation and phonetic context, while the diagonal "emerging" mark is used for a phoneme that is commonly used but omitted frequently enough to interfere with intelligibility.

The Association Phoneme-Unit Approach

The Association Phoneme-Unit approach was motivated by the need to devise an alternative for those children who by the methods previously described were not learning to talk. It has its origins in the ideas and experience of Mildred McGinnis at Central Institute for the Deaf and was intended for those whose hearing impairment was overlaid by conditions that would render conventional procedures unsuitable to the achievement of oral communication (205). A number of these conditions and the variety of symptoms ascribed to them were subsumed under the rubric "congenital aphasia." The issues related to etiology, nomenclature, and classification, or whether this clinical entity occurs at all, are beyond the scope of this book, as are any applications of the method to other "learning disabilities." What is pertinent to our purposes is that in our experience hearing-impaired children have acquired functional spoken language by this approach or its adaptations (307). Our brief exposition is based on McGinnis' elaboration of the method in her treatise on the identification and education of asphasic children and on our own observation and experience.

The more distinctive characteristics of the Association Phoneme-Unit approach are these: (1) *multisensory stimulation for speech production,* (2) *the individual phoneme is the basic unit for speech instruction,* (3) *the teacher applies direct efforts primarily in school toward the development of speech units* through (4) *emphasis on the third phase of speech development* (Table III-6), prompting the child to respond with speech in association with her speech and with other language modalities.

Multisensory Stimulation For Speech Production

As in the Multisensory Syllable Unit approach, all sensory channels are used selectively for speech development. Since precise speech production is desired, more stress, at least initially, is placed on visual stimulation in this approach. Once a child has successfully produced a speech unit, emphasis is placed on his memory of that production, rather than on continued sensory stimulation as a prompt. Auditory-only stimulation exercises (in which the mouth is hidden) are used in this approach, and may become the focus of perceiving speech for children with mild or moderate hearing levels.

The Phoneme Is the Basic Unit for Speech Instruction.

The single phoneme in isolation is the basic unit of instruction for speech production. Its precise articulation enhances the memory for the motor acts associated with it and its combinations. Voiceless sounds (such as **p, f, ch**) are said in isolation without a voice carrier and voiced stops are terminated with the vowel **-u-**. Since the written symbol is always associated with the spoken phoneme, the child and teacher develop a written inventory of the

Learning a single sound by the Association Phoneme Unit approach

phonemes which have been "mastered." Near-perfect production of a number of consonants and vowels is required before "blending" of two or more phonemes is attempted. Drills blend consonant and vowel sounds leading to the articulation of a word. Even after words are begun, the child continues to say the phoneme separately and blended in syllables. When he makes an error in a word, the child is instructed first to repeat the phonemes individually and then to "smooth" the sounds together. To direct attention to individual speech sounds within syllables, consonants are frequently written in one color and the vowels in another. Smoothing may be facilitated by cursive script. Advocates of cursive script point to its clarity in separating words while connecting letters within words.

From mastery of his first phoneme the child develops speech in small units progressing from the simple to the complex. A reasonable number of individual phonemes are developed before blending of consonants and vowels is attempted. When the child can blend with some confidence, two or more phonemes are combined into single-syllable words such as *pie* and *boat*. When a number of words are mastered, the child is ready to put a few together into simple sentences such as, "I see a boat."

Once the child has learned to recognize and produce a unit of spoken language, he is expected to recall and produce it without frequent prompting. When, for example, the child is asked to say aloud the phoneme associated with a written symbol, the teacher withholds clues until the child has exerted his best effort to respond correctly. The teacher encourages the child to remember and gives him sufficient time to "search his memory." This sort of practice in recall should gradually decrease the time and effort necessary to accomplish it.

For the child who has experienced failure and discouragement by other methods, the experience of success is especially to be stressed. The achievement of real success and its accompanying satisfactions are more probable when the required increment of learning is small.

Direct Development of Speech Units

As in the Multisensory Syllable-Unit approach, the teacher develops each of the phonemes and maintains an inventory of their status, whether emerging and mastered (see Tables IV-2 and IV-3). Even if a child should produce an acceptable phoneme by chance, he should be required to produce it carefully to be sure it is under conscious control. Duration and force of articulation of phonemes may need to be exaggerated in order to enhance their tactile and kinesthetic impression, and to give the child a clear auditory impression of the formant target of vowels and the spectral features of consonants.

The Association Phoneme Unit approach is based on the idea that speech perception is influenced by speech production. We tend to hear the speech of others as we produce it. For example, when we hear the Spanish bilabial voiced fricative consonant in *Havana* (a sound that does not occur in English), we hear it either as a **b** (which is a bilabial stop) or a **v** (which is a labio-dental fricative), both sounds which we produce.

The child is taught to produce each sound very precisely, thus developing a strong motor pattern which should be easy for him to remember. He learns to associate most of the speech he sees and hears with the patterns he has produced. No formal lipreading, listening, or reading is attempted in the Association Phoneme Unit approach except for words which the child can say.

When a child produces a sound correctly, it is immediately associated with other means of language expression and reception by the following specified steps, generally in the indicated sequence.

a. The child reads the symbol (General American) for the sound written by the teacher and pronounces it aloud.

b. He lipreads (and hears as he is able) the sound produced by the teacher and again pronounces it aloud.

c. He lipreads the sound produced by the teacher, writes the appropriate symbol himself, and once more pronounces it aloud.

d. He hears the speech sound—but does not "see" it—as the teacher says it near his ear, then writes it and again pronounces it aloud.

Writing is always associated with oral production. This association of speech with other language modalities is prescribed for a phonologic and linguistic range of increasing complexity from single phonemes, through individual words, to sentences and questions.

Of the four phases of the acquisition of speech and spoken language in Table III-6, this approach emphasizes phase 3, in which the child is prompted to respond, not by imitating but by answering with an appropriate vocal response. This stimulus-response paradigm begins by prompting the child to produce a single phoneme associated with its written symbol, advances to requiring the child to remember the word associated with an object or picture and to say and write that word, and then to prompting the child to say a sentence in response to the teacher's written or spoken question. The child's ability to retain and recall, and a long period of familiarity with the question-answer use of spoken language, are believed to lead to the initiation of spoken language.

The primary characteristics of the three basic approaches to developing speech are summarized in Table IV-4. Now we turn to the problem of choosing among these approaches for individual hearing-impaired children.

CHOOSING AN APPROACH

Recognizing the conditions affecting the acquisition of spoken language, the initial approach of choice should meet the following requirements:

1. The approach should be appropriate for very young children whenever they are identified.

We enthusiastically advocate appropriately planned measures to develop speech at the earliest possible time. Intervention for speech development could begin at birth. Unfortunately, the opportunity to do this is rare. Such procedures as are available for neonatal screening for hearing impairment are of questionable reliability, validity, and economy, and those that do show some promise are not widely used. Nor is screening routine in "well-baby" clinics or in conventional pediatric care. Even when hearing loss is recognized early, timely intervention does not always follow. Early education programs may not be conveniently available or parents may delay action. Some health care professionals still advise parents to "come back in six months" for more tests or to "wait until he is old enough" for school.

Organized as we now are, our imperfect system of early identification and delays in initiation of action result in the opportunity for intervention coming at different ages for children. In the past, apparent consistency in the age of intervention with deaf children was achieved by setting an arbitrary "age of admission" for enrollment in programs of early education. Such a policy cost

	Sensory Channel Emphasized	Basic Unit of Speech	Teacher Intervention Area	Acquisition Phase Emphasized
Auditory-Global Approach	Auditory	Connected Speech	Comprehensive Intervention	Stimulation
Multi-sensory Syllable Unit	Auditory Visual Tactile	Syllable	School with home carry over	Imitation Prompted Response
Association Phoneme Unit	Tactile-Kinesthetic Auditory Visual	Phoneme	Primarily School	Prompted Response

Table IV-4.   Summary of primary characteristics of alternative approaches to developing speech.

children valuable months and even years of waiting until they reached the designated age.

2. *The approach should provide maximum opportunity for each child to develop his hearing ability, regardless of early estimates of the nature and degree of hearing loss.*

Current procedures for assessing and describing the hearing ability of very young children do not yield the information related to speech development that we should like to have. Information about perception of patterns, the use of minimal auditory cues, attentiveness to sound, and sensitivity to changes in intensity, frequency, and duration would be helpful. The younger the child and the greater his hearing impairment, the less information about his hearing ability we can obtain. Many of our audiologic tests require complex directions and responses, previous experience with listening, and, to some extent, familiarity with speech. Firm decisions on the basis of premature and meager evidence should be scrupulously avoided.

Even when reasonably valid audiologic test results (primarily audiograms) are available, audiologists and educators have struggled over the problems of definition and classification for educational purposes. In the main they have resorted to "behavioral" definitions. In this context a *deaf child* is defined as one who "cannot understand and acquire speech and language through the sense of hearing, even with sound amplification," while the *severely hard of hearing child* "suffers delayed speech and language development." But such behavioral definitions are of little value for the young child who, fortuitously, has been identified at an early age. Before these definitions can be applied they require that the child has had some significant experience—has tried and either failed or succeeded. They may also lead to static classification of hearing impaired children into rigidly determined groups in response to conventional arrangements for educational placement.

3. The approach should provide an opportunity to identify other disabilities which might affect speech development.

Gross disorders such as cleft palate, blindness, and cerebral palsy are obvious. Neuromuscular incoordination, visual defects, and mental retardation may be revealed through testing or observation. Instructional experience is probably the only way to ascertain clues to milder but significant disabilities and to pervasive problems in language learning. The latter are often difficult to pinpoint and their precise definition is frequently elusive. A good illustration of this issue is the history of controversy surrounding the early identification of "congenital aphasia." Table II-2 shows additional handicapping conditions encountered in schools and classes for the deaf as reported to the Office of Demographic Studies at Gallaudet College (101).

Of course, when combined with hearing loss, disabilities may retard or in extreme cases prevent the acquisition of speech—this despite excellence of teaching in the context of an environment that promotes its use. Nevertheless, it is irresponsible to assume *at the outset* that certain disabilities, of whatever degree or kind, will preclude learning to speak. Confident prediction of their precise effect is indeed precarious and difficult. The child should have the benefit of appropriate and sufficient empirical tests of assumptions about his ability to learn to talk. To do otherwise is to arrive at an all too common self-fulfilling prophecy. If a child is treated as though he will not learn, he will not learn.

4. The approach should provide sufficient experience for assessing progress in speech development.

Knowledge of a child's previous experience with intervention for speech development can influence not only initial steps but also the efficacy of continuing with the previous approach or of changing to an alternate one. Specifically we should know the nature and duration of the experience and the progress in speech or speech-like behavior resulting from it. Two 30-month-old children with similar hearing levels cannot be compared for speech development when one has worn a hearing aid for 12 months and the other not at all, or when one has had guidance in his home environment through an early education program and the other has only been fitted with a hearing aid and given no treatment. Chapter II addresses ways to describe the nature of the child's experience.

In addition to the total time elapsed from beginning to end of the experience, the amount of time during which the child has been directly involved warrants attention. The duration of an experience that will influence the decision about change in approach is likely to vary with chronological age. The older the child the less time there is available for observing the progress resulting from initial procedures. Nevertheless, sufficient time should be allowed to make a reasonably confident judgment.

We are usually inclined to compare the young child's speech output with that of normal children of the same chronological age or with that of other deaf children of a similar age and hearing level. We may compare the rate of speech development and the amount, spontaneity, and intelligibility of speech. But when the child has had previous intervention, we should assess his speech production before and after that experience, comparing his progress with that of similar children who have undergone the same experience.

It is our considered judgment that the above requirements are best met by the Auditory Global approach and we recommend it as the initial approach of choice. Realistically we need to anticipate that the Auditory Global approach will not be satisfactory for all children. Careful regular assessment of the child's progress in learning to talk is essential as suggested by this simple flow chart.

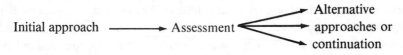

ASSESSMENT

Time for Assessment

With the initial approach, no hard and fast rules can be laid down for the best length of experience or for the age of the child before formal speech assessment, but Table IV-5 provides some general guidelines. A two- to three-year period of experience with the initial approach gives a reasonably good opportunity to judge a very young child's progress. On the other hand, by the time he is of kindergarten age it is important to have him placed in the kind of program he will find to best advantage. Regardless of age, though, the initial approach experience should probably not be less than six months. Even

Age at Beginning of Initial Approach	Age at Assessment
6 months	2 to 3 years
1 to 2 years	3 to 4 years
3 to 4 years	4 to 5 years
5 years	5.5 to 6 years
6 years	6.5 years

Table IV-5. *Guide to term of initial approach and age at assessment.*

before the formal assessment takes place, the teacher and parents should have been making continuous observations during the experience which will be helpful to gauge the child's progress.

Questions for Assessment

After a reasonable experience with the Auditory Global approach, assessment should address three basic questions:
1. What progress has the child made in speech development?
2. What special problems does the child have in learning speech?
3. Can an environment conducive to speech development be maintained?

1. What Progress Has the Child Made in Speech Development?

Progress in speech development should consider the aspects of speech discussed in previous chapters, *voice, rhythm,* and *articulation.* Now ready for assessment is speech *usage,* an additional important dimension. If the child is making good progress with the Auditory Global approach, the volume of his voice should be adequate to carry speech to the average listener and his voice quality should approximate that of a child of his age with normal hearing. The normal temporal features and intonation of connected speech, fundamental outcomes of the Auditory Global approach, should be emerging. These include patterning of questions, declarative sentences, exclamations, and serial words. Arhythmic speech, as evidenced by single words serving as the total utterance, or words in the same phrase but separated by pauses and having undifferentiated syllabic value, suggests the need for change in approach.

Articulation development should be well along. However, at an early age precise articulation is not critical. The Auditory Global approach does not stress precision in the early years. The child should have many words recognizable at least to parents and teachers, rather than a few words accurately pronounced. Vowel/consonant differentiation should be made easily. Manner and/or place of articulation along with coarticulation should be approximated or achieved. A pertinent question here is whether the child has formed an internalized phonological system similar to that of a normal talker. For example, in addition to emerging manner and place features, does the child produce normal durational differences resulting from phonetic context? Consider the duration of the vowels **ee** and **-i-** in the words *eat* and *ease,* and in *it* and *is.* Note the difference in duration of the same vowels determined by the consonant following. To assess articulation at this time, a picture description test which demands **connected speech** may be more useful than a single-word picture-naming test, but a combination of the two should not be ruled out.

In most situations, the child should be using speech to make his wants known, to respond to others, and to initiate communication. The utterances are likely to be accompanied by gestures just as with a normal child. Of course, semantic and syntactic development of spoken language should be noted. A promising guide for judging them is the Scales of Early Communication Skills for Hearing Impaired Children developed by Moog and Geers at Central Institute for the Deaf.

2. What Special Problems Does the Child Have in Learning Speech?

A reasonable amount of experience should reveal to the alert teacher any special problems in learning speech. The handicapping effects of obvious disabilities, such as vision or motor control and others listed in Table II-2, can be assessed. If a special problem in learning speech exists, change to another method may be indicated to accommodate that problem. Of course the child's progress, despite the disability, must be considered.

3. Can an Environment Conducive to Speech Development Be Maintained?

In Chapter II we outlined the requirements for an "oral environment," and earlier in this chapter we have stressed the need for comprehensive support for communication in the child's home and community. The parents' attitudes and interest in working with their child and in cooperating with the professionally directed program may influence the decision to discontinue the Auditory Global approach, even though the child has the potential for benefiting from it. For example, the professional staff may note that, despite counseling and reminders, the parents have not kept the child's hearing aid constantly operative, have not made and kept appointments for hearing examinations as advised, or have not provided speech stimulation. An impoverished auditory-oral environment, whatever its cause, will render ineffective the Auditory Global approach.

If assessment of experience with the Auditory Global approach is judged to be satisfactory we recommend its continuance beyond the preschool, keeping in mind the previously mentioned pragmatic points that need to be considered. Among the conventional options to accomplish this are:

a. No special assistance: One alternative is to place the hearing-impaired child in a regular class with no provision for special assistance. This assumes that auditory stimulation in the natural course of events will be sufficient to maintain continuing speech development; it is indicated generally for those children with moderate degrees of hearing loss who use hearing aids very effectively. Guidance for the parents and classroom teacher may be necessary to ensure a facilitating acoustic environment. Periodic reassessment should include an analysis of hearing, electro-acoustic measurements of the characteristics of the hearing aid, and, of course, evaluation of speech and language development. Lagging speech development may call for more intensive procedures.

b. Special tutorial assistance: Some children will require the support of tutorial assistance that supplements their placement in a regular full-time classroom. Such assistance may be obtained through the school speech and hearing program, from a community agency, or through a private tutor. The speech tutor should have the dual responsibility to foster speech development and to maintain maximal auditory stimulation through auditory training. For such a child speech deviations are likely to be articulatory, although voice and rhythm may require some attention. Here and there some special language instruction may be included in the supportive regimen.

c. Part- or full-time special class: A third alternative is to enroll the child in a special class part of his school day, providing regular classes the rest of the day. This situation should include a program of parental guidance, guidance for teachers of those regular classes in which the child is enrolled, and annual reassessment of hearing, of hearing aids, and of speech and language development. The special class should provide intensive communication instruction and assistance with other academic instruction. It may range from a resource room which the child attends for only one hour a day to a special class for most or all of the day.

The program should be flexible enough to enable a child to move from one to the other of these situations. Children commonly termed "mildly hard of hearing," "moderately hard of hearing," "moderately deaf," or "deaf" may be included. Such terms are irrelevant. The child's academic achievement, his social development, and his progress in language and speech—rather than his hearing level—should be the deciding factors.

If progress by the Auditory Global approach is judged to be unsatisfactory, then we recommend either the Multisensory Syllable-Unit approach or the Association Phoneme-Unit approach. Our choice between these two methods depends upon assessment of experience that addresses itself to the same questions posed for the Auditory Global approach. Obviously the answers to these questions need to take into account the child's age and the reasonableness of the length of experience.

What progress has the child made in speech development? In general this child requires multisensory stimulation to develop speech. Assessment, therefore, should focus on how the child responds to such stimulation. He should be able to respond by imitation to vibro-tactile and visual cues that may convey speech information about place, manner, voicing, duration, pitch, loudness, and patterning. Of course, auditory stimulation should always be available. Retention and retrieval of stored phonologic information should be demonstrated. Depending on the child's stage of development, this may be elicited by pointing to an orthographic symbol, a picture, or a written word or phrase. There should be evidence of the ability to produce increasingly longer combinations of segments of speech without abnormal motor effort. As the child learns orthographic symbols, he should be strengthening his power to attack the production of new vocabulary graphically presented—for example, oral reading of chart language. Fundamentally, as with the Auditory Global approach, speech should be developing as a vehicle for everyday communication, initiated by the child and not perceived by him merely as a classroom gymnastic.

By this time the retarding effects of the kinds of special problems cited during the early Auditory Global approach period will have been noted. It is important, too, that a continuing reinforcing oral environment be maintained and that the child's teachers be skilled in multisensory methods. If the assessment leads to a reasonably positive judgment, the Multisensory Syllable-Unit approach should be used. If not, the Association Phoneme-Unit approach should be tried with the expectancy that the child can "graduate" to one or the other of the approaches, or a combination of them.

From what we have said about choosing among approaches, it is evident that although exclusive, incontrovertibly valid techniques for making decisions are not immediately at hand, there are sufficient bases for making rational judgments. Furthermore, we repeat that sensible management requires periodic evaluation and that one should avoid an attitude of irrevocable commitment to a particular approach. The possibility of shift in method or of employing effective combinations of methods should always be kept in mind.

CHAPTER V

Improving and Maintaining Speech

In this chapter we shall assume that the foundation for speech development, as treated in Chapter IV, has been laid. We now turn our attention to the instructional activities that build upon it and lead to improvement. As we have said in the Introduction, speech must not only be developed; it must be improved or corrected, and maintained. It is difficult, and perhaps not too helpful, to attempt a fine delineation among the goals of improvement and maintenance. Here and there in this chapter we shall emphasize implicitly one or the other, but—realistically—instructional procedures are likely to be a blend of both and even include development. It is probable that the speech of deaf children may improve with usage and in response to social demands made upon them to communicate, but this is not likely to happen—particularly during school age—without planned intervention that derives from a child's individual speech program that is carefully thought-out. De-emphasis of speech instruction as a child advances through the grades not only risks the detrimental effect on acquired competence but also devalues its importance for him.

In general, improvement centers not only on specifically targeted aspects of articulation, voice, and rhythm, but also on closing the gap between performance in the disciplined context of speech instruction and in the everyday situation of oral exchange, frequently referred to as the "carry-over." For example, we noted in Chapter IV that in the disciplined context the child typically

157

produces units or segments clearly superior to his production in less organized situations. This stresses the need for alertness of the teacher in recognizing and responding to a child's capabilities. Furthermore, the quality of speech production when prompted or elicited by the teacher is likely to be better than when the child uses spontaneously initiated speech. We must keep in mind that in communicating orally the child must not only attend to the phonology of his message, he must also give thought to its semantic and syntactic requirements. This complex task may reduce the care with which his demonstrated ability in the production of single or small units is incorporated in flowing utterances.

Sensitivity and responsiveness of the teacher—and for that matter of all who are responsible for a child's development—to the need for carry-over should strengthen the child's confidence in his speech as a socially significant skill. This is necessary to foster, if not actually to determine, its social usefulness. We are less likely to avoid a task if we have confidence in our ability to perform it. Of course, in our efforts to expand the opportunities for speech usage, we must caution against shattering a child's confidence by placing him in situations where his failure to be understood may demoralize him. He benefits from practice in social situations with sympathetic listeners who may inform him tactfully that they do not understand but who give him an opportunity to "reach back" for the best performance of which he is capable.

Essential to the improvement of speech is the correction of deviations. Correction may require teacher-initiated measures or self-correction by the talker, but usually a combination of both. We shall deal first with the teacher's part.

TEACHER CORRECTION

The teacher needs to maintain a continuing, but not overly intrusive, attitude of awareness of the **deviation from acceptable speech**. Acceptability will vary with the state of speech competence of the talker. Here the teacher will need to take into account the expectancies for each individual child. The teacher's observation of deviations in a child's speech should guide the development of his individual program. She should not depend solely on her "daily running assessment" but should make a periodic organized assessment which will lead to planned measures for correction.

Improvement through the correction of speech, whether in response to its production in the variety of situations that occur in daily activities or in purposeful structured drills, can be conceptualized around an ordered sequence of the kind described in Chapter II in our discussion of methodology. The first steps in the sequence are likely to be more applicable in unstructured situations, the later steps more pertinent for work in "speech periods."

Signaling

The teacher conventionally signals an error, abnormality, or irregularity by some expression such as, "What did you say?" or, "I did not understand you." Facial expressions, even raising the eyebrows, frequently constitute signaling.

Specifying

Specification is achieved on a gradient ranging from the initial signal which may be ineffective to accomplish correction to a clearly specified particular deviation. The aim throughout is to avoid a uniform "style" of specification of deviation and to achieve talker self-correction, by his recall, whenever possible. Specification may be oral, written, or both. The progression along the gradient, with illustrative teacher responses, could go something like this:

1. *Communicate the locus of the deviation.* "I didn't understand the first part of your sentence."

2. *Indicate the type of deviation.*
   a. *Indicate* that a combination of phonemes or a single one is in error without identification. "You left out a sound."
   b. *Indicate* a voice abnormality. "Watch your voice."
   c. *Indicate* a rhythmic irregularity. "You forgot the accents."

3. *Identify the point of deviation.*
   a. *Identify* the phoneme or combination. "You can say **ch** better in _____."
   b. *Identify* voice abnormality. "I could not hear you."
   c. *Identify* rhythmic irregularity. "The accent in _____ should be on the first, not the second syllable."

4. *Describe the nature of the error.* "You said **b** through your nose" or "Your voice was too high."

The remaining items in the sequence require more active participation by the teacher.

Correcting

1. *Model the desired speech orally for the child to imitate.* The model should avoid exaggerated articulation or tension, either deliberate or unconscious.

2. *Demonstrate over whatever sensory channels and mode best accomplish the communication of the abnormality and its correction.*

   a. A useful paradigm is to communicate the child's deviation by exaggerating it and then to exaggerate in the desired direction of correction. For example, if the child seems to insert a superfluous neutral vowel between **ee** and **l** in *meal*, then the teacher may give a full-length vowel between the two

Clapping the hands to develop appreciation for accent.

sounds as illustration of what not to do and, for correction, give a voiceless l even though some voicing is required.

b. Use easily perceived analogies. For example, excessive or inadequate pressure for plosives may be indicated by pressing the thumb in the palm of the hand or blowing a strip of paper. Rhythm may be shown by tapping on the shoulder or clapping the hands.

c. In cases of poor visibility or audibility it may be necessary to depart from natural production to communicate, for example, place of articulation. The demonstration of a lingua-velar **k** in the combination **koo** would require opening the mouth wider than necessary in order to make the articulation visible. Care should be taken to avoid this as a recurring model which is likely to produce speech with inordinate pervasive jaw movement. If in a two-syllable word like *mother,* equal stress is given to both syllables, a very loud first syllable and an almost voiceless second syllable may be helpful.

d. Discriminate among abnormalities that are class-like—whether of manner, place, etc.—and those that are specific to a particular sound. Excessive pressure may be characteristic of all plosives, or lingua-dental positions may reveal inadequate control of the tip of the tongue. Demonstrations should, therefore, include all members of a class and lead to generalization.

e. Reduce phonetic complexity by demonstrating a sound out of context to focus attention on it. Affricates like **ch** frequently need concentrated demonstration of the relation between the stop and fricative components. Of course, the sound then needs to be demonstrated in a variety of phonetic contexts.

f. Demonstrate by whatever sensory aids are available and applicable (see Chapter II).

3. *Manipulate the speech mechanism.* This involves shaping accessible parts of the speech mechanism—rounding the lips, pressing the tongue down or forcing it up—all to achieve motor action or accurate placement. It should be a last resort in correcting.

DEVIATIONS OF SPEECH

Experience has demonstrated, at least by instructional methods employed up to the present, that certain deviations are likely to occur frequently enough to warrant checking for them in any formal assessment (139, 231). The conventional way of assessing for deviations is to attend to spontaneous speech and to elicit devised samples from written items, picture descriptions, or combinations of these. In the sense that a physician looks for common symptoms, diseases, and causes, the teacher bases her assessment on the possible *errors of articulation, abnormalities of voice,* and *irregularities of rhythm* described in this chapter as well on the review of individual phonemes in Chapter VI (37). These judgments will depend on the child's stage of speech and language development. In planning remedial measures the teacher needs to distinguish whether a deviation is a failure to carry over a skill that a child already possesses or whether the skill needs to be acquired or possibly improved. Failure to carry over—generally observed in connected speech—whether spontaneous or elicited, suggests that the teacher simply remind the child about the deviation according to the sequence presented earlier in this chapter. Acquisition and improvement require planned intervention. The reader is referred to Chapter VI for suggestions for remediation of specific articulatory errors of omission, substitution, distortion, and addition.

The following catalogue of possible deviations is definitely not all-inclusive. The teacher's *power of analysis* should be brought to bear on any deviation.

Errors of Articulation

In Chapter VI we describe errors in the production of individual phonemes and their correction. In Table V-1 we have rank ordered groups of phonemes on a scale of frequency of need for correction as judged by teachers at Central Institute for the Deaf. It is interesting to note the substantial agreement with the study by Hudgins and Numbers at the Clarke and Pennsylvania Schools for the Deaf (139). It is probable that the children in these studies were taught by what we have called the Multisensory Syllable-Unit approach.

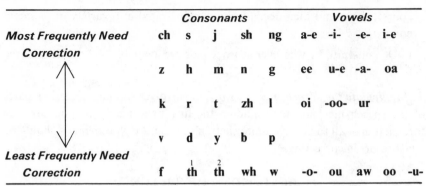

	Consonants					Vowels			
Most Frequently Need Correction	ch	s	j	sh	ng	a-e	-i-	-e-	i-e
	z	h	m	n	g	ee	u-e	-a-	oa
	k	r	t	zh	l	oi	-oo-	ur	
	v	d	y	b	p				
Least Frequently Need Correction	f	th¹	th²	wh	w	-o-	ou	aw	oo	-u-

Table V-1.   *Rank ordering of phonemes by frequency of correction needed.*

Errors of articulation are not confined to production of individual phonemes. They can and do occur because of the phonetic context in which the phonemes are imbedded. A child may be able to produce a perfect **s** in isolation but may omit or distort it in flowing speech. Furthermore, errors may be of a large-class or subclass variety. A large-class error may be voice-voiceless confusion that may reveal itself in a number of phonemes. Production of affricates may be a subclass error, as in the release of the **k** in the word *six* resulting in the intrusion of a neutral vowel between the **k** and **s** and producing a listener set for a two-syllable word. Furthermore, multiple causes may lead to single effects and single causes may lead to multiple effects, as we shall see in what follows.

1. Errors of Omission

a. Omission of s in all contexts: Because it is both a frequently occurring phoneme and one that is often omitted, we have singled out **s** for emphasis. As we have seen in Table I-4, **s** ranks low in internal feedback, and its poor visibility limits the child's exposure to it. It has been noted that omission of **s** is a prominent deviation in the speech of the adult whose hearing is failing.

b. Omission of the final consonant: Omission of final consonants by young deaf children is sometimes caused by forgetting to articulate the consonant, but in older speakers, the apparent omission of final consonants is more likely to be caused by one or more of three conditions of articulation distortion. These are:

(1) Reduced force on arresting consonants,

(2) Lack of coarticulation effect on preceding vowels, and

(3) Abnormal duration of the preceding vowels in relation to the final consonants.

In the syllable with an arresting consonant, important acoustic information about the consonant is conveyed by the duration of the vowel and its formant transitions (spectral changes as the vowel moves toward the consonant) as described in Chapter III. When the vowel is longer than it should be and "trails off" in expended energy, the listener is misled by the wrong cue. If in the word *beet* the **ee** is prolonged and the effects of coarticulation are lost as it trails off, the listener does not anticipate the final stop and judges that it is absent. When these effects are combined with reduced force on the final consonant, particularly on stops but not confined to them, it appears that the consonant has been omitted.

An instance of consonant omission worthy of mention is **ng** as in the word *sing*. This apparent omission is frequently caused by the production of **ng** with insufficient opening of the velopharyngeal port. The **ng** sounds like a continuation of the preceding vowel.

c. Omission of initial consonants: A consonant initiating a syllable may be perceived to have been omitted when it is distorted by reduced force. Plosive consonants are often released with insufficient force for the listener either to perceive its presence or to use the cue of the coarticulation effect on the formant transitions of the following vowel. Reduced force on the stop breath consonants **p, t,** and **k** also reduces their duration, and the listener may confuse them with their voiced cognates **b, d,** and **g,** or may even fail to perceive that they have been said at all.

2. Errors of Substitution

When the deaf child is developing speech, he is likely to have several consonant substitutions, much like the child with normal hearing who has not yet mastered the phonologic rules underlying spoken language. As he grows older these substitutions tend to diminish. Those remaining substitutions, some apparent, some real, are likely to be distorted productions of the intended consonants by the speaker, heard as different consonants by the listener.

a. Voice-voiceless consonant substitutions: An error considered uniquely typical of deaf speakers is the "surd-sonant," or the substitution of one sound for another when the sounds have the same place of articulation but differ in the voice-voiceless feature (146). Thus the voiceless (surd) stop consonant **p** may be heard as its voiced (sonant) stop consonant cognate **b,** or the reverse. Other cognates which are frequently confused are **t** and **d, k** and **g, f** and **v,** and $\overset{1}{\textbf{th}}$ and $\overset{2}{\textbf{th}}$.

As with the apparent omission of consonants, the substitution of these cognates for each other may be caused by articulation distortion (34,35,37). When a vowel precedes a voiceless consonant, for example, some deaf speakers continue the voice into the consonant. The resulting acoustic information suggests substitution of the voiced cognate of the intended voiceless consonant. Similarly, voicing for the following vowel may begin before the breath consonant has been completed, giving the listener voiced consonant information. Initiating and terminating voicing requires exquisite timing. In addition, as we pointed out previously, the surd-sonant error may have its roots in the inappropriate force of consonant articulation or in the abnormal duration of associated vowels **(eet-eed)**.

Our observations indicate that the surd-sonant error is not the simple substitution of one sound for another. It is an error of distortion by the deaf talker which influences the perception for the listener. In summary the causes of the distortion appear to be:

(1) Inadequate coordination of voicing and articulation. This point is supported by the ease with which deaf talkers can produce cognates accurately in isolation;

(2) Inappropriate force of articulation causing duration distortion of the consonant; and

(3) Distortion of the duration of vowels preceding consonants.

b. Nasal-oral consonant substitution: A nasal consonant may be substituted for its oral cognate (**m** for **b, n** for **d,** and **ng** for **g**). Deaf speakers, unlike hearing persons with palatal insufficiency, also reverse the substitution, so we have **b** for **m, d** for **n, g** for **ng**. Here again the nasal-oral consonant substitution rests primarily on improper coordination, in this case of the velopharyngeal closure. Compounding of surd-sonant and oral-nasal errors may result in **m** substituted for the breath **p, n** for **t,** and **ng** for **k**.

c. Low feedback substitutions: Production of some sounds is likely to provide little sensory feedback, while the substituted sound provides more perceivable feedback, especially tactile. For example, **w** or **l** may be substituted for **r**. The vocalized continuing nature of the consonant is appropriate, but the speaker seeks better feedback than a typical **r** provides. With the substituted **w** the speaker monitors the production from the kinesthetic impression of lip rounding. With the substituted **l** the tactile impression is strong for the tip of the tongue touching the palate.

Similarly **t** or **th** may be substituted for the low feedback **s**. The speaker seeks tactile feedback by touching the tongue and alveolar ridge for **t**, or seeks increased perception of friction by producing a **th**.

d. Vowel substitutions: The apparent substitution of vowels is caused largely by imprecision. As we have seen in Chapter I, exceedingly fine differences of mouth opening, rounding of lips, and place and height of tongue arching are required for accurate vowel formation. The differences among vowels give very little tactile or kinesthetic feedback. The vowel perceived is most likely to be one which adjoins the vowel intended, as represented on the vowel diagram (Figure I-7). A common vowel substitution, for example, would be -e- for -a- with the listener hearing *met* for the intended *mat*. The speaker is not likely to substitute a vowel with lip rounding (oo) for one without rounding (ee).

3. Errors of Distortion

a. Degree of force: Stop and fricative consonants are frequently made with either too much or too little force. Too little force gives the listener acoustic information of abnormally shortened duration and reduced intensity. He may hear the sound as a distortion of the intended consonant or as another consonant, or may sense the absence of an expected sound. Too much force gives the listener acoustic information of abnormally long duration and increased intensity. He may hear a distorted or a substituted consonant.

A frequent source of distortion is excessive force in producing stops p, t, k, b, d, and g. For example, p and t are often distorted by too much bilabial or lingua-alveolar pressure combined with excessive jaw movement. This may lead to breathiness of a following vowel as the residual air at the glottal sound source is insufficient to produce the vowel, or to diphthongization of the vowel as the jaw is returned to the required mouth opening.

b. Hypernasality: Deaf speakers, who experience difficulty with the fine coordination of rapid oral/nasal resonance changes in connected speech, produce hypernasal sounds. Consonants b, d, and g may be heard as substituted sounds m, n, and ng. Consonants l, r, w, v, th, and z, too, may be mistaken for one of the nasal consonants m, n, or ng, or may give the impression of a distorted and often non-targeted, indistinguishable sound (107). Nasal consonants may cause nasalization of the preceding or following vowel. In the syllable mo-, the -o- may be nasalized if the speaker fails to return the velum to its required position for vowel production. Vowels associated with a nasal consonant are vulnerable to nasalization particularly when the air flow to the oral cavity is restricted by the closeness of the velum and back of the tongue. High vowels oo and ee are examples of this.

The nasalization of certain vowels and consonants and their combinations should not be confused with pervasive abnormality of voice in which all voiced speech sounds are nasalized. As we shall see later, such nasalization is a general difficulty of voice production.

c. Imprecision and indefiniteness: We recall from Chapter I, and from our comments on substitutions, that vowels are produced by exquisitely slight variations in mouth opening, place and height of arching the tongue, and rounding of the lips. These variations in the vocal tract give rise to formant differences that constitute important, if not exclusive, listening cues, described in Chapter III. Deaf speakers may be slightly off target with respect to one or more of these required variations in the production of certain vowels, particularly those with low kinesthetic feedback. This applies especially to the front vowels **ee, -i-, -e-,** and **-a-** where lip rounding is not available as a monitoring production cue. On the other hand, some vowels are produced indefinitely and the listener has no class category cue at all. In the case of imprecision, **-i-** may be confused with **-e-,** and **-e-** with **-a-.** But the indefinite vowel is ambiguous for the listener. These observations apply also to vowel-like consonants **l, r, y,** and **w.**

d. Duration of vowels: The duration of vowels in connected speech should vary according to context. These systematic variations give the listener important acoustic cues to adjoining sounds. For example, vowels preceding voiceless consonants are typically shorter than the same vowels before voiced consonants (*beat-bead, leaf-leave*). The listener gets cues about the voicing and even identification of the consonant. Deaf speakers tend to produce vowels with undifferentiated duration. The tendency is likely to be in the direction of excessive duration (32).

e. Temporal values in diphthongs: Diphthongs combine two continuously phonated vowels, with the first portion (the nucleus) longer than the second (the glide), except for **u-e** where the relations are reversed. Deaf speakers may make the second portion longer than it needs to be. The effort to produce both elements accurately splits the diphthong, making two discrete vowels. *Buy* becomes **bo-ee,** *tape* becomes **te-eep** and *house* becomes **ho-oos,** giving the listener a message set for a two-syllable word. The error in the other direction either reduces the length of the glide or eliminates it entirely—*bait* becomes **bet,** *night* becomes **not,** and *cloud* becomes **klod.** Drills on vowels need to develop awareness of variations in their durational features and time relations. "Sing-song" drills that produce vowels of uniform duration should be avoided. Unless otherwise indicated, as in the case of a small increment approach, syllable drills should be of the consonant-vowel-consonant (CVC) type.

4. Errors of Addition

a. Insertion of a superfluous vowel between consonants: Adjoining consonants occur in various relations to each other. Among the important combinations of interest to us are *blends,* where **l** and **r** are preceded by consonants and the position for **l** and **r** is taken before the first consonant is produced (*blue, try*); *clusters* (*snow*), particularly affricates (*looks*); and *abutting consonants* (*football*), where they occur adjacent to each other but in separate syllables.

In these combinations the deaf talker may insert a superfluous neutral vowel that sounds almost like a brief **-u-** and the listener gets a misleading syllabic cue. In the case of blends this may be caused either by failure to take the position of **l** or **r** before articulating the preceding consonant (*blue*-**buloo**) or by voicing the **l** and **r** when preceded by a voiceless consonant (*try*-**turi-e**). In clusters the voiceless-voice sequence may be improperly coordinated and the voicing commenced in the transition from the voiceless to the voiced consonant (*snow*-**sunoa**). In affricates the stop may be completely released with voicing before the fricative is given (*looks*-**lookus**), and in the abutting consonants, too, the first consonant is released before the second consonant is given (*football*-**footubawl**, *good night*-**goodunite**).

b. Unnecessary release of final stop consonants: A distracting and frequently misleading insertion may be the forceful release of a final stop consonant as in "It's time to stop_____," or "Go to bed_____." The talker appears to have a static conception of the consonant produced in isolation and requires explosion at all times. Unfortunately, he may have been *taught* that this is the case.

c. Diphthongization of vowels: Certain vowel-consonant combinations require faster and smoother transitions than deaf talkers are likely to produce. Errors such as these result: *meat*-**meeut**, *feel*-**feeul**, *bed*-**beud**, *moon*-**mooun**. In **meeut,** for example, the transition of the movement of the tongue from the vowel to the lingua-alveolar position—from **ee** to **t**—is too slow, and voicing—again the brief **-u-** like sound—intrudes, giving rise to what appears to be a bisyllabic utterance.

d. Superfluous breath before a vowel: Vowels in English are all voiced. Deaf talkers, however, may precede a vowel by unnecessary aspiration, particularly a vowel that initiates an utterance. Apparently air is forcefully aspirated before the vocal folds approximate to produce phonation. The listener perceives the aspiration as an **h.** Incidentally, in combinations that require **h,** which always is produced in the position of the vowel that follows, the deaf talker may over-aspirate in a discrete position or he may omit the **h** as in cockney speech.

Abnormalities of Voice

It has been our observation that deviations in voice and irregularities of rhythm are posing less of a problem than heretofore, due perhaps to early application of hearing aids. As we have seen, "errors" of articulation are reasonably specifiable, whereas abnormalities of voice require judgments that are generally expressed by adjectives that do not always mean the same to those who use them. This supports the generalization that the less a science has advanced, the more its terminology tends to rest upon the uncritical assumption of mutual understanding. Our experience suggests that even teachers tend to use a variety of terms about "deaf voices," generally negative in their connotation. It has been found that frequently used terms included *dull, hollow, raspy, piercing, tense, flat, breathy, harsh, throaty,* and *shrieking* (32, 33, 35, 155). Never mentioned were terms such as *mellow, warm, smooth, full, vibrant, pear shaped,* or *clear.* For a penetrating review of parameters of voice quality, correlates of voice production, and a behavioral analysis of vocal function, the reader is referred to Chapters 17, 18, and 19 of the *Handbook of Speech Pathology and Audiology* (313).

Perhaps as useful a way as any to organize our presentation of abnormalities in voice is to discuss them in terms that are rather more descriptive of the observed vocal output than are some of the ambiguous adjectives mentioned above. These are *nasality, breathiness, stridency, inadequate loudness, fundamental pitch,* and *uncontrolled pitch.*

1. Nasality: We recall that English phonology includes only three nasal sounds, **m, n,** and **ng,** in which the velopharyngeal port is open. Hypernasality, the opening of the port when not necessary for the utterance, is unfortunately a frequent condition of deaf talkers (45, 63, 212, 213). It is interesting that in a cinefluorographic study comparing five typical deaf speakers producing oral syllables (not necessarily judged to be hypernasal), it was found that the experimental deaf group all exhibited velopharyngeal opening, which was not true of the normally-speaking control group (202). McClumpha found the deaf speakers to have shorter and thinner velums, which may result from lack of muscle activity involved in velopharyngeal closure and oral voice production. Of course, not to be overlooked as a cause of hypernasality may be an observable cleft or velar insufficiency.

When indicated, the improvement of voice—whether of nasality, breathiness, stridency, loudness, or pitch—should recognize the importance of conveying to the child what he is doing and what needs to be done. Sensory aids that display voice and rhythm parameters may be helpful and should be employed, but the alert ear of the teacher is still the major "error detector." The teacher must be able to imitate the child's deviation and to communicate it, frequently exaggerated, in order to give the child an unambiguous cue to the deviation. All principles of discriminating use of sensory channels, previously discussed, apply here. Trial and error invariably operate in the process of improving voice. The teacher needs to reinforce aggressively every satisfactory production. For hypernasality the child can feel the teacher's nose and the reduction of oral pressure. Exercises should concentrate on directing the breath stream through the oral cavity and giving the child the "feel" of velopharyngeal action. Just inhaling and exhaling through a wide open mouth and holding the position can communicate a feel of the velar movement. Then combining a nasal consonant—such as **ng**—with a vowel, both given with force, can accomplish this. These should form the basis for more elaborate nasal/non-nasal combinations.

2. Breathiness: The vowels of English require alternating closure of the glottis by contact of the vocal folds without unnecessary leakage of air. The inefficient control of this process leads again to a distracting voice quality and may actually degrade intelligibility. The closure of the folds may be either incomplete or too brief, or both. The condition may be reflected prominently in abnormally short phrased speech separated by unnecessarily frequent inhalations, sometimes referred to as "pumping." Recall, too, the excessive force on plosives preceding a vowel that may give it a breathy quality.

Breathiness can be communicated by having the child feel excessive air at the mouth during the phonation of a vowel and, of course, in connected speech, followed by the teacher's model of proper phonation. A strip of paper in front of the mouth can be observed to yield to the air stream, too. Sometimes a circle of moisture from the breath is visible on a chalk board or mirror. The child should try to produce vowels without bending the strip of paper, and he should also be required to count without taking a breath and continue to extend the number he attains by economizing on the use of air. For fluency, it should go "one-and-two-and-three-and-," etc. Holding a weight such as a stack of books, or pushing against a table while phonating, attains proper glottal action.

3. Stridency: The normal talker uses the muscles for articulation and voicing synergistically. The muscles "work together" without undue tension. Perhaps because he gropes for feedback or because he has been taught with overemphasis on the tactile impression gained from feeling a teacher's larynx, the deaf talker may speak with a great deal of generalized constriction and tension in both the glottal and supraglottal areas. The result is commonly termed stridency or, by some, harshness. Of course the teacher in her determination to develop good speech must be mindful to avoid tension in the model she presents to children.

The teacher can demonstrate stridency by letting the child feel her exaggerated muscle tension just above the larynx in saying a vowel and then feel the change that comes with return to normal muscle action. The child should not be expected to imitate the teacher's voice. He should be imitating her muscle action in those muscles that are accessible for demonstration. At times the bunching of the tongue in the back of the mouth needs to be explored and the child should be directed and shown to keep his tongue forward. When satisfactory production for a vowel has been achieved, additional vowels should be tried and then combined with sequences of familiar expressions.

4. *Loudness:* Normal talkers regulate loudness to accommodate to distance from a listener, to requirements of social situations, and to varying levels of ambient noise. Deaf talkers may be unaware of these conditions or may simply not be able to speak loud enough in any situation. Inefficient use of the air stream at the glottis may be responsible for the inability to speak loud enough. The suggestions for remediation of breathiness apply here.

5. *Fundamental pitch:* Both young male and young female deaf talkers tend to speak with a higher fundamental pitch than hearing persons with whom they have been matched in controlled investigations (115). In another acoustic analysis, Calvert (32) not only confirmed the higher fundamental frequency but also observed that deaf talkers exhibited a smaller separation of the fundamental frequency (higher than normal) and the first formant of the vowel -a- (lower than normal). While this higher fundamental pitch for deaf speakers may not interfere with intelligibility, it may intrude a characteristic that adds to listener effort. The higher fundamental pitch may be particularly noticeable for young adult deaf speakers when it should be getting lower as they grow older.

6. *Pitch control:* Control of pitch relates to reasonable maintenance of range of the fundamental pitch of a particular talker, and of the deliberate variations in pitch that express speaker intent and satisfy the linguistic requirements of stress—whether of accent or intonation. The lack of control of fundamental pitch by deaf talkers results in distracting random and wide fluctuations. This condition is frequently associated with high arched vowels. The upward movement of the tongue raises the larynx and may over-tense the vocal folds, like stretching a rubber band.

As in the case of stridency, deviations in fundamental pitch generally grow out of improper muscle action not suited to the particular physiological mechanism of a talker. The manner of communication to the child and the remediation suggested for stridency apply here. The ability to control pitch and to apply it to linguistic requirements and talker intent are interrelated and will be treated under irregularities of rhythm.

Irregularities of Rhythm

In Chapter I we discussed the aspects of speech that contribute to its rhythm growing out of the syllabic patterning of accent, emphasis, intonation, phrasing, and rate. The rhythmic features are achieved by appropriate coarticulation and by controlled variations of loudness, pitch, and duration, especially of the vowel components of syllables. Irregularities of rhythm in the speech of deaf persons appear to have their origins in the difficulty of a talker to control the mechanics of varying loudness, pitch, and duration; and even if the skills have been fairly well achieved, the talker may not know when to apply them to communicate the intent of his message or to satisfy its linguistic requirements. The examples of irregularities, cited in Chapter I, are pertinent to the speech of deaf talkers. These views are underlined by Hood (135), who observed that deaf speakers used about two-thirds as much variation in fundamental frequency, one-half as much variation in intensity, extended syllable duration more than twice that of normal speakers, and syllabic values which seemed to be monotonously uniform (115). Irregular rhythm not only may be esthetically unappealing but also affects intelligibility significantly. Hudgins and Numbers (139) and Hood (134) found a high correlation for both normal and deaf speakers between intelligibility and judgments of rhythmic quality.

As we have seen in Chapter I, a symbol system to indicate rhythmic parameters is helpful. Many are used, but there should be consistency within a program. The symbols should indicate pitch, loudness, duration, and phrasing. An example of such a system, illustrated below, uses a horizontal line above syllables to suggest loudness (height) and duration (length), and a curving line to indicate pitch glides. A connecting line beneath a phrase could indicate its limits, and the number of slash marks would be a cue to length of pause.

Yesterday was a beautiful day / but today // it's terrible.

Although we have speculated that early intervention may reduce irregularities of rhythm, it is useful here to treat the process of its improvement. When satisfactory fundamental pitch has been achieved, pitch change to three or four levels on single vowels should be demonstrated, in ways previously discussed, and imitated by the child. Then, high and low vowels should be combined and given with controlled fundamental pitch and then with variations. Some suggested combinations are:

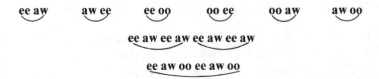

ee aw   aw ee   ee oo   oo ee   oo aw   aw oo

ee aw ee aw ee aw ee aw

ee aw oo ee aw oo

These should be followed by nonsense syllables and then by familiar expressions incorporating loudness and duration variations. Phrasing is aided by proper joining of words within phrases as well as by appropriate pauses. The following sentence, conventionally marked for phrasing, illustrates the point. "I don't think I can // but I want to try." The joining symbol ⌣ instructs the child to join the final sound of each word with the initial sound of the next word throughout the phrase. For example, the "I don't ---" is joined as though it were written "Idon't---"; the vowel i-e continues voicing as the position for d is taken. The sentence may also be marked for phrasing by using a continuous curved line under the entire phrase thus: "I don't think I can // but I want to try."

Consonants and vowels in adjoining words are joined in this example as follows:

"I don't think I can // but I want to try."

I don't — voicing on the vowel **i-e** continues as the position **d** is taken.

don't think — the stop consonant **t** is imploded and released into the position for **th,** as the tongue tip moves from the alveolar ridge to the edge of the upper teeth.

think I — **k i-e** blend is accomplished as though the **k** were the first sound of the syllable **ki-e.** To show this, the teacher may write the words in this fashion: "thing ki-e." Some teachers recommend that all syllables in a phrase be spoken with an initial consonant, even if the consonant is borrowed from the previous word.

I can — the vowel **i-e** is terminated by closure for the **k** stop consonant; the **n** is terminated by a pause.

but I — the **t i-e** blend is accomplished as though the final **t** of *but* were the first sound of the syllable **ti-e.**

I want — the **i-e** voicing continues as position is taken for the **w** and then the **aw,** almost like a triphthong.

want to — the abutting **t** sounds are blended into a single **t** sound which initiates the final syllable **too.**

to try — the vowel **oo** is terminated by closure for the **t** stop consonant in *try.*

On common short phrases, the teacher may demonstrate the joining of all phonemes, regardless of where words begin and end, by writing the phonemes of the phrase as though they were just one word. Some examples:

My name is	**mi-enameiz**
I live in	**i-elivin**
I am a	**i-eamu.**

Coding patterns of speech.

Accent on appropriate syllables within words and emphasis on appropriate words within phrases and sentences are best achieved through increases in the force or stress with which the accented syllable or emphasized word is uttered. This may be shown to the child by writing the syllable or word to be stressed in bold, large capital letters, as in the following examples:

PUM pum	pum pum **PUM**
BAby	**CAN**dy
you **ARE** the one.	I want to go **NOW.**

Also useful are stress marks, such as the following:

púm pum	pum pum púm
báby	cándy
You aŕe the one.	I want to go nów.

The teacher may also choose to underline words to be emphasized, as in the following examples:

You <u>are</u> the one.	I want to go <u>now</u>.

In all of the suggested exercises children should also be required to offer from their own repertoire matching linguistic patterns. For example, the teacher should ask the child to think of a pattern like "**CAN**dy." The patterns and uses of accents and emphasis were described in Chapter I.

In attempting increased force of articulation, the child is likely to make a change primarily in the loudness of his voice. Some increase in pitch will also result from increased force, but it may be best to emphasize only the increased loudness caused by the increased force in teaching stress production to the child.

Chapter I contains examples of linguistic requirements of English and patterns of speech that convey speaker intent. These form the basis for exercises in improvement of rhythm.

It is important to emphasize that although factors influencing the intelligibility of speech are treated differentially they are very much interrelated. Over-articulation can definitely contribute to abnormal voice quality and to irregular rhythm. An experiment by Calvert (33) relevant to this point is worthy of mention here. Experienced teachers of deaf children who were confident that they could identify a speaker as being deaf by just hearing his speech listened to samples from deaf speakers, normal speakers, speakers simulating deaf speech, and a person with a voice disorder. When the listeners heard only a steady voice cut from the center of a vowel sound, they could not tell accurately whether the speaker was deaf or hearing. As the articulatory complexity of the samples increased, the listeners became more accurate, reaching their highest accuracy on whole sentences. Table V-2 shows the percentage of deaf and normal speech samples which met a 70 percent criterion of correct identification by a group of experienced teachers. It appears that as the deaf speaker moves through articulatory strings he gives the listener speech information that identifies him as a deaf speaker. It is likely that characteristics of articulation and rhythm, as well as voice quality, have led to identification of "deaf speech."

MAINTENANCE OF SPEECH

Throughout this book our emphasis has been properly and understandably on the speech of children. The general considerations, principles, methods, analyses, and activities all combine to maintain speech. It is important, however, to concern ourselves with post-school maintenance of speech where conventional organized programs are not available or feasible. We need to prepare children for this situation and advise adults no longer in school (7). We make the following suggestions to accomplish this:

1. Constant usage: There is no substitute for continual use of speech in all situations, not only to practice self-correction but also to reinforce confidence in its value.

2. Maximum use of amplification: As we have stressed for children, the adult should maintain and use the best possible acoustic amplification. Hear-

Speech Complexity Level	Accuracy Percentage
Cut vowels (center portion)	48%
Whole simple vowels	65%
Whole diphthongs	85%
CVC syllables	85%
CVCVC bisyllables	93%
Whole sentences	100%

Table V-2. *Percentage of deaf and normal speech samples meeting the criterion of 70% agreement as to whether they were "deaf" or "normal" samples, at several levels of articulatory complexity* (33).

ing and hearing aid evaluation should be carried out periodically by professionally qualified persons, and promising new hearing aids should be tried.

3. Awareness of speaking situations: A deaf person can help his naive listener in a number of ways. Among these are:

a. *Helping the listener to lipread.* In any stressful listening situation, whether because of ambient noise, competing messages, or deviant speech of a talker, the listener seeks supplementary visual cues. The deaf talker should place himself in a position so that his face is clearly visible.

b. *Helping the listener to hear.* Develop sensitivity to the requirements of the acoustic situation frequently, but not always, detectable by a hearing aid. The masking effects of noise, of whatever origin, and the influence of distance from the listener should be understood. If it is necessary and practical, a quiet place should be sought for conversation.

4. Preparing the listener: The listener can be helped and even put at ease if at the outset he is given a sample of "small talk" such as, "I'm glad to meet you," "How are you?" or "Good morning."

5. A second chance: When a listener does not understand speech, a deaf speaker should not assume that the listener understood *none* of what was said. He probably understood part but not enough to "put the pieces together" for complete understanding. The item should be repeated with *exactly* the words as first spoken. The listener will have a second chance to fill in what was first missed. Of course, if the listener does not understand the repeated sentence, the speaker must change the wording and resort to intentional redundancy. Here is a situation where economy of verbalization should not apply. Of course, as we have mentioned previously, the talker should make use of his internalized catalogue of "error probabilities."

A deaf adult addresses a committee meeting.

6. Another ear: It is advisable for the deaf talker to develop a special relationship with a normally-hearing person or two who can act as a constructive and sympathetic critic of his speech. Care should be taken that the friend's judgment is not blunted by "getting used to" the speech. The other ear may, if desired, be a properly qualified professional who understands and is able to meet the distinctive speech needs of the adult deaf person.

7. Public speaking: It is encouraging that deaf persons are being called on to speak publicly. This requires suitable accommodation to public address systems. Among the sources of difficulty for the deaf speaker, as they may be for the hearing, are imperfections in the amplifying system, poor visibility of the face, and improper estimation of effects of distance from and angle to the microphone. These difficulties are best overcome by the use of a lavaliere microphone. We recommend testing a particular system before a speech is given, and enlisting the assistance of a hearing person and a monitor in the back of the room during the speech.

Chapter VI

Instructional Analysis of Consonants and Vowels

In this chapter we present information and suggestions about phonemes and combinations of phonemes that have direct application to the instructional process. Our treatment of phonemes on an individual basis does not imply a way of teaching. Rather it is to equip the teacher with an understanding of units basic to the production of speech and their dynamics as they are influenced by coarticulation, described in Chapter 1. For example, we are aware that the **p** that initiates a syllable is different from the **p** in the word *speech*. In the initiating case there is a discernible explosion, and in the other case the production is shorter and almost voiced—not quite exploded. Contrast the production of **p** in the words *peach* and *speech;* similarly, *tore* and *store, cool* and *school.*

For certain phonemes—particularly vowels—there may be variations in production, that is, the vowel boundaries related to sectionalisms may be quite extensive. Here our recommendation is to make the best approximation to General American production, and to accept that which is intelligible and which is easily produced by the child. For example, for the word *cent* some people may say **cint** and some may call it **cent**. Here we leave it to the teacher's judgment as to which can best be produced by the child. Another illustration is the diphthongization of vowels by Southern talkers. The general American talker pronounces the word *bed* as **bed** while the Southern talker may diphthongize it as **beud**.

177

What we have selected about phonemes for inclusion in this chapter, although not exhaustive, constitutes a broad and solid foundation to devise and apply techniques appropriate to a child's requirements, whether for development or correction of individual sounds or their combinations. For each phoneme there are symbols of the General American system, of the International Phonetic Alphabet, and of Webster's dictionary. Key words are presented along with some unusual spellings to remind the teacher about transformations to the primary spelling. We then describe the production of each phoneme, including conventional shorthand descriptions used in the phonetic literature.

This is followed by the internal sensory feedback readily available to the speaker, that is, what is available to the feedback system the child carries around with him. An example is the motor feedback he gets whenever he speaks, unlike the feedback he may get from a mirror which is not an integral part of him. Given our aim to have the child speak in real-life situations, which requires monitoring his own production, we emphasize the importance of internal feedback.

We then analyze instructional possibilities for communicating the properties of the phoneme visually, tactually, and, wherever possible, auditorily. Suggestions and alternative techniques for development grow out of these analyses. We then list the probable errors of deaf talkers and suggestions for remediation. The probabilities include *large class errors* such as voice and voiceless confusion, *subclass errors* such as those that may have to do with excessive pressure occurring in plosives, and errors that may be *singular for a particular phoneme* such as the place variations determined by phonetic context in the production of **k**.

h

KEY WORDS: **h**ad, a**h**ead
SPELLINGS: h, wh(o)

h   /h/   h-

Production *(lingua-velar/lingua-palatal voiceless fricative)*

Velopharyngeal port closes, breath is directed through the oral cavity—which assumes the configuration for the following vowel—with audible friction. The **h** has no oral cavity formation of its own but changes with the vowels that surround it (**h** is always followed by a vowel). In an intervocalic position (*ahead*), **h** is commonly produced as a voiced fricative. The production of audible friction, while the oral cavity assumes the position for surrounding vowels, distinguishes the **h** sound. Audible friction is caused by breath rushing through the oral cavity across the tongue, velum, and palate. The relative lack of constriction in most vowel formations requires that breath be emitted with greater force than for other fricatives in order to make **h** audible.

Internal Feedback Information

TACTILE: Some friction from restricted breath flow on the tongue, velum, and palate.

KINESTHETIC: Some thoracic muscular tensing in emitting breath with sufficient force for audibility.

Sensory Instructional Possibilities

TACTILE: Steady breath flow on skin of the hand.

VISUAL: Steady breath flow by movement of feather, flame, paper.

Suggestions for Development

1. Develop in syllables using different vowels following **h.** Have the student produce a series of **hee hee hee hee hee** on a single breath so that the **h** is audible, but without running out of breath. Then have him produce a series of **h** sounds with other vowels. When each vowel can be made in combination with

h in a series without running out of breath, have the student produce a series on a single breath, mixing vowel sounds as follows: **hee hoo haw ho- hu-.** Demonstrate by lines drawn under the written symbols that the **h** is relatively short in duration compared to the vowel sound.

2. Have the student feel the flow of breath on his hand. Associate with the written "h." Use a feather, strip of paper, or other visual aid only if necessary to demonstrate flow of breath. *Avoid* giving the impression of a sudden puff of breath, dropping the jaw, or exaggerating the force of production.

3. Develop in intervocalic positions as a voiced fricative. In such phrases as, "I have —," demonstrate that the voicing continues by drawing a continuous line under the phrase and let the student feel with his hand that the teacher's voice does not stop. Demonstrate the increased force of air emitted at the **h** position by letting the child feel the emission with his other hand. The voice **h** may be written "**h̬**" to remind the student of voicing.

4. Demonstrate the nature of the voiced friction by associating the **h̬** with other voiced fricatives; practice a series **v t̬h̬ h̬,** feeling the emission of slight breath on each.

Common Errors and Suggestions for Improvement

1. Excessive breath emitted: Use cool mirror close to student's mouth to show excess breath on **h** (by breath moisture condensation). Compare with teacher's acceptable production. Produce a series of syllables with **h** followed by a vowel (**hee hee hee**) for student to practice controlling breath emission. Increase the number of syllables with practice. For the intervocalic **h**, practice a continuously voiced string of syllables (**heeheeheehee**). Demonstrate graphically the need for a reduced **h** production by writing the "h" smaller than the vowel or by underlining the "h" and the vowel so that the "h" line is shorter.

2. Insertion of **-u-** *between* **h** *and the following vowel:* Have student practice taking position for the following vowel before producing **h**. Demonstrate graphically by substituting a dotted line symbol for the vowel in place of the "h" symbol, as in the word *ham* written as "⋅⋅am."

3. Excessive friction with lingua-velar restriction: To gain tactile feedback the student may elevate the back of the tongue to approximate the velum for **h**, giving a harsh or guttural sound (like clearing the throat). Redevelop with the vowel **ee** for which the front of the tongue is elevated. Let the student feel the inappropriate vibrations under the chin near the base of the tongue; contrast with **h** produced with no vibrations.

wh /ʍ/ hw

Production *(bilabial voiceless fricative)*

No voice, velopharyngeal port closes, the lips are rounded as in the vowel **oo** and slightly protruded. Breath is directed through the oral cavity and the constricted opening of the lips with audible friction. Lip protrusion and roundings are less tense than for the vowel **oo** or for **w-**. Rounding and protruding the lips tends to raise the back of the tongue.

Internal Feedback Information

TACTILE: Friction of restricted breath flow on the rounded lips.

KINESTHETIC: Rounding and protruding of lips.

Sensory Instructional Possibilities

TACTILE: Steady breath flow on skin of the hand.

VISUAL: Rounding and protruding of lips. Steady breath flow by movement of feather, flame, strip of paper.

Suggestions for Development

1. Imitate from teacher's model; *avoid* giving the impression of a sudden puff of breath.

2. Demonstrate the flow of breath by tactile impression on student's hand.

3. Demonstrate the flow of breath by visual impression with *steady* deflection of a strip of paper, feather, or candle flame.

4. With student and teacher seated side-by-side, show in a mirror the degree of rounding and protrusion of lips. *Avoid* giving the impression of tense lip rounding and protrusion.

5. To demonstrate steady but not excessive flow of breath, have the young student attempt to blow out a series of seven or eight candles on a single breath. *Avoid* having the student take a deep breath to accomplish this.

Common Errors and Suggestions for Improvement

1. Excess force of expelled breath: Have student feel the contrasted breath flow for acceptable and unacceptable production on his hand. Use a mirror to demonstrate that the cheeks are not puffed out. Develop in syllables showing with underlining that the **wh** is shorter than the following vowel. Have student produce a series of syllables, such as **whee whee whee whee whee whee**, on a single breath for breath control.

2. Excess tension of the lips: Redevelop using a narrow but not rounded lip opening for **wh** production.

p /p/ p

KEY WORDS: **p**ie, si**p**, sto**pp**ed
SPELLINGS: p, pp

Production *(bilabial, voiceless stop)*

STOP: No voice, velopharyngeal port closes, lips close, air is held and compressed in the oral cavity.

EXPLOSION: Air compressed in the oral cavity is exploded as audible breath between the lips. In connected speech, **p** is exploded in the initial position of words and syllables (*pie, helper*), and following **m** (*limp, ramp*) and **s** (*lisp, rasp*) in the final position of words. It is closed but not exploded preceding **s** (*lips, caps*) or another stop consonant (*apt, crept*) in the same syllable, and following s in the same syllable (*space, spot*). It is either not exploded or very lightly exploded in the final position (*sip, help*).

Internal Feedback Information

TACTILE: Lips touch with closure, exploded air between lips.

KINESTHETIC: Lips close with sufficient force to retain compressed air briefly.

Sensory Instructional Possibilities

TACTILE: Exploded air on skin of back of hand.

VISUAL: Lip closure and opening can be seen easily, explosion of air by movement of feather, flame, paper.

Suggestions for Development

1. Imitate from teacher's model; *avoid* dropping jaw with production.

2. Demonstrate manner of production by analogy from other stops (note: **p** is frequently the first stop developed).

3. Demonstrate explosion by tactile impression of breath on student's hand.

4. Demonstrate explosion by visual impression of sudden movement of strip of paper, feather, or candle flame; *avoid* exaggeration of force of explosion.

5. If necessary, manipulate for production by pushing on student's filled cheeks, press his lips together and open them rapidly, or stop his stream of blowing by occluding his lips and releasing.

6. Develop the closed **p** after the closed-exploded production is accomplished. Imitate from teacher's model of vowel interrupted by lip closure, as in **-op,** without release of the compressed air.

7. Demonstrate the lack of movement of a strip of paper, feather, or candle flame on the closed **p**; compare with exploded **p** with same visual aids.

8. Demonstrate by tactile analogy the difference between exploded **p** and closed **p** by having the student press his palms together and release them quickly (exploded) or release them very gently (non-exploded).

9. Written symbols may indicate whether the **p** is exploded or closed as follows: exploded "**p-**", closed "**-p**", closed **p** may be written in brackets as in "li[p]," may be outlined in dots, or may be written faintly; a short vertical "stop" line may be used for the non-exploded **p** as in "erup$_|$t" or "sip$_|$".

Common Errors and Suggestions for Improvement

1. Excess pressure on explosion of breath: If cheeks are puffed, show child appropriate production by mirror. Demonstrate reduced pressure by tactile impression of breath on student's hand. Contrast excess breath with appropriate amount. Have the student produce a series of rapid **p** sounds (**ppppppppp**) on the same breath; then a series of **pu- pu- pu- pu- pu-** syllables on a single breath.

2. Insufficient pressure on explosion of breath: Demonstrate increased pressure by tactile impression of breath on student's hand; use strip of paper or other visual aid. Contrast increased breath with insufficient amount. Demonstrate degree of pressure by pressing together student's thumb and forefinger or by pressing his hands together. Manipulate by lightly compressing child's lips together.

3. Escape of breath through nose on explosion: Demonstrate oral emission of breath by placing feather or strip of paper where it can be moved by oral but not nasal breath. Place card just under nose to separate oral and nasal breath emission; place bits of paper on top of card which will be moved by unwanted nasal breath. Place cool mirror under nose to show fogging with nasal breath. Having student close off both his nostrils with his thumb and forefinger while producing **p**, then produce **p** with nostrils open.

4. Dropping jaw on release of explosion: Use a mirror for imitation of teacher's correct production of **p** in isolation. Demonstrate student's faulty production by exaggeration; compare with appropriate production. Have the student produce series of syllables (**pee pee pee**), observing his productions in a mirror. There should be no dropping of the jaw. If necessary, the teacher may hold her hand under the student's jaw during production of **p** to prevent dropping of the jaw.

5. Substitution of **b** *for* **p**, *a sonant for surd error:* Write "b" and cross it out to make student aware of the nature of his error. Demonstrate the tactile difference by having student feel explosion of breath on **p** and voice vibration on **b**. Write a faint (or dotted) "h" in the space after "p" as in "p h ie." To extend duration of exploded **p**, demonstrate by writing the "p" with a line extended from it in a syllable, thus: "p____aw."

6. Blowing rather than exploded production: Demonstrate tactile difference on back of student's hand; demonstrate visual difference with feather or strip of paper.

t /t/ t

KEY WORDS: tie, sit, sitting
SPELLINGS: t, tt, -ed,
Th-(Thomas)

Production *(lingua-alveolar voiceless stop)*

STOP: No voice, velopharyngeal port closes, tip of the tongue closes against alveolar ridge and side of tongue against molars, air is held and compressed in the oral cavity.

EXPLOSION: Air compressed in the oral cavity is exploded as audible breath between alveolar ridge and point of the tongue through slightly open teeth and lips.

In connected speech, **t** is closed but not exploded preceding **s** (*eats, bits*) and following **s** in the same syllable (*stop, star*). It is exploded in the initial position of syllables when followed by a vowel (*tie, retain*), following other lingua-alveolar consonants (*want, salt*), and other breath consonants (ke*pt, act, fast, watched*) in the final position of words. It is either not exploded or very lightly exploded in the final position of words (*bracelet, sit*).

Internal Feedback Information

TACTILE: Tip of the tongue touches the alveolar ridge, exploded air is felt between tongue and alveolar ridge.

KINESTHETIC: Movement of tongue slightly upward to alveolar ridge.

Sensory Instructional Possibilities

TACTILE: Exploded air on skin of the hand.

VISUAL: Raised tongue tip through the slightly open teeth, explosion of air by movement of feather, flame, paper.

Suggestions for Development

1. Imitate from teacher's model; *avoid* dropping jaw with production.

2. Demonstrate manner of production by analogy from **p**.

3. Demonstrate explosion by tactile impression of breath on student's hand.

4. Demonstrate explosion by visual impression of sudden movement of strip of paper, feather, or candle flame; *avoid* exaggeration of force of articulation.

5. Demonstrate place of production by slowly giving a visual exaggeration of the formation: with teacher's mouth wide open, place tongue tip behind upper teeth, slowly narrow opening (keeping tongue in place) toward normal position, and produce exploded **t**. Have student attempt to imitate this production with a mirror if he cannot produce it without.

6. Demonstrate manner and place of production by giving a visually exaggerated step-by-step production: form **t** with the tongue tip outside the oral cavity making closure with front of the upper lip and explode; next make the closure with the tongue tip on the lower edge of upper lip and explode; next make the closure on the upper teeth and finally on the alveolar ridge. Have the student imitate each step as the tongue is drawn back into the oral cavity.

7. Develop the unreleased **t** after the exploded production is accomplished. Demonstrate with techniques that are similar to those suggested for the sound **p**.

Common Errors and Suggestions for Improvement

1. Excess pressure on explosion of breath: Demonstrate reduced pressure by tactile impression of breath on student's hand; contrast excess breath with appropriate amount. Demonstrate reduced pressure by tactile impression of teacher's thumb pressed against student's palm; contrast excess pressure with appropriate amount. Have the student produce a series of rapid **t** sounds (**tttttttttt**) on a single breath; then a series of **to-** syllables, (**to- to- to-**), or **tip** syllables, (**tip, tip, tip, tip, tip**) on a single breath.

2. Insufficient pressure on explosion of breath: Demonstrate increased pressure by tactile impression of breath on student's hand; use strip of paper, feather, or other visual aid. Demonstrate pressure by pressing together student's thumb and forefinger, or his hands, and releasing them.

3. Improper place of production (tip of tongue on back of upper teeth or mid-portion of tongue against alveolar ridge): Redevelop **t** using open mouth position to give visual information about position of tip of tongue against alveolar ridge. Use diagram or model to show correct placement; have student use mirror to produce **t** with appropriate placement.

4. Dropping jaw on release of explosion: Have student produce series of syllables **tee tee tee tee**, observing his productions in a mirror. There should be no dropping of the jaw. Demonstrate with teacher's production of **to- to- to-**, pointing out that the jaw does not drop. If jaw dropping persists, teacher may hold her hand under student's jaw as he produces syllables. Have student hold his own hand under his jaw for tactile feedback.

*5. Substitution of **d** for **t**, a sonant for surd error:* Write "d" and cross it out to make student aware of the nature of his error. Demonstrate the tactile difference by having student feel explosion of breath on **t** and voice vibration on **d**. To extend duration of exploded **t**, demonstrate by writing the "t" with a line extended from it in a syllable, thus: "t____oo."

6. Too wide a mouth opening on production: Have the student produce the series of syllables **tee tee tee** and **eet eet eet**, observing his productions in a mirror; there should be no movement of the jaw. The student may hold a pencil eraser between his teeth while producing these syllables to assure that the jaw does not drop. Practice production of **t** in association with **p** in syllables **ipitip, ipitip, ipitip**.

KEY WORDS: **k**ey, ba**ck**, be**c**ome
SPELLINGS: k, c, -ck, cc,
ch(school), -(a)lk

k /k/ k

Production (*lingua-velar voiceless stop*)

STOP: No voice, velopharyngeal port closes, back of tongue closes against front portion of velum or back portion of palate, air is held and compressed in the back of the oral cavity. *Note:* the point of contact on the velum-palate changes with surrounding vowels.

EXPLOSION: Air compressed in the back of the oral cavity is exploded as audible breath between the velum-palate and back of the tongue through slightly open teeth and lips.

In connected speech, **k** is stopped but not exploded preceding **s** (*cooks, talks*) or another stop consonant in the same syllable (*act, elect*), and following **s** in the same syllable (*skin, scat*). It is exploded in the initial position of words and syllables (*king, crow, declare*), and immediately following any consonant in the final position (*ask, bank, bark, milk*). It is either not exploded or very lightly exploded in the final position following a vowel (*like, sack*).

Internal Feedback Information

TACTILE: Closure of back of tongue on velum or palate gives little information.

KINESTHETIC: Raising of back of tongue to close against velum or palate gives little information.

Sensory Instructional Possibilities

TACTILE: Exploded air on skin of the hand.

VISUAL: Exploded air by movement of feather, flame, or paper; place of production visible only with exaggerated mouth opening.

Suggestions for Development

1. Imitate from teacher's model; *avoid* dropping jaw with production. *Note:*

fair to very poor sensory features make **k** a difficult sound to develop from imitation.

2. Demonstrate manner of production by analogy from **p** and **t**.

3. Demonstrate explosion by tactile impression of breath on student's hand.

4. Demonstrate explosion by visual impression of sudden movement of strip of paper, feather, or candle flame; *avoid* exaggeration of force of articulation.

5. Demonstrate place of production by slowly giving a visual exaggeration of the formation: with the teacher's mouth wide open, place the back of the tongue against the back portion of the palate (keeping the tip of the tongue behind the lower front teeth), slowly narrow mouth opening (keeping tongue in place) toward normal position and explode **k**. Have student attempt to imitate this production, using a mirror if necessary.

6. Demonstrate manner and place of production by giving a visually exaggerated step-by-step production: form **k** with the back of the tongue against the back of the upper front teeth (keeping the tip of the tongue behind the lower front teeth and explode (sound will be similar to **t**); next make the closure with the back of the tongue on the alveolar ridge and explode; next closure on the front portion of the palate and finally on the back portion of the palate. Have the student imitate each step as the back of the tongue is drawn back into the oral cavity.

7. Develop **k** in association with the **ee** vowel, a position in which the tongue is very close to the velum-palate, helping to avoid dropping the jaw on production of **k**. Closure of the **k** on syllables **eek** or **kee** is likely to be at the back of the palate rather than on the velum, avoiding unwanted noise of closure on the back of the velum and uvula.

8. While the student attempts to produce **t**, hold the tip of his tongue down (with finger or tongue blade) behind the lower front teeth (do not let the back of the tongue move forward). Associate the exploded sound he produces with written "k." After several repetitions with the teacher or student holding down the tip of the tongue, have the student attempt the production without this aid.

9. Have the seated student hold his mouth slightly open and breathe deeply through his nose (to accomplish this the velum and back of tongue must make closure). See that the tip of the tongue lies against the lower front teeth. While expelling breath through his nose, have student occlude his nostrils quickly with his thumb and forefinger, forcing the air to separate the velum and back of the tongue. Associate with written "k"; repeat.

10. Have the student lie on his back, relaxed (in this position the velum and

back of the tongue are very close together). Have student breathe through his slightly opened mouth and attempt **k** explosion. *Note:* production will occur far back on the velum and should later be brought forward.

11. Develop the unreleased **k** after the exploded production is accomplished. Demonstrate with techniques similar to those suggested for the sound **p**.

12. If necessary, place teacher's thumb and forefinger on student's throat just under back of the tongue; press upward and forward, then move down quickly. Demonstrate explosion on teacher's production and ask student to attempt the same using his own thumb and forefinger on his throat.

Common Errors and Suggestions for Improvement

1. Excess or insufficient pressure on explosion of breath: Demonstrate as with **p** and **t**. Reduce pressure by having student produce a series of rapid **k** sounds (**kkkkkkkkkk**) on one breath, then produce syllables **kee kee kee kee kee** on another single breath.

2. Lack of closure for stop: Demonstrate by analogy with **p** and **t**. Have student produce series of **ptk** (**ptkptkptkptkptk**) on a single breath. Demonstrate difference between steady breath and sudden explosion with strip of paper or other visual aid. Redevelop in syllables following **ng**: extend **ng** and stop with breath (whispered) explosion. Use visual aids as needed. If **k** closure is accomplished in syllables, tell student to make **ng** without voice and then produce **k** at the end of the syllable.

3. Closure made too far back on velum and tongue: With diagrams compare correct and incorrect placement. Have student keep tip of tongue against lower front teeth while producing **k**. Practice **k** in syllables with **ee** and other vowels with forward tongue placement.

*4. Substitution of **g** for **k**, a sonant for surd error:* Write "g" and cross out to make student aware of nature of error. Demonstrate tactile difference as with **b** for **p**, and **d** for **t**. Extend duration of exploded **k** as with **p** and **t**.

5. Mouth too far open: Redevelop, demonstrating that the jaw does not drop on production. Use mirror or, if necessary, place hand under student's jaw on production of a series of **kkkkkkkkkk**. Develop in association with vowel **ee**; use exercises such as **eekee, eekee, eekee,** using a mirror to show that the mouth opening is very slight. Place a pencil or tongue blade between the teeth and have student produce **k** without letting go of object.

6. Explosion made as glottal stop: Redevelop by analogy from **p** and **t**, moving back from **p** to **t** to **k**, and showing place of production by exaggerating if necessary. Redevelop by having student make explosion with closure made by back of tongue on alveolar ridge; gradually move tongue closure back in mouth until a good **k** is produced. Redevelop using development procedure #9, above.

f /f/ f

KEY WORDS: fan, leaf, coffee
SPELLINGS: f, ff, ph, -gh(rough)

Production (*Labio-dental voiceless fricative*)

No voice, velopharyngeal port closes, the lower lip approximates the upper front teeth, breath is continuously emitted between the teeth and lower lip as audible friction.

Internal Feedback Information

TACTILE: Lower lip lightly touches upper front teeth, friction of restricted breath flow across lower lip.

KINESTHETIC: Lower lip moves upward to approximate upper front teeth.

Sensory Instructional Possibilities

TACTILE: Steady breath flow on skin of the hand.

VISUAL: Approximation of lower lip and upper front teeth can be seen easily. Steady breath flow shown by movement of feather, flame, paper.

Suggestions for Development

1. Imitate from teacher's model; *avoid* excessive pressure on production. Use mirror, if necessary.

2. Demonstrate emission of steady breath with feather, strip of paper, or other visual aid; *avoid* excessive breath pressure or sudden emission.

3. Have student blow, press his lower lip gently upward to approximate the upper front teeth; associate with written "f ".

Common Errors and Suggestions for Improvement

1. Excess force of expelled breath: Demonstrate that cheeks are not puffed out in producing **f.** Use visual aids to demonstrate difference between appropriate and excess breath pressure. Have student produce and extend **f** on a single breath (but do not let student take a deep breath). Draw line after written "f" to show duration of student's production: "f____." Practice extending duration until the force of breath is reduced, then practice a short production, isolated and in syllables **fo-, fee, foo, faw.**

2. Excess pressure on contact of lower lip and upper teeth: Have student produce a rapid series of syllables **fo- fo- fo- fo-** on a single breath. Demonstrate degree of pressure by approximating student's index fingers one on top of the other; demonstrate undesirable pressure.

3. Insufficient breath flow: Use visual aids or student's hand to demonstrate breath flow. If caused by escape of breath through wide spaces between the teeth, have student approximate the inner surface of the lower lip with the edges and front surface of the teeth. If caused by excess pressure on contact of lower lip and upper teeth, use procedure #2 above.

4. Substitution of v *for* **f,** *a sonant for surd error:* Write "v" and then cross it out to make student aware of nature of error. Demonstrate the tactile difference by having student feel breath emission on **f** and voice vibration on **v.** Demonstrate greater duration of **f** than **v** by drawing a line to extend the **f:** "f____."

5. A stop plosive given in place of the fricative: The student may produce either a **p** sound or a labio-dental stop plosive in place of the fricative **f.** Compare visually, using a mirror if needed. With a strip of paper or other visual aid, show continuing nature of fricative compared to a plosive.

6. Insertion of **h-***like sound after final* **f,** *or between* **f** *and another breath consonant (sof* **h** *t):* Error on final **f** occurs because breath continues after **f** position is released. Practice **f** in final position of syllables **-of, eef, oof,** demonstrating with feather and mirror that breath emission ends before **f** position is released. Contrast inappropriate release to **h**-like sound. With **f** followed by breath stops (**p, t, k**) or affricate **ch,** have student practice terminating the fricative with the stop. With **f** followed by **t,** have student take position for **t,** then produce **ft** blend. Practice in syllables **-oft eft ooft.** With **f** followed by other breath fricatives (*half sole*), practice combinations in blended bisyllables **-afsa- awfsaw eefsee.**

7. Insertion of natural vowel **-u-** *between* **f** *and following voiced consonant:* With **f** followed by **r** or **l,** have student take tongue position for **r** or **l** before producing **f.** With **f** followed by voiced stop, have student practice terminating the fricative with the stop (*life belt*). With **f** followed by other voiced consonants or vowels, practice coarticulation in blended syllables.

KEY WORDS: **th**in, too**th**, no**th**ing

th /θ/ th

SPELLINGS: th

Production (*lingua-dental voiceless fricative*)

No voice, velopharyngeal port closes, the tip of the tongue (spread wide and thin) approximates the edge of the upper front teeth, breath is continuously emitted between the front teeth and tongue with audible friction.

Internal Feedback Information

TACTILE: Tongue lightly touches upper front teeth, friction of restricted breath flow across tongue.

KINESTHETIC: Tongue tip moves forward slightly.

Sensory Instructional Possibilities

TACTILE: Steady breath flow on skin of the hand.

VISUAL: Tip of the tongue approximating upper front teeth can be seen through the slightly open front teeth. Steady breath flow shown by movement of feather, flame, paper.

Suggestions for Development

1. Imitate from teacher's model: *avoid* excessive pressure on production. Use mirror if necessary.

2. Demonstrate emission of steady breath with feather, strip of paper, or other visual aid: *avoid* sudden emission of breath.

3. Demonstrate manner of production by analogy from **f.**

4. If necessary, demonstrate place of production by slowly giving a visual exaggeration of the formation: with the teacher's mouth wide open, protrude the tongue, spread it wide and thin, then slowly withdraw it toward position for **th** and produce the sound.

5. If the student is not able to develop **th** otherwise, have him produce it with the tongue protruded between the teeth for improved tactile-kinesthetic feedback. Then have him produce the **th** with the tongue gradually farther back.

Common Errors and Suggestions for Improvement

1. Excess pressure on contact of tongue and upper front teeth: Have student produce the rapid series of syllables **t̄ho- t̄ho- t̄ho- t̄ho-** or **t̄hee t̄hee t̄hee t̄hee** on a single breath. Demonstrate degree of pressure by approximating student's hands or index fingers one on top of the other; compare with undesirable pressure. Place student's fingertip between teacher's upper front teeth and tongue, and demonstrate appropriate pressure with teacher's tongue against student's fingertip.

2. Excess force on expelled breath: Demonstrate as with **f** sound.

3. Substitution of t̄h for t̄h, a sonant for surd error: Write "th" and then cross out to make student aware of nature of error. Demonstrate tactile difference as with **f.**

4. Tip of tongue protruding too far: Redevelop from imitation, using mirror if necessary.

5. Breath escapes from sides of tongue into cheek cavity: Give visual demonstration of the tongue flat and broad, making contact with molars on side. Show with mirror that cheeks are not puffed out on production. Use diagram to show frontal escape of breath. If necessary, gently press student's cheeks inward on production of **t̄h.** If caused by excess breath pressure or excess pressure of tongue contact on front teeth, demonstrate appropriate force as described above.

KEY WORDS: see, makes, upset
SPELLINGS: s, ss, c (e, i, y),
ps-, sc(e, i, y)

s /s/ s

Production (*lingua-alveolar voiceless fricative*)

No voice, velopharyngeal port closes, the tip of the tongue approximates the alveolar ridge, breath is continuously directed through the narrow aperture between the alveolar ridge and the grooved tip of the tongue against the closely approximated front teeth with audible friction.

Alternate formation: No voice, velopharyngeal port closes, the tip of the tongue is placed *against the lower front teeth,* the front of the tongue is elevated to approximate the alveolar ridge and is grooved to form a narrow aperture through which breath is continuously directed against the closely approximated front teeth with audible friction. The essence of **s** is the forcing of a constricted breath stream against the approximated front teeth; either formation will accomplish this. Both formations are used by normal speakers. Either formation can yield an acceptable **s** for deaf speakers. Some teachers believe the alternate formation impedes coarticulation with surrounding phonemes. Others find the superior tactile feedback from the tongue tip against the lower front teeth in the alternate formation helpful in developing and maintaining **s**.

Internal Feedback Information

TACTILE: Friction of restricted breath flow across tongue and alveolar ridge. Tip of tongue touches lower front teeth in alternate formation.

KINESTHETIC: Very little feedback from grooving and raising tongue. Because of limited internal feedback information, this is one of the first speech sounds to be affected by hearing loss and is one of the most difficult for deaf persons to monitor.

Sensory Instructional Possibilities

TACTILE: Steady breath flow on skin of hand.

VISUAL: Steady breath flow by movement of feather, flame, paper. Narrow aperture between lower and upper front teeth may be shown with a mirror.

Suggestions for Development

1. Demonstrate manner of production by analogy from **f** and **th**.

2. Develop in association with **th**. Beginning with the **th** position, produce friction gradually withdrawing tongue and approximating front teeth toward **s** production. Show by diagram that tongue tip moves up toward alveolar ridge as it is withdrawn.

3. Demonstrate emission of steady breath with feather, strip of paper, or other visual aid.

4. Demonstrate place of production by slowly giving a visual exaggeration of formation: with teacher's mouth open wide, show the tongue grooved in the center, then elevated toward the alveolar ridge; slowly narrow mouth opening (keeping tongue in place) toward normal position and produce **s**.

5. Develop in association with **f**. While the student produces a prolonged **f**, pull down his lower lip with two fingers; **s** may result as student tries to maintain restriction of breath flow with his tongue.

6. Develop in association with th: insert a tongue blade between his upper teeth and tongue and gently push tongue back.

7. For alternate formation, demonstrate place of production by slowly giving a visual exaggeration of formation: with teacher's mouth open wide, show the tongue tip behind the lower front teeth and grooved at the center; slowly narrow mouth opening (keeping tongue in place) toward normal position and produce s.

8. For alternate formation, develop in association with **ee.** Maintaining position for **ee,** giving a whispered production which can be felt on back of the hand. Show the student that the tongue is grooved centrally and that the front approximates the alveolar ridge.

9. Manipulate for appropriate lingua-alveolar openings by inserting a dull pencil point or other slender rounded object between the tongue and alveolar ridge. For the tongue-up s, begin with the position for **n.** For tongue-down s, begin with **ee.**

Common Errors and Suggestions for Improvement

1. Inadequate constriction of breath stream directed against teeth: Redevelop, taking care to show grooving of tongue and proximity of tongue to front teeth. Use a diagram to show position if necessary. Demonstrate with feather, strip of paper, or other visual aid that escape of breath is limited to the area of the central incisors and is directed primarily downward on production of an acceptable s. Compare to diffuse escape of air for unacceptable production. Use mirror for student to imitate acceptable production.

2. Insertion of t either before or after s production: In order to achieve better tactile feedback, some deaf speakers may make lingua-alveolar or lingua-dental closure perceived by the listener as a t sound. Write "t" in the position in which it is inserted and cross it out. If t is inserted between s and the following vowel, it may help to write the word with a faintly written "h" following the s to indicate continued breath.

3. Insufficient breath flow: The tongue may be tightly pressed against palate, alveolar ridge or teeth, not permitting a channel for breath. Redevelop showing manner of production by analogy with a series of **f,** then **th,** then **s.** Press midline of student's tongue with pencil or other rounded object to show a grooved central passage for air flow.

4. A sound close to **sh** *is produced:* This may be caused by positioning the tongue too far back so that breath flow is diffused. Show student that the tongue approximates the alveolar ridge. If the sound is the result of insufficient pressure of the sides of the tongue closing against the back teeth, have the student raise his jaw slightly for better closure. Pressing upward on both of the student's cheeks may raise the sides of the tongue sufficiently. If necessary, a tongue depressor may be inserted under the sides of the tongue, gently pressing upward to close against the teeth.

5. Omission of **s**, *especially in final positions of words:* One of the most common and universal errors in the speech of deaf persons, for apparently the **s** is highly dependent on auditory feedback. Frequently what appears to be an **s** omission is inadequate pressure on production so that friction is not audible. Demonstrate increased pressure on production, using visual aids. Practice **s** production in connected words, underlining all **s** sounds in a written text to be read. Constant reminders with rewards for correct **s** production. Coordinated school-home effort to emphasize **s** production in all connected speech. If omission continues, the alternate production (tongue-down or tongue-up) may be developed.

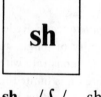

sh / ʃ / sh

KEY WORDS: **she**, fi**sh**, sun**sh**ine
SPELLINGS: sh, -t(ion), -c(ious)
ch-(chic), s(sure),
ch(machine),
c(ocean),
-ss-(tissue)

Production (*lingua-palatal voiceless fricative*)

No voice, velopharyngeal port closes, the sides of the tongue are against the upper molars, the broad front surface of the tongue is raised toward the alveolar ridge and palate forming a central aperture slightly broader and farther back than for **s**. Lips are protruded and slightly rounded (approximate lip formation for vowel **-oo-**) to direct the breath stream through and against the slightly open front teeth as audible friction.

Internal Feedback Information

TACTILE: Friction of restricted breath flow across tongue, palate, and alveolar ridge.

KINESTHETIC: Some feedback from grooving and raising the tongue. Rounding and protruding of lips.

Sensory Instructional Possibilities

TACTILE: Steady breath flow on skin of the hand.

VISUAL: Rounding and protruding lips seen with mirror. Steady breath flow shown by movement of feather, flame, paper.

Suggestions for Development

1. Imitate from teacher's model; *avoid* excessive pressure on production. Use mirror, if necessary, to show protruded lips and slight opening of teeth.

2. Demonstrate emission of steady breath with feeling on the back of hand, or with a feather, strip of paper, or other visual aid; *avoid* sudden emission of breath.

3. Demonstrate manner of production by analogy from **th** and **s**. Show student that the tongue is moved successively back from **th** to **s** to **sh** production.

4. Demonstrate place of production by slowly giving a visual exaggeration of the formation: with the teacher's mouth open wide, show the broad front of the tongue well behind the lower front teeth, slowly narrow mouth opening (keeping tongue in place) toward normal position, protrude and round the lips; produce **sh**. Have student attempt to imitate this production using a mirror, if necessary.

5. Develop in association with **ee**. Maintaining the mouth opening position for **ee,** protrude the lips and give a whispered production. Have the student feel the emission of breath on his hand. Similarly, develop in association with **r,** giving a whispered production with the lips rounded and protruded, and maintaining the tongue position for **r**.

6. Manipulate for appropriate position by using the following steps for production: have the student imitate the teacher opening the mouth (about two fingers' space between the teeth), protrude and point the tongue straight out, have the student place the tip of his index finger against the point of his tongue, have the student slowly push the point of his tongue back into the mouth well behind the lower front teeth (being careful not to let the tongue tip curl upward) until the broad front of the tongue is observed, have student slowly protrude his lips while the index finger maintains the broad front of the tongue in place. Close teeth gently on the index finger with upper and lower front teeth partly showing (not covered by lips), produce the **sh** approximation with the finger still holding the tongue in place. Remove the finger (keeping the tongue in place) and produce **sh** again. Teeth opening may be reduced further for improved production. Repeat until student has produced **sh**. Use a mirror if necessary.

7. Manipulate in association with the **th** sound. While the student produces an extended **th,** gently push the lip of the tongue back inside the mouth well

behind the lower front teeth. When an approximation of **sh** is reached, have the student attempt pulling back without help of the finger. Have student protrude and slightly round the lips on production.

Common Errors and Suggestions for Improvement

1. Inadequate constriction of the breath stream: Redevelop, taking care to show by teacher·example or diagrams that the tongue is raised high in the mouth, the sides of the tongue are against the upper molars directing the flow of breath centrally, and the teeth are only slightly open. Demonstrate by feeling on the hand, or by using a feather, strip of paper, or other visual aids, that the flow of breath is reduced. Compare to excessive breath emission. Demonstrate constriction of breath by analogy from **th** and **s**.

2. Excessive constriction of the breath stream: To achieve feedback, the student may seek to close the tongue point against the alveolar ridge or palate, causing lateral emission of breath, or he may press it against the lower front teeth, causing an **s**-like sound. Redevelop, using the procedures in development technique #6, above, emphasizing that the broad front of the tongue is well behind the lower front teeth. Redevelop, taking care to have student feel the sides of the tongue against the upper molars. If necessary, have the student close the lower molars gently up against the sides of the tongue, also, so that the flattened sides of the tongue are sandwiched between the upper and lower molars. In this position the steady emission of breath will not permit the tongue tip to close against the alveolar ridge or palate.

KEY WORDS: **ch**air, su**ch**, tea**ch**er
SPELLINGS: ch, -tch, -t(ure),
-t(ion)

ch /tʃ/ ch

Production (*lingua-alveolar, lingua-palatal voiceless affricate*)

No voice, velopharyngeal port closes, the sides of the tongue are against the upper molars, lips are protruded and slightly rounded (as for **sh**), the front of the tongue closes just behind the alveolar ridge; air held and compressed in the oral cavity is exploded as audible breath through the aperture between the alveolar ridge and tongue, and against the slightly open front teeth as audible friction.

The position is essentially that for the **sh** except that, instead of the steady flow of breath for friction, breath is imploded and exploded by the tongue closure slightly farther back on the alveolar ridge than for the **t** sound, and released more slowly but with greater pressure than for the **t**. This phoneme is produced with a single impulse of breath, even though it includes components of both the **t** and the **sh** sounds.

Internal Feedback Information

TACTILE: Point of the tongue touches the alveolar ridge; exploded air is felt across the tongue, palate, and alveolar ridge.

KINESTHETIC: Movement of tongue slightly upward to alveolar ridge, grooving of tongue on release of compressed air. Rounding and protruding of lips.

Sensory Instructional Possibilities

TACTILE: Exploded air on skin of the hand.

VISUAL: Rounding and protruding of lips seen with mirror. Explosion of air shown by movement of feather, flame, paper strip.

Suggestions for Development

Note: the **ch** is best developed after the **sh** can be produced well.

1. Imitate from teacher's model. Let student feel explosion of breath on back of his hand. *Avoid* excessive dropping of jaw on production.

2. Develop by analogy from **sh**. Have the student produce **sh** and write it on the chalk board. Now show the student the closure of the tongue against the alveolar ridge and produce **ch,** letting him feel the explosion of breath.

3. Demonstrate place of production by slowly giving a visual exaggeration of the formation: with the teacher's mouth open wide, show the tip of the tongue just behind the alveolar ridge, slowly narrow mouth opening toward normal position, protrude and round the lips; produce **ch** with a slight jaw dropping.

4. Develop in association with **sh**. Have the student produce an extended **sh** with interruptions of the continued breath flow for tongue closure as in **t**. Have the student imitate the teacher's pattern. The pattern may be represented by writing the "sh" on the chalk board with a tail interrupted as follows: "sh____/ /____/ /____/ /____," or as "sh____t____t____t," writing the "t" very small. When the **ch** is produced in these patterns, have the student produce it in isolation and with vowel sounds.

5. Develop by analogy from **t** and **sh**. Have the student produce the following series: **t sh tsh ch**. Demonstrate that the **ch** is made on a single breath impulse as compared to the **tsh** combination.

Common Errors and Suggestions for Improvement

1. Inadequate friction on production: Redevelop by analogy from **sh**. Have the student produce **sh** and write it on the chalk board. Show the student closure of the tongue against the alveolar ridge and produce **ch,** letting him feel the explosion of breath. Redevelop in association with **sh**. Follow suggested technique #4 for development of **ch**.

2. Failure to make the plosive tongue closure: The student may produce the **sh** sound in substitution for **ch,** or he may produce a short burst of breath by glottal closure and release. Redevelop place of production by slowly giving a visual exaggeration of the formation; follow suggested technique #3 for development. Emphasize position of tongue for closure and release. Have student imitate each step, using mirror if necessary, making certain that he accomplishes tongue closure on the alveolar ridge. Exaggerate the plosive manner of production, dropping jaw and letting student feel sudden explosion of breath on his hand. When student makes satisfactory production, demonstrate that **ch** should be produced without dropping the jaw. Demonstrate plosive manner of production by analogy; produce a series as follows: **p t k ch p t k ch.** Demonstrate plosive action by pressing the fingers of one hand on the palm of the other, and then release them suddenly.

*3. Production of two breath impulses as in **t** and **sh** combination:* Redevelop as **ch** on a single breath impulse. Contrast the **tsh** combination with the single impulse **ch,** letting student feel the difference on his hand. Write "tsh" and "ch" on the chalk board, comparing the two and then crossing out the "tsh." Write the "tsh" combination on the chalk board with the "t" written very small.

4. Extended duration of fricative finish: Practice repeated short productions of **ch** on a single breath (**ch ch ch ch ch ch**).

w-   /w/   w

Production (*bilabial resonant glide*)

With voice, the velopharyngeal port closes, the lips are rounded and slightly protruded. Lip protrusion is not so great as for **oo;** lip aperture is smaller than for **oo**. The **w-** is always released into a vowel; taking the lip rounded position described above, the **w-** is very brief, rapidly gliding into the formation of the following vowel.

Internal Feedback Information

TACTILE: Voicing may be felt.

KINESTHETIC: Rounding and protruding of lips.

AUDITORY: May be heard in a syllable but duration is very short.

Sensory Instructional Possibilities

TACTILE: Vibration of voicing with hand on lips or cheeks.

VISUAL: Rounding and protruding of lips.

Suggestions for Development

1. Develop **w-** in syllables using a wide variety of vowels; emphasize the relatively short duration of the **w-** in relation to the following vowel.

2. Imitate from teacher's model. Use mirror, if necessary. Show student that lip protrusion is not so great as for **oo**.

3. With student and teacher seated side-by-side, show in a mirror the degree of rounding and protrusion of the lips.

4. Develop by analogy to **wh**. Show student by tactile impression that breath is not expelled and that voice vibration is present.

5. Develop by analogy to **oo**. By underlining, show the student that **w-** is shorter than **oo** as follows: "w<u>oo</u>."

6. If the student has difficulty rounding the lips, trace a circle around his lips with the teacher's index fingertip. If the lips are not sufficiently protruded, the circle tracing finger may be held just beyond the lips, with teacher urging the student to touch her finger with his lips.

7. If necessary, manipulate the lips with teacher's thumb and index finger, pressing the corners of the mouth inward toward the rounded position.

Common Errors and Suggestions for Improvement

1. Duration too great (similar to duration of **oo***):* By underlining, show student that **w-** is shorter than **oo,** as in development suggestion #5 above. Write syllables with **w-;** underline the vowel and only the last part of the **w-** as follows: "<u>w- ee</u>."

2. Produced with audible breath friction (usually associated with extended duration); may be heard as **wh:** Reduce duration, as described above. Demonstrate the lack of breath flow by tactile impression on student's hand.

3. *Exaggerated rounding of the lips:* Redevelop in syllables using a narrow but not rounded lip opening.

b /b/ b

KEY WORDS: **b**oy, ca**b**, ra**bb**it
SPELLINGS: b, bb

Production *(bilabial voiced stop)*

CLOSURE: With voice, velopharyngeal port closes, lips close, air is held and compressed briefly in the oral cavity while voicing continues.

RELEASE: Lips, held together with less pressure and for shorter duration than for **p,** are opened; voicing continues.

In connected speech, "closure" and "release" more accurately describe the force of action for producing **b** than do "stop" and "explosion." The **b** is closed but not released with voicing as the final sound of an utterance or immediately before a breath consonant (*lab coat*). As the initial sound of an utterance or immediately following a breath consonant, voicing begins with the lips closed and the **b** is released into the following voiced sound. As a sound between two voiced sounds, **b** is a brief closure and release with voicing continuing. The sound **b** cannot be produced in isolation; it is often identified as a phoneme in a syllable preceding the natural vowel, as in **bu-.**

Internal Feedback Information

TACTILE: Lips touch with closure, voicing may be felt.

KINESTHETIC: Lips close lightly with less force than on **p.**

AUDITORY: In a syllable with a vowel, can be heard but duration is very brief.

Sensory Instructional Possibilities

TACTILE: Vibration of voicing with hand on lips or cheeks.

VISUAL: Lip closure and opening seen easily.

Suggestions for Development

1. Imitate from teacher's model in syllables; *avoid* dropping jaw and produc-

ing excess pressure. Produce a series of **b** closures with continuing voice (**bubububububu-**).

2. Have student use mirror to monitor his production if he cannot imitate the teacher's pattern otherwise.

3. If necessary, develop **b** by analogy to **p,** demonstrating the absence of explosion for **b** and the presence of voicing. *Avoid* producing the sounds **b** and **p** with equal force.

4. Develop the unreleased **b** after the released production is accomplished. Imitate from teacher's model of vowel interrupted by lip closure as in **-ub;** use a series of **-ubububububub** and contrast with **bububububu-** where final **b** is released.

5. If necessary, demonstrate that the final **b** is not released by teacher placing her finger over her lips to apparently prevent release. The unreleased sound may be written "-b" compared to the released "b-."

Common Errors and Suggestions for Improvement

1. Excess pressure on release: Demonstrate reduced pressure by tactile impression of absence of breath on student's hand. Contrast with excess breath explosion. Have the student produce a series of relaxed syllables (**bubububu-bubububu-**) on the same breath.

2. Substitution of **p** *for* **b,** *a surd for sonant error:* Write "p" and cross it out to make student aware of the nature of his error. Demonstrate the tactile difference by having student feel voice vibration on **b** and explosion of breath on **p.** Instruct student to reduce pressure on release; write "b" faintly or with dotted writing to show reduced pressure on production. Instruct student to make **b** of shorter duration or say it faster; contrast with **p** duration using written symbols: "<u>b</u>" vs. "<u>p   </u>."

3. Substitution of **m** *for* **b,** *a nasal error:* With breathy emission, show with strip of paper or other visual aid. Demonstrate inappropriate nasal emission by having student feel vibration on his nose with **m** but not with **b.** Have student produce a series of syllables on a single breath (**bubububububu-**), interrupting the series by occluding the student's nostrils. Have student attempt the series occluding his own nostrils, then without occlusion.

4. Release of final **b** *and* **b** *before voiced consonants:* Redevelop the unreleased **b** in syllables (**-ubububububub**). If necessary, place finger over the lips at conclusion of the series to prevent release. With vowel following **b,** practice production of coarticulated **b** and vowel in a series (**beebeebeebeebeebee**), (**bawbawbawbawbawbaw**) using mirror, if needed. With **l** or **r** following **b,** practice production for coarticulation by having student first take the tongue position for **l** or **r**, then produce the **b** in combination with **l** or **r** and a vowel, as in **bloo, blo-, blee,** or **broo, bro-, bree.** For timing, duration of syllable **bloo** should be not much (if at all) longer than **boo**; have student practice series of syllables (**boo boo boo bloo bloo bloo boo boo boo**), attempting the same duration on each syllable. Repeat with other vowels.

d /d/ d

KEY WORDS: **d**ay, mu**d**, la**dd**er
SPELLINGS: d, dd

Production *(lingua-alveolar voiced stop)*

CLOSURE: With voice, velopharyngeal port closes, tip of the tongue closes against alveolar ridge and side of tongue against molars, air is held and compressed briefly in the oral cavity while voicing continues.

RELEASE: Closure of tip of tongue on alveolar ridge (held with less pressure for shorter duration than for **t**) is released; voicing continues.

In connected speech, "closure" and "release" more accurately describe the force of action for producing **d** than do "stop" and "explosion." The **d** is closed but not released with voicing as the final sound of an utterance (*mud, sad*) or immediately before a breath consonant (*bedtime*). As the initial sound of an utterance or immediately following a breath consonant, voicing begins with the lingua-alveolar closure and the **d** is released into the following voiced sound. Between two voiced sounds, **d** is a brief closure and release with continued voicing. The sound **d** (like **b**) cannot be produced in isolation; it is usually identified as a phoneme in a syllable preceding the natural vowel, as in **du-**.

Internal Feedback Information

TACTILE: Tip of the tongue touches the alveolar ridge, voicing may be felt.

KINESTHETIC: Movement of tongue slightly upward to alveolar ridge, closure lighter than for **t**.

AUDITORY: In a syllable with a vowel can be heard but duration is very brief.

Sensory Instructional Possibilities

TACTILE: Vibration of voicing with hand on lips or cheeks.

VISUAL: Raised tongue point seen through the slightly separated teeth.

Suggestions for Development

1. Imitate from teacher's model in syllables; *avoid* dropping jaw and producing excess pressure. Produce a series of **d** closures with continuing voice **(dudududududu-)**.

2. Have student use mirror to monitor his productions, if necessary.

3. If necessary, develop **d** by analogy to **t,** demonstrating the absence of explosion for **d** and the presence of voicing. *Avoid* producing the sounds **d** and **t** with equal force.

4. Develop the unreleased **d** after the released production is accomplished. Imitate from teacher's model of vowel interrupted by lingua-alveolar closure as in **-ud;** use a series such as **-ududududud;** contrast **dudududu-** where the final **d** is released.

5. If necessary, demonstrate that final **d** is not released by teacher's placing her finger over her lips to prevent release. The unreleased sound may be written "**-d**" compared to released "**d-.**"

Common Errors and Suggestions for Improvement

1. Excess pressure on release: Demonstrate reduced pressure by tactile impression of absence of breath on student's hand. Contrast with excess breath explosion. Have the student produce a series of relaxed syllables **(dududududu-)** on the same breath.

2. Substitution of **t** *for* **d,** *a surd for sonant error:* Write "t" and cross it out to make student aware of the nature of his error. Demonstrate the tactile difference by having student feel voice vibration on **d** and explosion of breath on **t.** Instruct student to reduce pressure on release; write "d" faintly or with dotted writing to show reduced pressure on production. Instruct student to make **d** of shorter duration or say it faster; contrast with **t** duration using written symbols: "d___" vs. "t____."

3. Substitution of **n** *for* **d,** *a nasal error:* With breathy emission of **n,** demonstrate inappropriate nasal emission with strip of paper or other visual aid. Demonstrate inappropriate nasal emission by having student feel vibration on his nose with **n** but not with **d.** Have student produce a series of syllables on a single breath **(dududududu-),** interrupting the series by occluding the student's nostrils. Have student attempt the series occluding his own nostrils, then without occlusion.

4. Release of final **d** *and* **d** *before voiced consonants:* Redevelop the unreleased **d** in syllables (**-udududududud**). If necessary, place hand over the mouth opening at conclusion of the series to prohibit release. With vowel following **d,** practice production of coarticulation in a syllable series (**deedeedeedee-deedee**), using mirror, if needed; see that jaw does not move appreciably with syllables.

With lingua-alveolar consonants **n** or **t** following **d,** practice coarticulation on syllables without moving tongue position *(had not, had to).* With lingua-alveolar **l** following **d,** practice keeping tongue tip on alveolar ridge, narrowing tongue for lateral emission *(badly, would let).* With lingua-alveolar fricatives **s** and **z** following **d,** practice coarticulation with only slight movement of tongue for release into the fricative *(could see, good zoo).* With lingua-dental th following **d** *(had the, hid them),* produce the **d** with closure forward on the back of the upper front teeth opening slightly for release into the fricative with only slight tongue protrusion for the th. For the **dr-** blend, practice making the sound in syllables, moving the tongue back on the alveolar ridge as the **d** is being formed, releasing the closure into the **r.**

5. Too wide a mouth opening: Have the student produce a series of syllables **dee dee dee** and **eed eed eed,** observing his productions in a mirror; there should be no movement of the jaw. The student may hold a pencil eraser between his teeth while producing these syllables to assure that the jaw does not drop.

g /g/ g

KEY WORDS: **g**o, lo**g**, be**gg**ed
SPELLINGS: g, gg

Production *(lingua-velar voiced stop)*

CLOSURE: With voice, velopharyngeal port closes, back of the tongue closes against front portion of velum or back portion of palate, air is held and compressed briefly in the back of the oral cavity while voicing continues. *Note:* the point of contact on the velum-palate changes with surrounding vowels.

RELEASE: Closure of back of tongue and velum-palate—held together with less pressure and for shorter duration than the **k**—is released; voicing continues.

In connected speech, "closure" and "release" more accurately describe the force of action for producing **g** than do "stop" and "explosion." The **g** is closed but not released with voicing as the final sound of an utterance (*bag, rag*) or immediately before a breath consonant (*rag time*). As the initial sound of an utterance or immediately following a breath consonant, voicing begins with the lingua-velar closure and the **g** is released into the following voiced sound. As a sound between two voiced sounds, **g** is a brief closure and is released with continued voicing.

Internal Feedback Information

TACTILE: Closure of back of tongue on velum or palate gives little information; voicing may be felt.

KINESTHETIC: Raising of back of tongue to close against velum or palate gives little information; closure lighter than for **k**.

AUDITORY: In syllable with a vowel, can be heard but duration is very brief.

Sensory Instructional Possibilities

TACTILE: Vibration of voicing with hand on lips, cheeks, or throat.

VISUAL: Place of production visible only with exaggerated mouth opening.

Suggestions for Development

1. Imitate from teacher's model in syllables; *avoid* dropping jaw and producing excess pressure. Produce a series of **g** closures with continuing voice (**gugugugugugu-**).

2. Demonstrate manner of production by analogy from **b** and **d**. If necessary to demonstrate place of production as well as manner, show the analogy to the **k** sound. Produce the series **p t k,** then **b d g.**

3. Demonstrate place of production by slowly giving a visual exaggeration of the formation as with **k**.

4. Demonstrate manner and place of production by giving a visually exaggerated step-by-step production as with **k**.

5. Develop **g** in association with the **ee** vowel, a position in which the tongue is very close to the velum-palate, **eeg** or **gee**. Develop **g** in association with **ng,** using such syllables as **eeng g.**

6. While the student attempts to produce **d,** hold tip of his tongue down (with finger or tongue blade) behind the lower front teeth (do not let the back of the tongue move forward). Associate the sound he releases with written "g." After several repetitions with the teacher or student holding down the tip of the tongue, have the student attempt the production without this aid.

7. Have the student produce and extend **ng**. While this is being produced have student occlude his nostrils quickly with thumb and forefinger while voicing continues, forcing a separation of the velum and back of the tongue. Associate the resulting release sound with the written "g."

8. Develop the imploded (unreleased) **g** after the released production is accomplished. Demonstrate the techniques similar to those for **b** and **d**.

Common Errors and Suggestions for Improvement

1. Excess pressure on release: Demonstrate reduced pressure by tactile impression of absence of breath on student's hand. Contrast with excess breath explosion. Have student produce a relaxed series of syllables (**gugugugugugu-**) on the same breath. If **b** and **d** have appropriate pressure and release, associate **g** with these sounds in a syllable series of **budugu-budugu-budugu-** on a single breath.

2. Closure made too far back on velum and tongue: With diagrams compare correct and incorrect placement. Have student keep front of tongue against lower front teeth while producing **g**. Practice **g** in syllables with **ee** and other vowels with forward tongue placement.

*3. Substitution of **k** for **g**, a surd for sonant error:* Write "k" and cross it out to make student aware of nature of error. Demonstrate tactile difference as with **p** for **b** and **t** for **d**. Instruct student to reduce pressure and duration as with **b** and **d**.

*4. Release of final **g** and of **g** before voiced consonants:* Redevelop the unreleased **g** in syllables (**-ugugugugugug**). If necessary, place hand over mouth opening at conclusion of the series to prevent release. With a vowel following **g**, practice production of coarticulation in a syllable series of **go-, go-, go-, go-;** see that the jaw does not drop on syllable production.

With **k** following **g** in connected speech (*big king*), practice coarticulation on syllables without moving tongue position. With **gr-** and **gl-** blends, practice positioning tongue tip for **r** and **l** sounds before the **g** is produced; release **g** into the **r** or **l**. Then produce syllables such as **gloo, glee, groo**. For timing, duration of syllable **gloo** should be not much (if at all) longer than **goo;** have student practice series of syllables **goo goo goo gloo gloo gloo goo goo goo** attempting the same duration on each syllable.

5. Mouth too far open: Redevelop, demonstrating that the jaw does not drop on production in isolation. Use mirror or, if necessary, place hand over child's jaw on production of a series of **gggggg**. Develop in association with vowel **ee**; use exercises such as **eegee, eegee, eegee** using a mirror to show that the mouth opening is very slight. Place a pencil or tongue blade between the teeth and have student produce **g** without letting go of object.

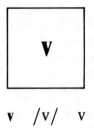

KEY WORDS: vine, give, every
SPELLINGS: v, -f(of),
-ph-(Stephen)

v /v/ **v**

Production *(labio-dental voiced fricative)*

With voice, velopharyngeal port closes, the lower lip approximates the upper front teeth, voice is continuously emitted with escape between the teeth and lower lip as combined voice and audible friction. Duration is shorter and produced with less force than for **f.** In termination of an utterance the **v** has a voiceless finish.

Internal Feedback Information

TACTILE: Lower lip lightly touches upper front teeth, friction of restricted breath flow across lower lip. Voicing may be felt.

KINESTHETIC: Lower lip moves upward to approximate upper front teeth.

AUDITORY: Acoustically weak, and duration is very short.

Sensory Instructional Possibilities

TACTILE: Slight flow of breath on skin of the hand. Vibration of voicing by hand on lips or cheeks.

VISUAL: Approximation of lower lip and upper front teeth can be easily seen.

Suggestions for Development

1. Imitate from teacher's model; *avoid* excessive pressure on production. Use mirror, if necessary.

2. Develop by analogy from **f,** demonstrating the absence of escaping breath flow and the presence of voicing. *Avoid* producing **v** with pressure equal to **f.**

3. Demonstrate vibration of lower lip by having student feel teacher's lip as she produces **v.**

4. Have student produce and extend the vowel **-u-,** press his lower lip gently upward to approximate the upper front teeth; associate with written "v."

Common Errors and Suggestions for Improvement

1. Breath flow insufficient for audible friction: Use visual aids or tactile impression on student's hand to demonstrate breath flow. If caused by escape of breath through side spaces between the teeth, have student approximate the inner surface of the lower lip with the edges and front surface of the teeth. If caused by excess pressure on contact of lower lip and upper teeth, demonstrate degree of pressure by approximating student's index fingers one on top of the other; demonstrate undesirable pressure.

2. Substitution of **f** *for* **v**, *a surd for sonant error;* Write "f" and then cross it out to make student aware of nature of error. Demonstrate the tactile difference as described for **f**. The **v** may be improved by having the edge of the upper front teeth contact just inside the lower lip, rather than on the top surface of the lower lip as with **f**.

3. Nasal emission of voice: Demonstrate tactile impression of vibration on the lower lip and absence of voice vibration on the nose with **v**. Redevelop by analogy from **f**; have student produce extended **f** blending into extended **v** (**f___v___f___v**) on a single breath.

4. Release of final **v** *with -**u*** *- sound.* Voicing continues after **v** is released. Contrast released and unreleased **v**, demonstrating tactile and visual differences. Have student release final **v** sound with a soft breath release. Write as "-vf" with the "f" written faintly.

5. Extended duration: Draw line after "f" to show its duration ("f_____"), compare with **v** drawing a much shorter line ("v__"). Practice a series of short syllables (**veeveeveeveeveevee**) on a single breath.

th /ð/ ~~th~~

KEY WORDS: **th**e, smoo**th**, bo**th**er
SPELLINGS: th-, -th(er),
-th(s), -th(e)

Production *(lingua-dental voiced fricative)*

With voice, velopharyngeal port closes, the tip of the tongue approximates the edge of the upper front teeth, voice is continuously emitted with escape between the front teeth and tongue as combined voice and audible friction.

Duration is shorter and produced with less force than for th[1]. In termination of an utterance the th[2] has a breath finish.

Internal Feedback Information

TACTILE: Tongue lightly touches upper front teeth, friction of restricted breath flow across tongue. Voicing can be felt.

KINESTHETIC: Tongue tip moves forward slightly.

AUDITORY: Acoustically very weak, and duration is very short.

Sensory Instructional Possibilities

TACTILE: Slight flow of breath felt on skin of the hand. Vibration of voicing can be felt by hand on cheeks, or by fingertips on extended tongue tip.

VISUAL: Tip of the tongue approximating upper front teeth can be seen through the slightly open front teeth.

Suggestions for Development

1. Imitate from teacher's model; *avoid* excessive pressure on production. Use mirror, if necessary.

2. Develop by analogy from v for manner of production. Develop by analogy from th[1] for place of production; demonstrate absence of escaping breath flow and the presence of voicing for th[2]. Avoid producing th[2] with pressure equal to th[1].

3. Demonstrate voice vibration by having the student feel the protruded tip of the teacher's tongue as she produces th[2].

4. Have the student produce and extend the vowel -u-, extending his tongue tip beyond the edge of the upper teeth. Gently press his tongue upward against the edge of the upper teeth as voicing continues.

Common Errors and Suggestions for Improvement

1. Substitution of th[1] for th[2], a surd for sonant error: Write "th" and then cross it out to make student aware of nature of error. Demonstrate the tactile difference of reduced breath flow and presence of voicing on production of th[2] compared to th[1]. The th[2] may be improved by having the tip of the tongue approximate the upper front teeth just inside the edge (slightly less tongue protrusion than for th[1]).

2. Nasal emission of voice: Demonstrate the tactile impression of vibration on the slightly protruded tongue and the absence of voice vibration on the nose with th[2]. Redevelop by analogy from th[1]. Gently close off the nostrils, if necessary.

z   /z/   z

Production *(lingua-alveolar voiced fricative)*

With voice, the velopharyngeal port closes, the tip of the tongue approximates the alveolar ridge, voiced breath is continuously directed through the narrow aperture between the alveolar ridge and the grooved tip of the tongue against the closely approximated front teeth as combined voice and audible friction. Duration is shorter and produced with less force than for **s.** The initial **z** requires more breath pressure than do the voiced fricatives **v** and **t̊h.** In termination of an utterance *(runs)*, the **z** has a voiceless finish.

Alternate formation: see description of tongue-down formation for **s.**

Internal Feedback Information

TACTILE: Slight friction of restricted breath flow across tongue and alveolar ridge. Voicing may be felt.

KINESTHETIC: Very little feedback from grooving and raising the tongue.

AUDITORY: Acoustically weak, and duration is short.

Sensory Instructional Possibilities

TACTILE: Vibration of voicing can be felt by hand under chin near base of the tongue, or by finger tips on teeth. Slight flow of breath on skin of the hand.

VISUAL: Narrow aperture between lower and upper front teeth may be shown with a mirror.

Suggestions for Development

1. Develop by analogy from **s,** demonstrating the presence of voicing with **z.** Let student feel vibration of teeth and chin. Modify suggestions for developing **s.**

2. Demonstrate manner of production by analogy from **v** and **t̊h.** Contrast **v** with **f, t̊h** with **t̊h,** then **z** with **s.**

3. Develop in association with **t̊h.** Beginning with the **t̊h** position, produce

voiced friction, gradually withdrawing tongue and approximating front teeth toward **z** production. Show by diagram that the tongue tip moves up toward the alveolar ridge as it is withdrawn.

4. Demonstrate place of production by slowly giving a visual exaggeration of formation: with teacher's mouth wide open, show the tongue grooved in the center then elevated toward the alveolar ridge (tongue tip behind the lower front teeth for alternate formation), slowly narrow mouth opening toward normal position and produce **z**.

5. *Note:* When it is the terminating consonant preceded by a voiced sound (*tabs, goods, bags, knives*), the teacher may choose to develop the **z** as an **s** in order to reduce voicing at the finish.

Common Errors and Suggestions for Improvement

1. Inadequate breath flow on production: Redevelop by analogy from **s**, emphasizing the flow of breath on both sounds; exaggerate the breath flow on **z**, if necessary. Relax excessive pressure to permit escape of breath stream if production is inhibited by too much constriction.

2. Inadequate voicing in the production: Redevelop by analogy from **v** and **th**.² Develop in association with **ee**, producing alternate sounds **z** and **ee** on a single breath (**eezeezeezeezeezeez**).

3. Excessive voicing and duration as a terminating sound: Demonstrate the voiceless finish by writing the sound as "**z-s**," as in the word *goods*. Point out that the breath finish has diminished pressure by writing the **s** finish small or in dotted lines. The teacher may choose to develop this terminating sound as **s** following voiced sounds. Voicing from the preceding sound will infiltrate the **s** to give the acoustic impression of a final **z** sound.

zh

zh /ʒ/ zh

KEY WORDS: measure, vision, usual
SPELLINGS: -s(ion), -s(sure),
-g(e)(loge)

Production *(lingua-palatal voiced fricative)*

With voice, the velopharyngeal port closes, the sides of the tongue are against the upper molars, the broad front surface of the tongue is raised toward the alveolar ridge and palate forming a central aperture slightly broader and farther back than for **s**. Lips are protruded and slightly rounded (approximate lip formation for vowel **-oo-**) to direct the voiced breath stream through and against the slightly open front teeth as combined voice and audible friction.

Internal Feedback Information

TACTILE: Slight friction of restricted breath flow across tongue, palate, and alveolar ridge. Voicing can be felt.

KINESTHETIC: Some feedback from grooving and raising the tongue. Rounding and protruding of lips.

AUDITORY: Acoustically weak, and duration is short.

Sensory Instructional Possibilities

TACTILE: Vibration of voicing can be felt by hand on sides of neck and under chin near the base of the tongue.

VISUAL: Rounding and protruding of lips can be seen with mirror.

Suggestions for Development

Note: this sound does not typically occur in children's early vocabulary.

1. Development by analogy from **sh**, demonstrating the presence of voicing with **zh**.

2. Demonstrate manner of production by analogy from **v**, $\overset{2}{\text{th}}$ and **z**. Contrast **f** and **v**, $\overset{1}{\text{th}}$ and $\overset{2}{\text{th}}$, **s** and **z**, then **sh** and **zh**. Show student that the tongue is moved successively back from $\overset{2}{\text{th}}$ to **z** to **zh**.

3. Demonstrate place of production by slowly giving a visual exaggeration of the formation, as with **sh**.

4. Develop in association with **ee**. Maintaining the mouth opening position for **ee**, protrude the lips and produce **zh**. Have the student feel the emission of breath on his hand.

5. Manipulate in association with the $\overset{2}{\text{th}}$ sound, as for development of **sh** from $\overset{1}{\text{th}}$.

6. As a terminating consonant (*garage*) the **zh** has a voiceless finish. Demonstrate by writing the sound as "zh__sh." Point out the breath finish has diminished pressure by writing the **sh** finish small or in dotted lines.

Common Errors and Suggestions for Improvement

1. Inadequate breath flow on production: Redevelop by analogy from **sh**, emphasizing the flow of breath on both **sh** and **zh**; exaggerate the breath flow on **zh**, if necessary, letting student feel tactile impression on his hand. Redevelop, taking care to show by teacher example or diagram that the tongue is raised high in the mouth, the sides of the tongue are against the upper molars directing the flow of breath centrally, with a fairly broad aperture.

2. *Inadequate voicing in production:* Redevelop by analogy from **v, th**, and **z**.

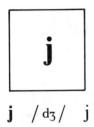

j / dʒ / j

KEY WORDS: **jam, edge**, enjoy
SPELLINGS: j, -dg(e), -g(e)

Production *(lingua-alveolar/lingua-palatal voiced affricate)*

With voice, the velopharyngeal port closes, the sides of the tongue are against the upper molars, lips are protruded and slightly rounded (as for **sh**), the front of the tongue closes just behind the alveolar ridge; air held and compressed briefly in the oral cavity is released as breath and voice combined through the aperture between the alveolar ridge and tongue, and against the slightly open front teeth as audible friction. The position is essentially that for the **ch**, except that voicing is involved. It may also be considered a single impulse production of combined **dzh**. The explosion is released with less pressure than for **ch** but with greater force than for **d**. Tongue placement for closure is slightly farther back on the alveolar ridge than for **d**.

Internal Feedback Information

TACTILE: Point of the tongue touches the alveolar ridge. Voicing may be felt; slight friction of restricted breath flow across tongue, palate, and alveolar ridge.

KINESTHETIC: Movement of tongue slightly upward to alveolar ridge, grooving of tongue on release of compressed air. Rounding and protruding of lips.

AUDITORY: In a syllable with a vowel, can be heard but duration is very brief.

Sensory Instructional Possibilities

TACTILE: Vibration of voicing felt by hand under chin near base of the tongue.

VISUAL: Raised tongue point can be seen through the slightly open teeth. Rounding and protruding of lips can be seen with mirror.

Suggestions for Development

Note: the **j** is best developed after the **d** and **ch** can be produced well.

1. Imitate from teacher's model; *avoid* dropping jaw on production.

2. Develop by analogy from **ch,** demonstrating the presence of voicing with **j.**

3. Demonstrate manner of production by analogy from other voiced plosives. Have student produce a series of **b, d, g, j.** Contrast **p** and **b, t** and **d, k** and **g,** and then **ch** and **j.**

4. Develop by analogy from **zh** (if the student can produce a good **zh**), using techniques suggested in developing **ch** by analogy from **sh.**

Common Errors and Suggestions for Improvement

1. Inadequate friction on production: Redevelop by analogy from **zh.** Have the student produce **zh** and write it on the chalk board. Show student closure of the tongue against the alveolar ridge and produce **j,** letting the student feel the explosion of breath.

2. Production of two voice impulses as in **d** *and* **zh** *combination:* Contrast the **dzh** combination with the single impulse **j,** letting student feel the difference on his hand.

3. Extended vocalization as a terminating consonant: Demonstrate that **j** has a breath finish as a terminating consonant by writing it as "d__sh," writing the "sh" in small letters or dotted lines to show that it is de-emphasized.

```
┌──────────────┐
│              │
│      m       │
│              │
└──────────────┘
```

m   /m/   m

KEY WORDS: meat, team, camera
SPELLINGS: m, -mb, -lm, -mn

Production *(bilabial nasal resonant)*

The lips close, voice is directed through the open velopharyngeal port to the nasal cavity and out the nostrils. The tongue lies flat in the mouth or is prepared for the following vowel sound providing opening for resonation of the voice in the entire oral cavity closed off by the lips, as well as resonation in the opened nasal cavity. The teeth are slightly opened.

Internal Feedback Information

TACTILE: Lips touch with closure. Voicing may be felt.

AUDITORY: Voicing may be heard.

Sensory Instructional Possibilities

TACTILE: Vibration of voicing easily felt on the lips, nose, or cheeks. Some emission of breath from nostrils.

VISUAL: Lip closure is easily visible.

Suggestions for Development

1. Imitate from teacher's model; *avoid* producing with lips pressed tightly together.

2. Let the student feel voice vibration on the sides of the nose and on the lips. Vibration may also be felt on top of head.

3. If the student can produce oral resonant vowels but cannot imitate **m**, have him produce **-u-** and extend it. While the vowel is being sounded, have the student close his lips and continue phonating.

Common Errors and Suggestions for Improvement

1. Excessive pressure of lips during production: Contrast formation with excessive pressure to that of appropriate pressure. Have student imitate teacher's production of a series of **mumumumumumumu-** uttered at a slow rate with obvious relaxation of the facial muscles. Have the student produce an extended **m**; flick down his lower lip rapidly to give the idea of relaxing his lips. Place the student's finger between your lips giving different degrees of pressure; indicate pressure which is appropriate for **m** closure.

2. Tongue closure reducing the volume of the oral cavity for resonance: Redevelop the **m** showing student that the tongue lies flat in the mouth. Use a diagram, showing that the tongue does not make closure either at the alveolar ridge, or at the palate or velum. Let the student feel vibration on the lips with correct production of **m**. With tongue closure, lip vibration will be reduced.

*3. Extended duration of **m** in connected speech:* Practice **mumumumumumu-** uttered rapidly on a single breath.

*4. Smacking of lips or insertion of **b** following **m** before a vowel:* Write "b" between **m** and vowel; cross it out to show nature of error. Have student produce syllables with **m** in a very relaxed way. Produce a series of **mumumumu-mumu-** very rapidly. Have the student produce an extended **m**; gently move his jaw downward to open for a vowel. Write a small "h" between the **m** and following vowel to show a relaxation between the sounds as "m___ h ee___."

*5. Substitution of **b** for **m**, an oral for nasal error:* If substitution is caused by excessive pressure of lips on closure, reduce pressure as described in #1 above. Write the letter "b" and cross it out to show the nature of the error. Develop in a syllable **mee**, extending the duration of **m**. Develop in a syllable **eem** with extended duration of **m**.

6. Non-vocalized breath emitted through nose before or during **m** *sound:* Practice prolonged humming on a single breath. Demonstrate that there is little noticeable breath emission in appropriate production on back of student's hand; contrast with unacceptable breath emission.

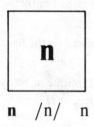

n /n/ n

KEY WORDS: **n**ew, ti**n**, a**n**y
SPELLINGS: n, kn-, pn-, gn-, -gn

Production *(lingua-alveolar nasal resonant)*

The tip of the tongue closes against the alveolar ridge and the sides of the tongue against molars, the teeth and lips are open, voice is directed through the nasal cavity and out the nostrils. The back of the tongue is open to the oropharynx both for resonation of voice in the oral cavity closed off by the tip of the tongue at the alveolar ridge, and for resonation in the opened nasal cavity. Tongue pressure at the alveolar ridge is less than for the **t** or **d**. The acoustic difference between **m** and **n** depends on the differences in size and shape of the oral cavity, closed at the lips for **m**, and closed by the tongue and alveolar ridge for **n**.

Internal Feedback Information

TACTILE: Tip of the tongue touches the alveolar ridge. Voicing can be felt.

KINESTHETIC: Movement of the tongue slightly upward to the alveolar ridge.

AUDITORY: Voicing may be heard.

Sensory Instructional Possibilities

TACTILE: Vibration of voicing can be easily felt on the nose. Some emission of breath from nostrils can be felt.

VISUAL: Raised tongue point can be seen through the slightly open teeth.

Suggestions for Development

1. Imitate from teacher's model; let student feel voice vibration on the nose.

2. Develop by analogy from **m** for manner of production. Show the student the closure of the point of tongue and alveolar ridge. By diagram show that

the back of the tongue does not close with the velum or palate. Have **m** and **n** repeated in close succession.

3. Develop by analogy from **d** for place of production. Have student take the tongue position for **d** if he has already developed that sound. Let him feel voice vibration on the nose as the tongue position is held.

4. If good tongue closure is not made, **n** can be developed in steps of gradually withdrawing the tongue tip. First have the **n** produced with the tongue tip protruding slightly between the closed lips; a sound between the **m** and **n** will result. Next have student pull the tongue in just inside the lips to produce the sound. When this is successful, have student open his lips, making the tongue closure with the upper lip. Then make the closure just behind the teeth, and finally on the alveolar ridge.

Common Errors and Suggestions for Improvement

1. Back of the tongue raised to close off the oral cavity; sound produced will be between **ng** *and* **n**: Show student by diagram that the back of the tongue is down leaving the oral cavity open in the back. Redevelop by analogy from **d**, as described above. Have student produce a series of **nu-nu-nu-nu-** syllables with the mouth wide open. When the **n** is produced, have student narrow opening of mouth.

2. Inadequate closure of the tongue and alveolar ridge: Redevelop by analogy from **d** or **t**. Redevelop following steps of #4, above. Demonstrate with mirror that the tongue is spread wide for complete closure.

3. Tongue pressure too great on closure: Practice rapid repetitions of **n** with a vowel as in **nunununununu-**, on a single breath. Demonstrate reduced pressure by showing appropriate pressure with teacher's thumb on palm of student's hand.

```
┌─────────────┐
│             │
│   ng        │
│             │
│             │
└─────────────┘
```

ng / ŋ / ng

KEY WORDS: so**ng**, si**ng**er
SPELLINGS: -ng, -n(k),
-n(g) (single),
-n(x)

Production *(lingua-velar nasal resonant)*

The back of the tongue closes against front portion of velum or back portion of palate, the teeth and lips are open, voice is directed through the nasal cavity and out the nostrils. The tip of the tongue rests just behind the lower front teeth forming a resonating cavity in the front of the open mouth.

Internal Feedback Information

TACTILE: Closure of back of tongue on velum or palate gives little information; voicing may be felt.

KINESTHETIC: Raising of back of tongue to close against velum or palate gives little information; closure lighter than for **k** or **g**.

AUDITORY: Voicing can be heard.

Sensory Instructional Possibilities

TACTILE: Vibration of voicing with fingers on nose, some nasal emission of air.

VISUAL: Place of production visible only with exaggerated mouth opening.

Suggestions for Development

1. Demonstrate the position of the tongue by opening the mouth wide, then slowly narrowing the opening; produce the **ng**, letting the student feel the voice vibration on the nose.

2. Develop by analogy from **m** and **n** for manner of production. Point out that closure of the mouth moves back from **m** to **n** to **ng**. Use the analogy of **b** to **d** to **g** to show the position of lips and tongue closure for **m, n,** and **ng,** respectively.

3. With the mouth slightly open, have student emit breath through the nose; then have student vocalize the breath.

4. Have the student produce **n** while the teacher holds down the tip of his tongue with the tip of her finger or a tongue depressor.

5. With thumb and forefinger on either side of the student's neck below the base of the tongue, press gently upward and hold the position; indicate nasality by touching the side of the nose.

Common Errors and Suggestions for Improvement

1. Closure made too far back on velum and tongue: With diagrams compare correct and incorrect placement. Have student keep front of tongue against lower front teeth while producing **ng**. Practice **ng** in syllables with **ee** and other vowels with forward tongue placement.

2. Inserting the sounds **k** *or* **g** *after the* **ng**: Demonstrate by tactile impression on the back of the hand that no explosion of breath is present. Redevelop by analogy from **m** and **n**, using syllables such as **mee nee ngee** to show transition from nasal consonant to following vowel. Then produce syllables initiated by a vowel such as **eem een eeng**.

3. Preceding vowel is given nasal resonance: Practice syllables beginning with another consonant blended with the extended vowel and concluded by **ng**: as **weeeeeeng, woooooong**.

4. Following vowel is given nasal resonance: Write a small "g" after the **ng** to show that the tongue/velum contact is discontinued as in "sing g ing."

l /l/ l

KEY WORDS: low, bowl, color
SPELLINGS: l, ll, -le, -el

Production *(lingua-alveolar lateral resonant)*

The velopharyngeal port closes, the point of the tongue is closed with slight pressure against the alveolar ridge with opening on both sides, voicing escapes on both sides of the tongue between the tongue and molars, and out the oral cavity. The mouth opening is that for the preceding and following vowels. The **l** is voiced when it initiates a syllable and when it is preceded by a voiced consonant (**bl-, gl-,** as in *blue* and *glass*). The **l** is given without voice when it is preceded by a voiceless consonant (**pl-, kl-, sl-, fl-,** as in *play, clean, slow,* and *fly*), modifying the flow of air from the previous breath consonant. In most consonant blends, the **l** tongue position should be taken before the previous consonant is initiated.

When **l** follows sounds articulated by the tongue in approximately the same place as **l** (examples: **t, d, n**), the tongue tip maintains its position for the preceding sound which is released into the **l** position by opening the sides of the tongue (*bottle, cradle, channel*).

When **l** is the final consonant following another consonant (as in *cable, angle, bottle, gavel*), the **l** becomes a semi-vowel and is produced as a syllable. With the tongue touching the alveolar ridge as described above, the mouth opening and lip position are those as for the vowel **-u-**.

Internal Feedback Information

TACTILE: Point of the tongue touches the alveolar ridge. Voicing can be felt.

KINESTHETIC: Movement of the tongue slightly upward to alveolar ridge.

AUDITORY: Voicing may be heard.

Sensory Instructional Possibilities

TACTILE: Vibration of voicing felt on the cheeks.

VISUAL: Raised tongue point can be seen through the slightly open teeth.

Suggestions for Development

1. Imitate from the teacher's model on syllables **lo- lo- lo- lo-;** avoid moving the jaw on producing these syllables.

2. Demonstrate the place of production by opening the mouth wide, showing the tongue point against the alveolar ridge; point out the apertures on both sides, reduce the mouth opening to normal and produce a steady **l.**

3. Demonstrate the position of the tongue by placing its point on the upper lip, point out the apertures on both sides of the tongue, draw it back slowly to position on the alveolar ridge and produce a steady **l.** Let the student imitate, using a mirror if necessary. *Note:* in normal position the tongue point would be broader than its fine point as it closes against the alveolar ridge.

Common Errors and Suggestions for Improvement

1. Duration too great: Practice production in a quick series of repetitive syllables as **lo- lo- lo- lo- lo-.** Produce a series with different vowels in sequence as **lo- loo lee li-e** on a single breath. Practice in blends with **l** followed by a stop breath consonant as in *help, built, milk.*

2. Vowel sound -u- between **l** *and following vowel:* Have student first take the position for the following vowel and then elevate the tongue for **l.** Produce the blend without dropping the jaw on **loo, lee, law.**

3. Substitution of **n** *for* **l,** *a nasal/oral error:* Demonstrate the tactile difference by having the student feel vibration on the nose for nasalized **l.** Practice a series of syllables beginning with a vowel as in **-olololo-.** Have the student point his tongue outside the mouth; demonstrate that it may be slowly pulled back inside the mouth to touch the alveolar ridge, keeping the tongue pointed and narrow. If necessary, have the child occlude his nostrils making a series of **lo-** syllables.

4. Tongue raised in back of the mouth for production: Have the student point his tongue outside the mouth, slowly pulling it inside the mouth, keeping it pointed and narrow as it touches the alveolar ridge; reduce mouth opening toward normal and produce a series of **lo-** syllables. Use a mirror to help student with this exercise.

r /r/ r-

KEY WORDS: red, bar, oral
SPELLINGS: r, rr, wr-, -rrh

Production *(lingua-palatal resonant)*

The velopharyngeal port closes, the tongue tip is turned up toward the palate just behind the alveolar ridge but without touching, the sides of the tongue are against the upper molars, voicing escapes between the tongue and palate and out the oral cavity. Duration is short. The lips are not rounded but may be slightly protruded as with **-oo-;** lips generally take the position of surrounding vowels. The tongue may be curled back—retroflexed.

The **r** is voiced when it initiates a syllable and when it is preceded by a voiced consonant (**br-, dr-, gr-,** as in *brown, dry, grow*). The **r** is given without voice when it is preceded by a voiceless consonant (**pr-, tr-, kr-, fr-, thr-** , as in *pry, try, cry, fry, three*), modifying the flow of air from the previous voiceless consonant. In most consonant blends, the **r** tongue position should be taken before the previous consonant is initiated.

In Southern and Eastern U.S. dialects, the **r** following a long vowel (**ee, oo**) or a diphthong is generally replaced with the vowel **-u-**. The final **-er** is also replaced with the vowel **-u-** in words of more than one syllable. In monosyllable words ending in "r," the **r** is dropped but the vowel is slightly prolonged. When **r** is followed by another consonant (*park, bird, surd*), the **r** is dropped but the vowel is slightly prolonged.

Internal Feedback Information

TACTILE: Voicing can be felt.

KINESTHETIC: Movement of the tongue toward the palate can be perceived. If retroflexed, the **r** provides considerable kinesthetic feedback.

AUDITORY: Voicing may be heard.

Sensory Instructional Possibilities

TACTILE: Vibration of voicing felt on cheeks and under chin near base of the tongue.

VISUAL: Elevation of tongue can be seen through the slightly open teeth.

Suggestions for Development

1. Imitate from teacher's model in syllables; demonstrate place of production by opening mouth wide, show the tongue raised but not touching the palate, narrow mouth opening to normal, produce **r** followed by various vowels.

2. Diagram tongue position with the tip slightly turned back. Using one hand to designate the palate and the other the tongue, show that the tongue tip is raised for initial **r** and then lowered for formation of the following vowel.

3. Develop by analogy from **l**. Have the student produce extended **l**, gradually pulling his tongue back. Use diagram to show positions for **l** and for **r**.

4. Develop by analogy from **t̆h** and **z**. Show student that the tongue is pulled back successively for production of **t̆h** to **z** to **r**. *Avoid* letting the student produce **r** with fricative quality resulting from excessive breath flow.

5. Develop voiceless **r** in association with **p, k, f, t, t̆h** on blends. On **pr-** and **fr-** blends, the tongue position for **r** can be taken before the **p** or **f** is produced. Practice these voiceless blends first without a vowel following. When they can be produced easily, add a vowel for syllables such as **proo, pro-, pree**. Contrast syllables **proo/broo, pro-/bro-,** and **pree/bree**.

6. For the student who cannot raise his tongue adequately for **r** production because of muscular control problems, an alternate formation is to produce **r** with the tongue against the upper molars on one side.

7. Have the student produce **zh**; push the tongue up and back with tongue depressor or pencil eraser while the **zh** continues.

Common Errors and Suggestions for Improvement

1. Substitution of **w** *for* **r**: Redevelop showing that the tongue is raised toward the palate; do not let student protrude and round the lips.

2. Vowel sound **-u-** *inserted between* **r** *and following vowel:* Have student first take the position for the following vowel and then elevate the tongue for **r**. Produce the blend without dropping the jaw on **roo, ree, raw**.

3. Vowel sound **-u-** *inserted between* **r** *and preceding consonants:* Develop **r** as a voiceless consonant after **p, t, k, t̆h, f**. To blend with **b**, student should take the lip position for **b** (closure) while the tongue is in the **r** position, as in *brown*.

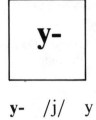

y- /j/ y

KEY WORDS: yes, canyon
SPELLINGS: y

Production *(lingua-palatal resonant glide)*

With voice, the velopharyngeal port closes, the lips are slightly pulled back; the tip of the tongue remains behind the lower front teeth and the front of the tongue is raised toward the palate. Tongue/palate aperture is slightly smaller and farther back than for **ee**. The **y** is always released into a vowel; taking the tongue and lip formation above, the **y** is very brief, rapidly gliding into the formation of the following vowel.

Internal Feedback Information

TACTILE: Voicing may be felt.

KINESTHETIC: Raising of tongue and pulling back of lips.

AUDITORY: May be heard in a syllable, but duration is short.

Sensory Instructional Possibilities

TACTILE: Vibration of voicing felt by hand on cheeks or under chin.

VISUAL: Slight pulling back of lips.

Suggestions for Development

1. Develop **y** in syllables using a wide variety of vowels; emphasize the relatively short duration of the **y** in relation to the following vowel.

2. Imitate from teacher's model. Show student with mirror that **y** is similar to **ee**, but demonstrate that the duration is shorter.

3. In the syllable **yee**, demonstrate by diagram that the raised tongue is slightly farther back for **y** than for **ee**, and that in the blend of **y** and **ee** the raised tongue moves slightly forward.

Common Errors and Suggestions for Improvement

*1. Duration too great (similar to duration of **ee**):* By underlining, show student that **y** is shorter than **ee** as follows: "y<u>ee.</u>" Write syllables with **y** underlining the vowel and only the last part of the **y** as follows: "y<u>oo.</u>"

2. Produced with audible breath friction, heard as **h**: Reduce duration. Demonstrate the lack of breath flow by tactile impression on student's hand.

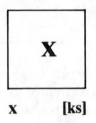

x   [ks]

KEY WORDS: box, taxi
SPELLINGS: -x, -ks, -cks

Production (*lingua-velar, lingua-alveolar voiceless affricate*)

This sound is essentially an affricate combining **k** and **s**. The position for stop **k** is taken and released into the **s** position with a single impulse.

Suggestions for Development

Have the student take mouth opening for **s** before producing the **k** portion. If the **k** and **s** are written, connect the two with a line to show they are one sound.

qu   [kʍ]

KEY WORDS: **qu**een, li**qu**id
SPELLINGS: qu-

Production (*lingua-velar, bilabial voiceless affricate*)

This sound is essentially an affricate combining **k** and **wh**. The position for stop **k** is taken and released into the **wh** position with a single impulse.

Suggestions for Development

Have the student take mouth and lip position for **wh** before producing the **k** portion. If the "k" and "wh" are written, connect the two with a line to show they are one sound.

Front Vowels

```
┌─────────────────┐
│                 │
│  ee      -i-    │
│                 │
│  -e-     -a-    │
│                 │
└─────────────────┘
```

ee	/ i /	e	**KEY WORDS:** east, beet, be
			SPELLINGS: -e, ea, -ee, -ey, -ie-, (c)ei-
-i-	/ ɪ /	i	**KEY WORDS:** if, bit
			SPELLINGS: i-, -y-, -ee-
-e-	/ ɛ /	e	**KEY WORDS:** end, bet
			SPELLINGS: e-, -ea-, -ue-, -ei-, -e(r)e
-a-	/æ/	a	**KEY WORDS:** at, mat
			SPELLINGS: a-, -au(gh), -ai-

Production

The middle and front portion of the tongue is raised high with the tip of the tongue touching behind the lower front teeth. The sides of the back of the tongue touch the upper molars laterally. The lips are not directly involved but tend to retract at the corners as the front of the tongue is raised. For **ee** the tongue is arched high almost to the palate and the upper and lower front teeth nearly contact each other. For **-i-** the tongue arch is not so high and the opening between the teeth is increased slightly. The tongue height decreases and teeth opening increases further for **-e-** and further still for **-a-**. The lateral contact of the tongue and upper molars may be broken for **-a-**.

Suggestions for Development

Develop in syllables with initial and final consonants. The forward arching of the tongue is essential for the definitive production of these vowels. Emphasize the tongue position with a mirror, first exaggerating the mouth opening for tongue visibility and then closing the mouth opening for production of the vowel. Demonstrate the forward arching of the tongue by projecting the middle of the tongue forward of the teeth while the tip remains behind the lower front teeth; then slowly withdraw the tongue inside the mouth while decreasing the mouth opening and produce the vowel **ee**.

Give a similar demonstration for **-i-, -e-,** and **-a-,** lowering the tongue successively for each of the vowels. Develop **-i-, -e-, -a-** by analogy from **ee**. Using a mirror, imitate a series of **ee, -i-, -e-, -a-,** pointing out the difference in mouth opening. Draw a series of diagrams showing both the lowering of the tongue arching and the increasing mouth opening successively for each of the vowels.

Develop **ee** in association with **h**. If the student can produce **h**, have him do so with the mouth opening for **ee**, adding voice to the **h**. Practice a series of **h, h, hee**. To restrict breath flow sufficiently to feel the friction of **h**, the student will tend to raise his tongue toward the palate approximating the position for producing **ee**. Retracting the corners of the mouth will tend to raise the front of the tongue to the appropriate position for **ee**. If necessary, use this device to raise the tongue, but later show the student production of **ee** without lip retraction which can cause tension.

Develop **ee** in association with **sh**. The position for **sh** is similar to the **ee**. Practice in syllables **shee, shee, shee.**

Common Errors and Suggestions for Improvement

1. Imprecision (a common error of vowels where production is slightly off target so that **-e-** sounds like **-a-**): show student openings of mouth contrasting one position with another in isolation and in various combinations.

2. Indefiniteness (another common error for vowels, with tongue arching lacking or inadequate so that these vowels sound something like **-u-,** the neutral vowel): Redevelop vowels demonstrating the frontal arching of the tongue. Use a mirror, a model, or diagrams as necessary to show the position of the tongue for these vowels. With the tongue tip behind the lower front teeth, practice with a mirror, arching and protruding the tongue, then returning it inside the mouth still arched toward the palate. Let the student insert his finger into the teacher's mouth to feel proximity of tongue to palate and degree of upward pressure.

3. Rigidity (in attempting to arch the tongue upward, the lower jaw may be held rigidly with teeth clenched and lips drawn back too far): Using a mirror, demonstrate the child's exaggerated tension compared to the appropriate level of relaxation. Conduct tongue exercises taking care to see that there is not excess tension of lips and jaw.

Back Round Vowels

oo -oo- aw

oo /u/ o͞o

KEY WORDS: **boot, too**
SPELLINGS: -oo, -ou, -ui, -o,
-oe, -ew, -ough

-oo- /ʊ/ o͝o

KEY WORDS: **book, put**
SPELLINGS: -o-, -u-, -ou-

aw /ɔ/ ô

KEY WORDS: **awful, caught, law**
SPELLINGS: au-, aw, a(ll), -o-,
ough(t), -augh(t)

Production

The back of the tongue is raised high with the tip of the tongue touching behind the lower front teeth. The lips are rounded and slightly protruded. For **oo** the lip aperture is rounder and smaller than for any other vowel, and is almost imperceptibly wider than for **w** (compare in syllable **woo**). For **-oo-** the tongue is slightly lower, the jaw is slightly more open, and the lips round but more open. For **aw** the tongue is slightly lower yet, with the jaw and lips slightly more open, and the lips still rounded.

Suggestions for Development

Develop in syllables with initial and final consonants. Emphasize the lip rounding and protrusion which can be seen since this action will tend to raise the back of the tongue. Contrast **oo** with **-o-** in series of **-o-oo, -o-oo, -o-oo, -o-oo**; if necessary, have student round his lips around a pencil eraser for **oo** aperture.

Develop **-oo-** by contrast with **oo.** Using a mirror if necessary, imitate a series of **oo -oo- oo -oo- oo -oo- oo -oo- oo.** Practice **-oo-** with initiating and terminating consonants since it generally occurs only between consonants.

Develop **aw** by contrast with **oo** and **-oo-**. Using a mirror if necessary, imitate a series of **oo -oo- aw oo -oo- aw oo -oo- aw**. Point out differences in lip opening but continue protrusion and rounding.

Common Errors and Suggestions for Improvement

1. Imprecision and indefiniteness, as in the case of front vowels.

2. Exaggerated or inadequate lip rounding: An exaggerated demonstration for development and the student's quest for tactile-kinesthetic feedback may lead to exaggerated tension on lip rounded vowels. Contrast correct and inappropriate lip tension with a mirror and by having the student feel the teacher's lips.

Mid Back Vowels

```
┌─────────────────┐
│                 │
│     -o-         │
│                 │
│        -u-      │
│                 │
└─────────────────┘
```

-o-   /ɑ/   a(r)

KEY WORDS: odd, father, park
SPELLINGS: o-, a(r), a(l),
o(rr), ah

Occurs in Northeastern and Southern U.S., and in England as sound for **ar** in **car, farm, bar** without the glide **r**.

-u-   /ʌ/   u
/ə/   ə

KEY WORDS: up, cup, above, lemon, cobra
SPELLINGS: u-, o-e, ou, oe, oo (stressed)

Production

The tongue is relaxed and lies low in the mouth with the tip touching behind the lower front teeth and slightly arched at the back of the mouth. The lips are open and unrounded. The **-u-** requires only a small jaw opening with the tongue and lips relaxed. Because of the little effort required, -u- is referred to as the natural or the neutral vowel. The -o- is made with the tongue relaxed but the jaws and lips open wider than for any other vowel.

Suggestions for Development

Develop in syllables with initial and final consonants. The -o- is commonly chosen as a first vowel to develop. Develop in a series of syllables **lo- lo- lo- lo- lo-.** Develop as a separate vowel, showing student that the tongue lies flat in the mouth. Develop **-u-** by contrast to **o-,** demonstrating the reduced mouth opening for **-u-.** Practice **-u-** in syllables with initial and final consonants rather than as an individual sound. When **-u-** is unstressed, its duration should be brief.

Common Errors and Suggestions for Improvement

1. Tongue withdrawn from front teeth and arched high in mouth: This error may be accompanied by nasal emission if tongue arch touches velum or palate. Open the mouth wide, show student that the tongue touches the lower front teeth and lies flat in the mouth; reduce mouth opening and phonate. Have student protrude tongue beyond front teeth, then pull it back, touching back of lower front teeth. If nasal emission is present, have student feel difference in vibration on nose. If necessary, close off student's nostrils to force oral emission.

2. Mouth opening too wide: Relax the jaw and demonstrate reduced opening. Practice in syllables **bu- bu- bu- bu- bu-** and **bo- bo- bo- bo- bo-** at a fast rate using a mirror to show that the jaw does not drop excessively.

Mixed Vowels

ur / ɝ / er
/ ɝ /
/ ɜ /

KEY WORDS: **urn, burn, fur**
SPELLINGS: -er, ur, ir, -or-,
ear-, -ar, -re

Production

In the United States the **ur** is made with tongue positions ranging from the / ɜ / to a very strongly retroflexed / ɝ /. Its production and development vary greatly.

General American / ɝ / *stressed,* / ɚ / *unstressed:* See the formation for **r-**. The **ur** is of greater duration than **r-**, carrying full syllable duration (compare *trait/obliterate*). Following consonant **r-**, the **ur** requires movement of the tongue from and again toward the **r-** position (compare *bore/borer*) so that the **ur** approaches a diphthong. Initial **ur** (*irk, urn, urban*) stressed also has diphthong quality as the tongue moves toward the raised position. The **r** coloring may be produced by either raising the tip of the tongue or by holding the central part of the tongue slightly higher than for the vowel / ɜ /.

Southern U.S., Eastern U.S. / ɜ / *stressed:* This is produced without the **r** glide. The tongue lies flat and low in both the front and back. The mouth opening is less than for **-u-** with only a slight opening of the teeth (compare *bud/bird*). The / ɜ / may be combined with / ʌ / on stressed syllables to form a diphthong / ɜʌ /. The unstressed **ur** is very close to the neutral vowel / ə /.

Suggestions for Development

If it is desired to develop the sound with a glide **r,** the / ɚ / should follow development of **r** (see suggestions for development of **r-**). Develop / ɜ / by comparison with **-o-** and **-u-**, showing the decreasing mouth opening from **-o-to -u-** to **ur.** Demonstrate the narrow separation of the teeth by inserting a flat tongue blade between the teeth, having the student produce **ur** while holding the tongue blade.

Common Errors and Suggestions for Improvement

1. Substitution of **w-** *or* **-oo-** *for* **ur** (/ ɚ /): Redevelop showing that the tongue is raised toward the palate; do not let student protrude and round the lips.

2. Indefiniteness: Develop as with **r-**, demonstrating the tongue tip up toward the palate.

Diphthongs

```
┌─────────────────────┐
│                     │
│  a-e  i-e  oa       │
│                     │
│  ou  oi  u-e        │
│                     │
└─────────────────────┘
```

		Nucleus	*Glide*	
a-e	/eɪ/	ā -i-/-e- /e/	ee	KEY WORDS: able, made, may SPELLINGS: ai-, -ay, ei-
i-e	/aɪ/	ī -o-	ee/-i-	KEY WORDS: ice, mice, my, eye SPELLINGS: -i-, i-e, -y, ie, -igh, -ui-
oa	/ou/	ō aw/-oo- /o/	oo	KEY WORDS: old, boat, no, owe SPELLINGS: -o-, o-e, ow, oa-, ough, -ew
ou	/au/	ou -o-	-oo-/oo	KEY WORDS: out, now, loud SPELLINGS: ou-, ow, -au-, -ough
oi	/ɔɪ/	oi aw	ee/-i-	KEY WORDS: oil, coin, boy SPELLINGS: oi-, -oy

		Glide	*Nucleus*	
u-e	/ju/	y͞oo ee	oo	KEY WORDS: use, cute, few, ewe SPELLINGS: u-e, u-, -ue-, -ew, -ou

Production

Diphthongs have two parts, a short portion called a glide or vanish, and a longer portion called a radical or nucleus. The prime characteristic in formation of the diphthong is movement from one part to the other within a single syllable. Diphthongs **a-e, i-e, oa, ou,** and **oi** feature movement from the nucleus to the glide, while **u-e** moves from the glide to the nucleus.

Suggestions for Development

Develop in syllables with initial and final consonants. Develop by imitation as new vowels, emphasizing the movement from nucleus to glide or glide to nucleus, and associating the diphthong with its written symbol. If necessary, develop as two simple vowels the student has already learned, emphasizing the continuous movement from one to the other. Demonstrate the connection by joining the two portions with a continuous line as "ee____oo" for **u-e.** If diphthongs are developed as two vowels, we suggest the following simple vowel combinations for diphthongs:

$$a\text{-}e = \text{-e-} + ee; i\text{-}e = \text{-o-} + ee; oi = aw + ee;$$
$$oa = aw + oo; ou = \text{-o-} + oo; u\text{-}e = ee + oo.$$

To demonstrate the two positions of a diphthong, draw two sets of parallel lines representing lip openings for the nucleus and glide; connect the lines to show the continuous movement from one opening to the other as follows:

$$i\text{-}e = \text{-o-} \quad \overline{ee}$$

To suggest the difference in duration, make the glide portion shorter than the nucleus. To suggest the difference in intensity, write the nucleus portion of the diphthong in strong solid lines and the glide portion in softer dotted lines, or write the nucleus portion larger than the glide.

Common Errors and Suggestions for Improvement

1. Omission of the glide: Redevelop, emphasizing the two positions of the diphthong. If necessary, exaggerate the duration and intensity of the glide.

2. Prolongation of the glide: Redevelop demonstrating the short duration and reduce intensity of the glide with diagrams as suggested for development. Practice in syllables terminated with stop consonants.

3. Overall duration of diphthong too great: Seeking to achieve the two positions of the diphthong, the student may extend the overall duration beyond that of a typical syllable. Practice diphthongs in a series of syllables with simple vowels such as **boot, b-oo-t, boat, bawt,** having student keep equal duration on each of the syllables. The teacher may use a metronome or have the student move his arm in cadence to attempt equal duration.

CHAPTER VII

Thoughts on Evaluation of Speech

In the preceding six chapters we have woven into the text material that may properly be considered to be concerned with the "evaluation" of speech competence and performance. The integration of such material into various contexts, rather than to accord it discrete emphasis, has been intentional. Our aim was to stress the idea that the give-and-take of instruction, whether explicitly or implicitly, involves *continuing evaluation* and realistically is not a thing apart. In teaching speech, it may be given expression by student, by instructor, by both together, or by any listener. Nevertheless, given the content and organization of the preceding chapters, and the current concern of our society for individualized planning and accountability, it is logical and useful to address here the subject of evaluation as a deliberate purposeful activity, consistent with our overall aim to suggest "points of departure" for action that may be helpful to teachers.

PURPOSES OF EVALUATION

The benefits of formal evaluation of speech are likely to be enhanced or increased to the extent that its purposes are clarified and taken into account in developing and applying procedures to achieve them. In this section we consider the broad purposes of evaluating speech for *prognosis* and prediction, for *diagnosis* of present abilities and problems, for measuring *progress* from time to time, and for *comparison* of one's achievement with that of others.

At some early state in a child's development, decisions need to be reached about appropriate instructional programming and school placement. How much and what kind of speech training is required? Is it likely to be accessible in a special school, in a special class, in the "mainstream," in a context of total communication or exclusively oral communication? These types of questions suggest evaluation that has as its purpose *prognosis:* determination of a child's *aptitude* for learning speech and *prediction* about suitability of programs and placement. The demand here is for establishing criteria for placement and change that are validated as well as possible by measures and judgments, and which accommodate factors other than speech needs that are pertinent to the comprehensive planning for the child's education. In Chapter IV we suggested procedures and timing for choosing approaches to teaching speech based on observation during a period of instruction. Premature decisions based on such unvalidated preinstructional criteria as pure-tone threshold audiogram, demonstrated intelligence, family constellation, socioeconomic status, and even formal tests, are hazardous since they may lead to a self-fulfilling prophecy.

Diagnosis is a purpose that differs appreciably from prognosis. Here the purpose is to determine a child's performance on a variety of identifiable speech skills in order to formulate a reasonably detailed instructional plan, whether immediate or long range. What is the child's speech status, and what needs to be taught? What is he ready to learn and what should the teacher's next steps be? The basis may be an *error analysis* approach that targets for attention certain deviations or gaps in his speech production, or a *developmental* approach that describes where a child's speech performance fits in an anticipated sequence that points to a next logical step in speech training, or a combination of these. Note, for example, a useful guide for determination of where a child stands in his overall speech development is the four sequential phases described in Chapter III, Table III-6, beginning with an "absorption" phase and proceeding through phases of imitation, responsive talk, and finally self-initiated spoken language. For development of particular phonemes, we have included in Chapter IV an inventory of phonemes in Tables IV-2 and IV-3 that may be useful for diagnosis.

There is currently a discernible trend toward more structured diagnostic procedures than had been the case in the past. Monsen (216) has suggested segmental and prosodic evaluative indices of speech mechanics. The segmental indices would seek to establish coordination of laryngeal and oral articulatory gestures, accuracy of articulatory movement, and distinctiveness of phoneme images. Also included would be location of phoneme targets in phonologic space, coarticulation of phonemes and control of duration. Prosodic evaluation would consider pitch, duration and intensity control. Ling

(183) has produced a detailed protocol that evaluates segmental and nonsegmental aspects of speech at both phonetic and phonologic levels. It should be very helpful for "lesson planning" for speech exercises.

Another distinctive purpose for evaluation is to assess a child's *progress* in speech. At a refined analytical level, diagnostic protocols may be applied to this purpose. Periodic check of the needs therein assessed can indicate whether and to what extent specific objectives established by them have been achieved. However, less easily evaluated is progress in the "carry over" from formal speech training during a particular training period. Has the intelligibility of a child's speech improved in and out of the classroom? Is speech an increasingly vital mechanism of social relations, with those familiar to him, with strangers? Has the circle of people with whom he attempts to converse increased appreciably (see Figure 1. of the Introduction to this book)? Has his attitude toward requests for repetition of utterances been affected? Has confidence in his ability to talk decreased or increased, and consequently his desire to do so?

As we evaluate speech progress, realistic answers to these and similar questions need to be sought conscientiously. They may cause us to examine aspects of speech training not revealed by conventional measures of competence and performance. They are, nevertheless, important because they contribute to global decisions about such matters as "mainstreaming," modes of communication, and even ultimately to career choice.

Improvement in speech intelligibility may be evaluated by periodic tests, but the available tests are not as objective or as valid as our corresponding tests of many other skills or of a child's mastery of subject matter (140). Popular procedures require a child to read a selection as auditors indicate the extent to which the selection has been understood, or carefully selected word samples are read and scored by the auditors. In a sense, these tests determine the extent to which the deviant talker imposes a loss of discrimination of speech on a normal listener. Although this may yield a limited but fairly reasonable appraisal of the mechanics of the child's speech, it does not simulate the pattern of usual oral intercourse that takes place without benefit of a printed or written visual aid. What is being evaluated is a form of oral reading and not "speech" in broad social terms. The translation of a child's own thoughts into intelligible spoken language is an ability neglected by this type of evaluation.

The use of memorized material without visual aid is subject to similar criticism since the thoughts expressed usually are not the child's own; or, if they are, they have been memorized. This furnishes the child an advantage which he does not have in a normal social situation.

The interview, in which the child is stimulated to talk freely, may yield a fairly accurate appraisal of speech if it is conducted skillfully. Very often, however, the interview questions influence the message set of a listener. Furthermore, the technique fails to appraise the child's ability to initiate speech. The use of speech recordings for periodic evaluation has considerable value. However, the limitations of printed or memorized selections and of the question-and-answer type of sample should be kept in mind.

Of course, it would help to capture for study the casual conversation of children. We should always be cautious, though, about inferences that relate tests of talker intelligibility to the social usefulness of speech. The two are not always linearly related. Attitudes of talker and listener having to do with confidence, encouragement, frustration, motivation—all these play their role in the use a deaf person makes of his speech.

FORMULATION OF THE ORAL MESSAGE

Another aspect of speech training, intimately related to diagnostic assessment and evaluation, is worthy of special note. This is the process involved in a child's formulation of an oral message. Consider the task of the deaf child in so doing. As we have said in Chapter III, first he must have something that he wishes to convey. Then he must produce the language appropriate to his purpose mindful of its syntactic, semantic and phonologic requirements. We know, too, that the phonology requires attention to segments frequently complicated by articulatory dynamics, to phonation that may be influenced by acoustic ambience, and to prosody involving proper mechanics applied to the speaker's intent. Sensitivity to her ultimate goal of functional speech, demands of the teacher that she needs to be aware that a complete description of what children are doing when they speak includes not only the actual forms produced and their context, but the social uses of that speech—its "pragmatics." Formulation of the oral message does indeed require coherence in satisfying the multiple demands of speech production.

All of this has to be taken into account by the teacher as she extends her evaluation and subsequent instructional planning beyond the analysis of mechanical speech skills. In so doing, she needs, for example, to attend to a child's revisionary behavior since it is reasonable to assume that the deaf speaker will frequently be asked by a listener to repeat an utterance when it has not been understood when first spoken. The query may be in the form of a simple "What?", a quizzical facial expression or whatever. In investigation of listener uncertainty with normal hearing children, it has been found that interaction between speaker and listener may contribute as much to articulatory inconsistency as phonetic context. In language performance, revisions appear to be more frequent than repetitions in answer to the question "What?"

For her speaking deaf pupil, the teacher needs to ask what he has internalized concerning what needs to be changed when he is not understood. Does he change the language? And if so, does he change its structural, lexical or phonologic features? If the latter, does he change articulation, phonation or prosody? Does this change derive from an internalized phonologic system including a catalogue of "error probabilities" as suggested in Chapter V. The answers to such questions should influence the teacher's response to revision, or lack thereof. In seeking to encourage self-monitoring and self-correction, careful judgment is required at the level of specificity of intervention as discussed in Chapter V. If, for example, the teacher has decided that a particular phoneme needs correction, does she identify the phoneme for the child? Does she say a phoneme needs correction but does not identify it? Or does she merely say to the child "Say that again and watch your speech."

A recent experience of ours illustrates the significance of the problem of revisionary behavior. In the course of a lesson in a class of six-year-olds which he was observing, the teacher responded with "What did you say?" to the child's oral production of a sentence. The child's language was not only structurally perfect, but it was impressively rich for a six-year-old. The intent of the teacher's question was to improve the speech but, in response, the child changed her superb language. Perhaps, this occurred because the lesson was emphasizing language or because the child was simply not aware that revision of speech mechanics may be the response of choice to the frequently encountered "what" question.

The entire question of self-monitoring, of which revisionary behavior is an essential aspect, should command the earnest attention of teachers. As suggested by Vegeley (320), it is the fundamental process which is initiated when a person compares his speech to certain standards of correct speech. The deaf person can do this only by indirect comparisons based on his knowledge, gained through training, that in order to be understood certain sounds have to be produced in certain ways. *This is supplemented by the reinforcement he received in communicating orally with normal-hearing people.*

TEACHER SELF-EVALUATION

In this chapter we have stressed that continuing evaluation of a child's spoken language is inextricably bound up in the instructional process, whether spontaneous, in the context of classroom exchange, or deliberately formalized and structured. Obviously, the effectiveness of the evaluation and the instructional measures to which it leads depend on the teacher's own skills. We need to recognize that however experienced and competent we are, or others judge us to be, we can always benefit from examining the state of our skills with the aim of improving them. In the outline below we suggest some skills that we consider central to the performance of the teacher of speech and that should be helpful as a guide to self-evaluation.

1. **Assessment of speech needs**
    Interpret audiological data as applied to speech production
    Evaluate or judge responsiveness
      a) Sensory responsiveness, including auditory, visual, tactile
      b) Imitative skills
      c) Memory
      d) Motivation
    Screen special problems, e.g., motor, perceptual
    Evaluate oral environment
    Analyze
      a) Articulation—including phoneme mastery, coarticulation, sampling of frequently occurring clusters and combinations
      b) Voice quality including identification of nasality, breathiness, harshness—also develop ability to imitate deviant voices
      c) Patterning—status of production of supra-segmental features—and responses to symbols of prosody (pitch, duration, loudness)
    Estimate language level

2. **Instruction**
    Develop individualized plan based on assessment including intermediate (weeks) and long range (year) objectives, procedures, materials and evaluation
    Apply appropriate orthographic system, e.g., diacritical marks, General American symbols
    Develop reasonable hypotheses as a basis for choice of approach
    Develop any phoneme or combination based on analysis
    Apply criteria for change in approach
    Choose appropriate sensory channels or combinations thereof for speech development or improvement—also choose and judge value of sensory aids
    Develop appropriate purposeful drills
    Apply correction paradigm along with determination of proper level of intervention
    Apply appropriate reinforcement of speech production
    Adapt material to language levels
    Identify and locate useful instructional materials

Communicate expectations and guidance to other teachers, lay educators and parents

3. Evaluation

Apply test material—other methods
Judge social usefulness of speech
Keep appropriate records of achievement
Write clearly such reports as may be required

TEACHER'S EAR

This outline of essential teacher skills would not be complete without emphasizing that the teacher's ear is one of the most fundamental factors that contributes to the effectiveness of speech instruction, particularly its evaluation. Obviously her responses, whether to an isolated segment or to a complex message, depend on what she thinks she has heard. This, in turn, determines whether in a particular instance and for a particular child she reinforces the production by acceptance or by some form of reward, or whether and how she intervenes to "fix" or to change what is being said. What she thinks she has heard influences decisions related to the reasons for intervention. Does she intervene because she does not understand the child despite her "reverse auditory training" in listening to deaf speakers, to call attention to something that is being stressed in the child's program at that time, or to make a judgment that a naive listener would not understand the speech?

Pertinent to these questions, Vegeley (320) found that normally hearing listeners were consistently better than deaf talkers in their ability to predict the intelligibility of the speech of deaf talkers. Vegeley's results underline the fact that people with normal hearing serve as a vital part of the deaf talker's feedback loop for speech. This is obvious. Nevertheless, the feedback, depending so heavily on the ear of the listener, may be imperfect and may on occasion actually reinforce a speaker's mistakes and thus jeopardize some of his better speech. Increased emphasis on ear training of all who have to do with the speech of hearing-impaired children should reduce, if not avoid, the occurrences of such situations.

As we stated at the beginning of this chapter, the level of specificity dealing with evaluation has been dictated by our aim to provide the teacher with a sensible, flexible "point of departure," a theme we have stressed throughout this book. Hence, we have avoided here the inclusion of meticulously devised check lists, rigidly structured procedures and rigorously organized protocols. These are available elsewhere. This is not to say that they have no value. They most assuredly do. But they do not replace the spontaneous "evaluations" and the responses growing out of them that constitute the "real life" ongoing activity of the classroom. It is on this context of the instructional process that we have centered our intention.

Nevertheless, knowledge—however well organized, documented, and mastered—is not likely to be the exclusive ingredient for success. What eludes precise specification is the relationship that a teacher develops between herself and a student. Does the student feel "bad" when he is corrected or does he feel that the correction is made by someone who cares for him and in whom he has confidence? Does the teacher sense that too frequent interruption of an enthusiastic flow of language and thought, in order to correct speech, may degrade motivation for oral expression and, in the process, contribute to an abrasive teacher-student relationship? Does the worthwhileness of the effort to achieve spoken language permeate the atmosphere of the classroom? Does the lack of instant success lead to despair, resignation, or challenge? The answers to these and similar questions constitute the ingredient frequently referred to as "artistry" which, coupled with a sound scientific and empirical base, is the hallmark of the great teacher. In the face of the discouraging, the puzzling, the difficult, the unknown, and the deviant, the great teacher seeks and is likely to find a way to constructive action.

Bibliography and Suggested Readings

In the bibliography and suggested readings that follow, we have retained the entries from the first edition, including selected annotations. This conserves the historical continuity of the concerns expressed in the literature dealing with speech for the deaf. Entries added in the second edition do not contain annotations since most of these are now available in the abstract literature. We believe we have chosen representative entries that illustrate the kinds of helpful material available in the professional and scientific literature.

1. Alcorn, S. K. The Tadoma method. *The Volta Review,* 1932, **34,** 195–198.
2. Alcorn, S. K. Speech development through vibration. *The Volta Review,* 1938, **40,** 633–637.
3. Alcorn, S. K. Development of speech by the Tadoma method. In *Report of Proceedings of the 32nd Meeting of the Convention of American Instructors of the Deaf, 1941.* Washington, D.C.: U.S. Government Printing Office, 1942, 241–243.

   These three articles (also see Gruver) are brief descriptions, supplementing each other, of the Tadoma method, an approach to teaching speech in which much importance is given to the pupil's placing his hand on the teacher's face to feel vibrations and muscle movement.
4. Angelocci, A. A. Some observations on the speech of the deaf. *The Volta Review,* 1962, **74,** 403–405.
5. Avery, C. B. Orthographic systems used in education of the deaf. *The Volta Review,* 1967, **69,** 208–210.

6. Avondino, J. The babbling method. *The Volta Review,* 1918, **20,** 667–671, 767–771; 1919, **21,** 67–71, 142–145, 224–228, 273–282.

    The rationale and the procedures of a technique for developing, perfecting, and maintaining speech by drilling on nonsense syllables. A graded series of drill exercises, in which phonemes occur in a wide variety of contexts, is presented. The exercises aim at leading gradually from elemental and easy syllables to complex and difficult combinations. Explanations and teaching suggestions accompany the exercises.

7. Barefoot, S. M. Speech Improvement by the deaf adult: Meeting communicative needs. In *Deafness and Communication,* Sims, D. G., Walter, G. G. and Whitehead, R. L. (Eds.), Baltimore MD.: Williams & Wilkins, 1982, 209–221.

8. Becking, A. G. T. Perception of airborne sound in the thorax of deaf children. In *Proceedings of the International Course in Paedo-audiology,* Groningen, Verenigde Drukkerijen Hoitsema, N. V., 1953, 88–97.

9. Beckwith, L. Relationships between infants' vocalizations and their mothers' behaviors. *Merrill Palmer Quarterly,* 1971, **17,** 211–216.

10. Beebe, H. H. *A guide to help the severely hard-of-hearing child.* Basel, Switzerland: S. Karger, 1953.

    One of the original books on the auditory approach. Available through the Alexander Graham Bell Association, Washington, D.C.

11. Bell, A. G. *The mechanism of speech.* New York: Funk and Wagnalls Company, 1907.

    Lectures to teachers by A. G. Bell. "When the lectures were originally delivered, the teachers present were encouraged to ask questions concerning difficulties experienced in imparting the power of articulate speech to deaf children. In this volume the questions and answers have been appended to the lectures, in the hope that the replies may be of assistance to other teachers engaged in this difficult and laborious work."

12. Bench, J. & Bamford, J. (Eds.) *Speech-Hearing Tests and the Spoken Language of Hearing-Impaired Children.* London: Academic Press, 1979.

13. Bennett, C. & Ling, D. Discrimination of the voiced-voiceless distinction by severely hearing-impaired children. *Journal of Audiological Research,* 1973, **13,** 271–279.

14. Bess, F. H. Condition of hearing aids worn by children in a public school setting. In *The Condition of Hearing Aids Worn by Children in a Public School Program.* HEW Publication No. (OE)77–05002. Washington, D.C.: U.S. Government Printing Office, 1977.

15. Bess, F. H., *Audiology, Education, and the Hearing-Impaired Child.* St. Louis, MO: C. V. Mosby Co., 1981.

16. Bess, Fred H., Freeman, Barry A. & Sinclair, J. Stephen (Eds.), *Amplification in Education,* Washington, D.C.: Alexander Graham Bell Association for the Deaf, 1981.

17. Bishop, M. E., Ringel, R. L., & House, A. S. Orosensory perception, speech production, and deafness. *Journal of Speech and Hearing Research,* 1973, **16**, 257–266.

18. Black, J. W. Experimental phonetics: What experimental phonetics has to offer the teacher of the deaf. *The Volta Review,* 1960, **62**, 313–315.

19. Blanton, R. L., Nunnally, J. C., & Odom, P. B. Graphemic, phonetic, and associative factors in the verbal behavior of deaf and hearing subjects. *Journal of Speech and Hearing Research,* 1967, **10**, 225–231.

20. Blasdell, R., & Jensen, P. Stress and word position as determinants of imitation in first-language learners. *Journal of Speech and Hearing Research,* 1970, **13**, 193–202.

21. Boothroyd, A. Some experiments on the control of voice in the profoundly deaf using a pitch extractor and storage oscilloscope display. In C. P. Smith (Ed.), *Conference on Speech Communication and Processing.* Air Force Cambridge Research Laboratories, Cambridge, Massachusetts, AFCRL–72–0120 Special Report No. 131, 1972.

22. Boothroyd, A. Speech perception and sensorineural hearing loss. In M. Ross and T. Giolas (eds.), *Auditory Management of Hearing Impaired Children.* Baltimore, MD.: University Park Press, 1978.

23. Boothroyd, A., Archambault, P., Adams, R. E., & Storm, R. D. Use of a computer-based system of speech training aids for deaf persons. *The Volta Review,* 1975, **77**, 178–193.

24. Borden, G. J. and Harris, K. S., *Speech Science Primer: Physiology, Acoustics, and Perception of Speech.* Baltimore, MD: Williams and Wilkins, 1980.

25. Braeges, J. L. and Houde, R. A. Use of Speech Training Aids. In *Deafness and Communication,* Sims, D. G., Walter, G. G. and Whitehead, R. L. (Eds.), Baltimore, MD: Williams & Wilkins, 1982, 222–244.

26. Brannon, J. B., Jr. Visual feedback of glossal motions and its influence on the speech of deaf children. Doctoral dissertation, Northwestern University, 1964.

27. Brannon, J. B., Jr. The speech production and spoken language of the deaf. *Language and Speech,* 1966, **9**,127-135.
   A rapid survey of the speech and language defects of deaf persons.

28. Brodnitz, F. S. Semantics of the voice. *Journal of Speech and Hearing Disorders.* 1967, **32**, 325-330.

29. Brown, R. *A first language: The early stages.* Cambridge, Massachusetts: Harvard University Press, 1973.
   Draws on psychology and linguistics to treat first stages of language acquisition. Starts with the threshold of syntax when children begin to combine words to make sentences and then moves on to modulations of basic structural meanings and acquisition of morphemes.

30. Brown, R., & Bellugi, U. Three processes in the child's acquisition of syntax. *Harvard Education Review,* 1964, **34**, 133-151.

31. Calvert, D. R. General American speech and phonic symbols. *American Annals of the Deaf,* 1982, 127, 405-410.

32. Calvert, D. R. Some acoustic characteristics of the speech of profoundly deaf individuals. Doctoral dissertation, Stanford University, 1961.

33. Calvert, D. R. Deaf voice quality: A preliminary investigation. *The Volta Review,* 1962, **64**, 402-403.
   A brief summary of research which indicates that "deaf voice" is not simply a matter of unnatural fundamental frequency and unusual harmonics.

34. Calvert, D. R. Speech sound duration and the surd-sonant error. *The Volta Review,* 1962, **64**, 401-402.
   A short discussion of differences in the duration of segments of some of the consonants in the speech of deaf talkers compared with the speech of normally-hearing talkers.

35. Calvert, D. R. An approach to the study of deaf speech. *Report of Proceedings of the International Congress on Education of the Deaf and the 41st Meeting of the Convention of American Instructors of the Deaf, 1963.* Washington, D.C.: U.S. Government Printing Office, 1964, 242-245.

36. Calvert, D. R., *Descriptive Phonetics.* New York, N.Y.: Thieme-Stratton, Inc. 1980.

37. Calvert, D. R. Articulation and hearing impairment. In *Speech, Language, and Hearing,* Vol. II, Lass, N. J., McReynolds, L. V.,

Northern, J. S. and Yoder, D. E. (eds.), Philadelphia: W. B. Saunders Company, 1982, 638–651.

38. Campbell, Mary E. Amplification in the classroom for the deaf student. In *Deafness and Communication,* Sims, D. G., Walter, G. G. and Whitehead, R. L. (Eds.), Baltimore, MD: Williams & Wilkins, 1982, 416–423.

39. Carr, J. Early speech development of deaf children. *Report of Proceedings of the International Congress on Education of the Deaf and the 41st Meeting of the Convention of American Instructors of the Deaf, 1963.* Washington, D.C.: U.S. Government Printing Office, 1964, 261–267.

40. Cazden, C. B. Some implications of research on language development for preschool education. In R. D. Hess & R. M. Bear (Eds.), *Early education: Current theory, research and practice.* Chicago: Aldine Press, 1967.

41. Chen, M. Vowel length variation as a function of the voicing of the consonant environment. *Phonetics,* 1970, **22,** 129–159.

42. Clarke School for the Deaf. *Auditory training.* Special Study Institute, Curriculum Evaluation and Development Program, Auditory Training Handbook, Curriculum Series, Northampton, Massachusetts, 1971.

43. Clarke School for the Deaf. *Speech.* Special Study Institute, Curriculum Evaluation and Development Program, Speech Development, Curriculum Series, Northampton, Massachusetts, 1971.

44. Cohen, M.L. The ADL sustained phoneme analyzer. *American Annals of the Deaf,* 1968, **113,** 247–252.

45. Colton, R. H., & Cooker, H. S. Perceived nasality in the speech of the deaf. *Journal of Speech and Hearing Research,* 1968, **11,** 553–559. Concludes that much of the perceived nasality in the speech of deaf persons may be a natural consequence of unnaturally slow speaking tempo.

46. Conklin, J., Subtelny, J. and Walter, G. Analysis of the communication skills of young deaf adults over a two year interval of technical training. *American Annals of the Deaf,* 1980, **125,** 388–393.

47. Connor, L.E. (Ed.). *Speech for the deaf child: Knowledge and use.* Washington, D.C.: Alexander Graham Bell Association for the Deaf, 1971.
A monograph addressed to teachers and allied workers interested in speech for the deaf. Includes sections on speech science, speech

development and disorders, speech teaching, and organizational patterns.

48. Conrad, R. Short-term memory processes in the deaf. *British Journal of Psychology,* 1970, **61,** 179–195.

49. Conrad, R. Short-term memory in the deaf: A test for speech coding. *British Journal of Psychology,* 1972, **63,** 173–180.

50. Conrad, R. Some correlates of speech coding in the short-term memory of the deaf. *Journal of Speech and Hearing research,* 1973, **16,** 375–384.

51. Cooper, F. S., Abramson, A. S., Swashima, M., & Lisker, L. Looking at the larynx during running speech. *Annals of Otology, Rhinology, and Laryngology, 1971,* **80,** 678–682.

52. Cornett, R. O. Cued speech. In *Report of Proceedings of the 43rd Meeting of the Convention of American Instructors of the Deaf,* 1967. Washington, D.C.: U.S. Government Printing Office, 1968, 112–113.
    Brief, very general descriptions of cued speech, a system of hand signals whose purpose is to make lipreading easier.

53. Cornett, R. O. Oralism vs. manualism, the method explained, cued speech. *Hearing-Speech News,* 1967, **35,** 7–9.

54. Craig, W. N., Craig, H. B., and DiJohnson, A. Preschool verbotonal instruction for deaf children. *The Volta Review,* 1972, **74,** 236–246.

55. Cruttenden, A. A phonetic study of babbling. *British Journal of Communication Disorders,* 1970, **5,** 110–117.

56. Cued Speech. *The Australian Teacher of the Deaf,* 1970, **11,** 153–165.
    Assessments of cued speech, by principals of schools for the deaf where it has been tried.

57. Curran, J. R. Aspects of contemporary hearing aids. In *Speech, Language, and Hearing,* Vol. III, Lass, N. J., McReynolds, L. V., Northern, J. L. and Yoder, D. E. (Eds.), Philadelphia, PA: W. B. Saunders Company, 1982, 1108–1129.

58. Davis, H. "Acoustics and psychoacoustics," Chapter 2 in Davis, Hallowell & Silverman, S. Richard (Eds.), *Hearing and Deafness,* (4th ed.), New York, N. Y.: Holt, Rinehart and Winston, 1978.

59. DeFilippo, C. L. Tactile aids for the deaf: Design and evaluation strategies. In D. McPherson, *Advances in Prosthetic Devices for the Deaf: A Technical Workshop.* Rochester, New York, NY: NTID, 1978, 189–197.

60. Denes, P. B. Speech science and the deaf. *The Volta Review,* 1968, **70,** 603–607.
   Describes the thus far insoluble problems which scientists have encountered with speech aids which transform speech into light patterns.

61. Denes, P. B., & Pinson, E. N. *The speech chain.* New York Bell Telephone Laboratories, Inc., 1963. New York: Doubleday, 1973. An easy to understand, simplified but accurate account of communication by speech and hearing, including linguistics, physiology, anatomy, and acoustics.

62. DiCarlo, L. S. Speech: Deed or dream. In L. S. DiCarlo (Ed.), *The deaf.* Englewood, N.J.: Prentice Hall, 1964. (Chapter 4, pp. 88–116.)

63. Dickson, D. R. An acoustic study of nasality. *Journal of Speech and Hearing Research,* 1962, **5,** 103–111.

64. DiSimoni, F. G. Evidence for a theory of speech production based on observations of the speech of children. *The Journal of the Acoustical Society of America,* 1974, **56,** 1919–1921.

65. Doehring, D. G., & Ling, D. Programmed instruction of hearing-impaired children in the auditory discrimination of vowels. *Journal of Speech and Hearing Research,* 1971, **14,** 746–753.

66. Durity, R. P. Auditory training for severely hearing-impaired adults. In *Deafness and Communication,* Sims, D. G., Walter, G. G. and Whitehead, R. L. (Eds.), Baltimore, MD: Williams & Wilkins, 1982, 296–311.

67. Eguchi, S., & Hirsh, I. J. Development of speech sounds in children. *Acta Oto-Laryngologica,* 1969, Supplement, **257,** 5–51.
   Spectrographic analysis of changes in the accuracy of phonemes in the speech of normally-hearing children as their ages increased from 3 to 13 years old. These normally-hearing children's precision of timing in a plosive-vowel syllable did not reach a maximum until about age 9; accuracy of the children's vowels reached a maximum by about age 11.

68. Eilers, R. E., & Minifie, F. D. Fricative discrimination in early infancy, *Journal of Speech and Hearing Research,* 1975, **18,** 158–167.

69. Eimas, P. D., Siqueland, E. R., Jusczyk, P., et al. Speech perception in infants. *Science,* 1971, **171,** 303–306.

70. Eisenberg, R. B. *Auditory Competence in Early Life.* Baltimore, MD: University Park Press, 1976.

71. Elliott, L. L., & Armbruster, V. B. Some possible effects of the delay of early treatment of deafness. *Journal of Speech and Hearing Research,* 1967, **10**, 209–224.

72. Elliott, L. L., & Niemoeller, A. F. The role of hearing in controlling voice fundamental frequency. *International Audiology,* 1970, **9**, 47–52.

73. Engelmann, S. and Skillman, L. Developing a tactual hearing program for deaf children. *Research Conference on Speech Processing Aids for the Deaf,* Washington, DC: Gallaudet College, 1977.

74. Erber, N.P. Interaction of audition and vision in the recognition of aural speech stimuli. *Journal of Speech and Hearing Research,* 1969, **12**, 423–425.

75. Erber, N. P. Effects of angle, distance, and illumination on visual reception of speech by profoundly deaf children, *Journal of Speech and Hearing Research,* 1974, **17**, 99–112.

76. Erber, N. P. Visual perception of speech by deaf children: Recent developments and continuing needs. *Journal of Speech and Hearing Disorders,* 1974, **39**, 178–185.

77. Erber, N. P. The use of audio-tape cards in auditory training for hearing-impaired children. *The Volta Review,* 1976, **78**, 209–218.

78. Erber, N. P. Vibratory perception by deaf children. *International Journal & Rehabilitive Research,* 1978, **1**, 27–37.

79. Erber, N. P. Speech perception by profoundly hearing-impaired children. *Journal of Speech and Hearing Disorders,* 1979b, **44**, 255–270.

80. Erber, N. P. Speech correction through the use of acoustic models. In J. D. Subtelny (Ed.), *Speech Assessment and Speech Improvement for the Hearing Impaired.* Washington, D.C.: Alexander Graham Bell Association for the Deaf, 1980b, 222–241.

81. Erber, N. P. *Auditory Training.* Washington, D.C.: Alexander Graham Bell Association for the Deaf, 1982.

82. Erber, N. P., & Greer, C. W. Communication strategies used by teachers at an oral school for the deaf. *The Volta Review,* 1973, **75**, 480–485.

83. Erber, N. P., & Hirsh, I. J. "Auditory training," Chapter 12 in Davis, Hallowell and Silverman, S. Richard (Eds.), *Hearing and deafness,* (4th ed.) New York, N.Y.: Holt, Rinehart and Winston, 1978.

84. Erber, N. P., & Zeiser, M. L. Classroom observation under conditions of simulated profound deafness. *The Volta Review,* 1974, **76**, 352–360.

85. Ewing, A. Speech—some teaching methodology. *Proceedings of the International Conference on Oral Education of the Deaf.* Washington, D.C.: The Alexander Graham Bell Association for the Deaf, 1967, 556–563.

86. Ewing, A., & Ewing, E. C. *Teaching deaf children to talk.* Manchester, England: Manchester University Press, 1964.

87. Ewing, I. R., & Ewing, A. W. G. *Speech and the deaf child.* Washington, D.C.: The Alexander Graham Bell Association for the Deaf, 1954.

    The authors are strong proponents of oral communication. This book is a general presentation of their approach to teaching speech. Speech in their view is the capacity to understand the spoken word, to use it, and to take part in conversation. Includes sections on the history of the teaching of speech to the deaf, needs of the deaf child, and methods of developing speech.

88. Fairbanks, G. *Voice and articulation drillbook* (2nd ed.). New York: Harper and Brothers, Publishers, 1959.

    Drill materials and instructions for improving pronunciation, breathing, timing, loudness, pitch, intonation, voice quality, and general expressiveness. Not addressed specifically to the speech of the deaf. Contains suggestions on how to evaluate speech quality, and a section on articulation describes the common phonemes of English in terms of their place and manner of articulation and their spellings.

89. Farb, P. *Word play: What happens when people talk.* New York: Alfred A. Knopf, 1974.

    A popular treatise on speech and language and their relation to human behavior. Draws on work of modern linguists.

90. Fellendorf, G. (Ed.). *Proceedings of the International Conference on Oral Education of the Deaf.* (2 vols.) Washington, D.C.: The Alexander Graham Bell Association for the Deaf, 1967.

    Report in two volumes (2211 pages) of a conference observing the centennial of oral education of the deaf in the United States. Includes papers by world experts on identification of deafness, organization and administration of services, speech, auditory training, preparation of professional personnel, instruction in language, curriculum development, and educational trends. The following papers from these proceedings pertain to speech for hearing impaired children.

    90.1 Numbers, M. E. A plea for better speech, **1**, 543–555.

90.2 Ewing, A. W. G. Speech—some teaching methodology, **1**, 556–563.

90.3 Calvert, D. R. A descriptive outline of the act of teaching speech, **1**, 581–598.

90.4 Thomasia, M. Speech, **1**, 599–613.

90.5 French, S. L. Implications of information theory for speech for the deaf, **1**, 614–628.

90.6 Nicholas, M. Speech methodology at St. Mary's School for the Deaf, **1**, 629–643.

90.7 Harrell, H. Speech: An integrated subject, **1**, 644–651.

90.8 Lorenz, M. L. A speech program for deaf children from ten to fifteen, **1**, 652–663.

90.9 Krijnen, A. Developing the voices of very young deaf children, **1**, 664–671.

90.10 Schmaehl, O. Speech education for mentally retarded deaf children, **1**, 672–679.

90.11 Rozanska, E. V. D. An approach to teaching speech to the deaf, **1**, 680–684.

90.12 Carr, J. The role of the teacher educator in improving speech for the deaf, **1**, 685–704.

90.13 Berg, F. S., & Fletcher, S. G. The hard-of-hearing child and educational audiology, **1**, 874–885.

90.14 Woodward, H. M. E. Intonation and the teaching of speech, **1**, 886–907.

91. Fleming, K. J. Guidelines for choosing appropriate phonetic contexts for speech-sound recognition and production practice. *Journal of Speech and Hearing Disorders,* 1971, **36**, 356–367.
Directed to speech clinicians trying to correct the articulation of clients whose hearing is presumably normal. Though the author did not have deafness in mind, many of her ideas could be helpful to teachers of the deaf. The article summarizes the effects which neighboring sounds are likely to have on the case or difficulty of recognizing or producing a particular "problem" sound. Lists and explains a number of general characteristics of contexts which are worthy of consideration in devising articulation and recognition exercises.

92. Folkins, J. W. & Kuehn, D. P. Speech production. In *Speech, Language, and Hearing,* Vol. I, Lass, N. J., McReynolds, L. V., Northern, J. S. & Yoder, D. E. (Eds.), Philadelphia, PA: W. B. Saunders Company, 1982, 246–285.

93. Forner, L. L. and Hixon, T. J. Respiratory kinematics in profoundly hearing-impaired speakers. *Journal of Speech and Hearing Research,* 1977, **20**, 373–408.

94. Foust, K. O. & Gengel, R. W. Speech discrimination by sensorineural hearing-impaired persons using a transposer hearing aid. *Scandinavian Audiology,* 1973, **2**, 161–170.

95. Francis, H. Structure in the speech of a two-and-a-half-year-old. *British Journal of Educational Psychology,* 1969, **39**, 291–302.

96. Fry, D. B. The development of the phonological system in the normal and deaf child. In F. Smith & G. A. Miller (Eds.), *The genesis of language: A psycholinguistic approach.* Cambridge, Massachusetts: Massachusetts Institute of Technology Press, 1966, 187–206.
    Presents a theory of how the normal child develops a phonological system, starting with the earliest exposure to speech and continuing to the child's establishment of a complete repertory of phonemes by about 7 years of age. Discusses the roles of auditory tactile, and kinesthetic feedback; the contribution of babbling; and the importance of imitation and social reinforcement. Relates these ideas to the problem of speech acquisition by the deaf and outlines an approach for teaching deaf children based on auditory stimulation through speech, starting in infancy.

97. Fry, D. B. Phonemic system in children's speech. *British Journal of Communication Disorders,* 1968, **3**, 13–19.

98. Fry, D. B. Acoustic cues in the speech of the hearing and the deaf. *Proceedings of the Royal Society of Medicine,* 1973, **66**, 959–969 (Section of Otology, 31–41).

99. Fujimura, O. Analysis of nasal consonants. *Journal of Speech and Hearing Disorders,* 1957, **22**, 190–204.

100. Gallagher, T. M. Revision behaviors in the speech of normal children developing language. *Journal of Speech and Hearing Research,* 1977, **20**, 308–318.

101. Gallaudet College. *Additional handicapping conditions among hearing impaired students: United States:* 1971–1972, Data from the Annual Survey of Hearing Impaired Children and Youth. Washington, D.C.: Gallaudet College, Office of Demographic Studies, 1973.

102. Gault, R. H. The use of the sense of touch in developing speech. *The Volta Review,* 1934, **36**, 82–83.
    The author developed an aid which amplifies speech and presents it to the fingers through a vibrator. This article is a very brief sum-

mary of the aspects of speech which such a tactile device can help a deaf person to perceive.

103. Gay, T., & Harris, K. S. Some recent developments in the use of electromyography in speech research. *Journal of Speech and Hearing Research, 1971,* **14,** 241–246.

104. Geldard, F. A. Pattern perception by the skin. In D. R. Kenshalo (Ed.), *The skin senses.* Springfield, Illinois: Charles C Thomas, 1968.

105. Gengel, R. W., Pascoe, D., and Shore, I. A frequency-response procedure for evaluating and selecting hearing aids for severely hearing-impaired children. *Journal of Speech and Hearing Disorders,* 1971, **36,** 341–353.

106. Gibson, E. J., Shurcliff, A., & Yonas, A. Utilization of spelling patterns by deaf and hearing subjects. In H. Levin & J. P. Williams (Eds.), *Basic studies on reading.* New York: Basic Books, 1970.

107. Gilbert, H. R. Simultaneous oral and nasal airflow during stop consonant production by hearing-impaired speakers. *Folia Phoniata,* 1974, **27,** 423–437.

108. Gilbert, J. H. The learning of speechlike stimuli by children. *Journal of Experimental Child Psychology,* 1970, **9,** 1–11.

109. Gilbert, J. H. Formant concentration positions in the speech of children at two levels of linguistic development. *Journal of the Acoustical Society of America,* 1970, **48** (Part 2), 1404–1406.
    Shows no significant difference in vowel production accuracy between 4-year-olds with normal language development and 4-year-olds with retarded language development. Both groups of children had normal hearing.

110. Giolas, T. G., Owens, E., Lamb, S. H., and Schubert, E. D. Hearing performance inventory. *Journal of Speech and Hearing Disorders* 1979, **44,** 169–195.

111. Goldman, R., & Dixon, S. D. The relationship of vocal-phonic and articulatory abilities. *Journal of Learning Disabilities,* 1971, **4,** 251–256.

112. Goldstein, M. A. *The acoustic method for the training of the deaf and hard-of-hearing child.* St Louis, Missouri: The Laryngoscope Press, 1939.
    An early treatment of systematic auditory training. Author's quote: "It is my sincere opinion that the principal reason for the many unsuccessful attempts and indifferent results in the use of the acoustic method are due to the desultory, aimless, and unsystematic form of

procedure which has discouraged teacher and pupil alike and which has given rise to so many misconceptions and misunderstandings about this particular special pedagogy."

113. Graham, L. W., & House, A. S. Phonological oppositions in children: A perceptual study. *Journal of the Acoustical Society of America,* 1971, **49** (Part 2), 559–566.

Investigation of the ability of normally-hearing 3- to 4½-year-olds to tell whether the members of various pairs of speech sounds were both the same or were different. Discusses the relevance of several linguistic classification systems to the problem of understanding the actual process of perceiving differences between sounds.

114. Gray, W. G., & Wise, C. M. *The bases of speech* (3rd Ed.) New York: Harper and Brothers, 1959.

A textbook on speech. Not specifically concerned with the speech of the deaf, but encompasses it. Provides basic information on the nature of speech from the points of view of its social basis, its genesis, physics, physiology and neurology, psychology, phonetics, linguistics, and semantics.

115. Green, D. S. Fundamental frequency characteristics of the speech of profoundly deaf individuals. Doctoral dissertation, Purdue University, 1956.

116. Greenberg, S. R. *An experimental study of certain intonation contrasts in American English.* Working Papers in Phonetics No. 13. Los Angeles, California: University of California (Los Angeles) Press, 1969.

117. Griffiths, C. (Ed.) *International Conference on Auditory Techniques.* Springfield, Illinois: Charles C Thomas, 1974.

118. Gruber, J. S. Playing with distinctive features in the babbling of infants. In C. A. Ferguson & D. I. Slobin (Eds.), *Studies of child language and development.* New York: Holt, Rinehart, and Winston, 1973.

119. Gruver, M. H. The Tadoma method. *The Volta Review,* 1955, **57,** 17–19.

A description of the Tadoma method and a favorable report on its use at a school for the deaf.

120. Guberina, P. Verbotonal method and its application to the rehabilitation of the deaf. *Report of Proceedings of the International Congress on Education of the Deaf and the 41st Meeting of the Convention of American Instructors of the Deaf, 1963.* Washington, D.C., U.S. Government Printing Office, 1964, 279–293.

Largely devoted to the presentation of theoretical ideas about speech perception which provide the author's rationale for his Verbotonal Method.

121. Haber, R. N., & Hershenson, M. *The psychology of visual perception.* New York: Holt, Rinehart, and Winston, 1973.

122. Harris, K. S. & McGarr, N. S. Relationships between speech perception and speech production in normal hearing and hearing impaired subjects. In J. D. Subtelny (Ed.), *Speech Assessment and Speech Improvement for the Hearing Impaired.* Washington, D.C.: Alexander Graham Bell Association for the Deaf, 1980.

123. Hawes, M. D. Tactile perception of stress and intonation. *Journal of Audiological Research,* 1978, **18,** 141–145.

124. Haycock, G. S. *The teaching of speech.* Washington, D.C.: The Alexander Graham Bell Association for the Deaf, 1942.

First published in 1933 and repeatedly reprinted but not substantially revised, this book continues to be a basic reference for teachers of speech to the deaf, despite its predating the widespread use of electronic hearing aids. Contains systematic sets of procedures for teaching speech to deaf children. It emphasizes that "speech is movement" and outlines approaches for developing natural speech, at the same time not ignoring the need—sooner or later—for specific articulation work. To this end, each English sound is described, and practical advice is given on how to elicit it, drill on it, and correct it if it is faulty.

125. Hilgard, E. R. *Theories of learning* (2nd ed.) New York: Appleton-Century-Crofts, Inc., 1956. (pp. 486–487.)

126. Hirsh, I. J. Auditory perception of temporal order. *Journal of the Acoustical Society of America,* 1959, **31,** 759–767.

127. Hirsh, I. J., & Sherrick, C. E. Perceived order in different sense modalities. *Journal of Experimental Psychology,* 1961, **62,** 423–432.

128. Hirsh, I. J. Communication for the deaf. *Report of Proceedings of the International Congress on Education of the Deaf and the 41st Meeting of the Convention of American Instructors of the Deaf, 1963.* Washington, D.C.: U.S. Government Printing Office, 1964, 164–183.

A description in broad strokes—based on phonetics, psychoacoustics, and psychology—of what the task of teaching speech to the hearing handicapped consists of. Various definitions of deafness are considered, and the difficulties of using audiograms to describe and classify hearing impaired persons are explained. Examines some of the relations between different types of hearing losses and the acoustic properties of speech, discussing the nature of the acoustic information in speech which may be available—or may be made available—to the hearing impaired. Provides insight into the rationale of various approaches toward teaching speech to the deaf—for example, approaches which stress auditory training, or rhythm, or frequency shifting hearing aids, etc.

129. Hirsh, I. J. Teaching the deaf child to speak. In F. Smith & G. A. Miller (Eds.), *The genesis of language: A psycholinguistic approach*. Cambridge, Massachusetts: The Massachusetts Institute of Technology Press, 1966, 207–216.

130. Hochberg, I., Levitt, H. and Osberger, J. J. (Eds.). *Speech of the hearing impaired: research, training, and personnel preparation*. Baltimore, MD: University Park Press (submitted, 1981).

131. Holbrook, A. Procedures for conditioning deaf infants with speech teaching machines. (Paper presented at Norrkoping, Sweden, for the European Association for Special Education, July, 1971; and at the World Federation of the Deaf, Paris, France, August 1971.)

132. Holbrook, A. & Crawford, G. H. Modification of speech behavior in the speech of the deaf—hypernasality. (Excerpts from a paper presented to the Conference of Executives of American Schools for the Deaf, and included in its proceedings. St. Augustine, Florida, April 1970.)

133. Holbrook, A., & Crawford, G. H. Modifications of vocal frequency and intensity in the speech of the deaf. *The Volta Review*, 1970, **72**, 492–497.

Describes an operant conditioning apparatus (FLORIDA) using a timer and on-off lights to signal whether speech is within acceptable pitch and intensity ranges. Procedures for using it to modify the speech of deaf persons are outlined.

134. Hood, J. D. & Pooie, J. P. Influence of the speaker and other factors affecting speech intelligibility. *Audiology*, 1980, **19**, 434–455.

135. Hood, R. B. Some physical concomitants of speech rhythm of the deaf. *Proceedings of the International Conference on Oral Education of the Deaf*. Washington, D.C.: The Alexander Graham Bell Association for the Deaf, 1967, 921–925.

136. House, A. S. (Ed.). *Communicating by language: The speech process*. Proceedings of a conference, Princeton, New Jersey, 1964. Bethesda, Maryland: U.S Department of Health, Education, and Welfare, National Institute of Child Health and Development.

Report of a conference of investigators and clinicians dealing with the perception of speech, speech behavior, the structure of the linguistic code, development and deficits in language skills, production of speech, disorders of speech production and perception, neural mechanisms and models, man-machine communication, and machine analogies of human communication.

137. Hoverston, G. (Coordinator) *Auditory Skills Curriculum*. Los Angeles, CA: Foreworks, 1980.

138. Hudgins, C. V. A comparative study of the speech coordinations of deaf and normal subjects. *Journal of Genetic Psychology,* 1934, **44,** 1–48.

The author measured and compared the air pressures and muscle movements in the speech breathing of hearing impaired and normally-hearing children. The report is rich in background information and clear explanations about speech breathing, syllabification, accent grouping, phrasing, the releasing and arresting functions of consonants, breathiness, nasality, and voice-unvoiced consonant contrasts. Sheds light on a wide range of defects in the speech of deaf children which have little to do with the accuracy of individual element articulation but rather are related to poor coordination of the total speech producing system.

139. Hudgins, C. V., & Numbers, F. C. An investigation of intelligibility of speech of the deaf. *Genetic Psychology Monographs,* 1942, **25,** 289–392.

Analysis of the speech of 192 pupils in two schools for the deaf, with two main purposes: to identify speech errors, classify them, and determine their frequency of occurrence; and to determine the relative effects of each type of error on speech intelligibility. Two major classes of errors were considered: errors of articulation and errors of rhythm. Articulation errors were found to fall into seven categories for consonants and five categories for vowels. In addition to examining the importance of each category of error with reference to intelligibility, the authors correlate the various kinds of errors with degree of hearing loss and age of speakers. The authors also rank the phonemes of English according to their difficulty as determined by frequency of error in the speech of the deaf. This monograph continues the discussion of many of the ideas of Hudgins, particularly those concerning speech breathing, releasing and arresting functions of consonants, and the concept that unintelligibility results from incoordination of the total speech system.

Argues strongly against basing the teaching of speech on the teaching of individual element articulation.

140. Hudgins, C. V. Speech intelligibility tests: A practical program. *The Volta Review,* 1943, **45,** 52–54.

A description of a Clarke School for the Deaf speech intelligibility testing program based on the intelligibility of whole sentences.

141. Hudgins, C. V. Speech breathing and intelligibility. *The Volta Review,* 1946, **48,** 642–644.

Discusses the importance of controlling breath to form the syllable groupings and rhythms of normal-sounding speech. Types of speech rhythm defects related to improper breath control are listed, and their destructive effect on intelligibility is stressed. A type of teaching which fosters improper breath control, and is therefore to be avoided, is described; and a teaching approach which would help develop proper speech breathing is outlined.

142. Hudgins, C. V. A method of appraising the speech of the deaf. *The Volta Review,* 1949, **51,** 597–601, 638.

Describes a test in which deaf children are scored on the intelligibility of their pronunciation of lists of PBF (Phonetically Balanced Familiar) words. The method of testing is an application of the Bell Telephone Laboratories "Articulation Testing Method" commonly used to test speech intelligibility but not necessarily involving deaf speakers. The selection and training of judges is discussed, and the effects on their judgments of experience gained during the testing program are considered. A graph is presented showing a relationship which the author found between intelligibility scores on word list tests and on whole sentence tests; the possibility of predicting the score on the one kind of test from the score of the other kind is indicated.

143. Hutchinson, J. and Smith L. Aerodynamic functioning in consonant production by hearing-impaired adults. *Audiology and Hearing Education,* 1976, **2,** 16–25.

144. Huntington, D. A., Harris, K. S., & Shankweiler, D. Some observations on monosyllable production by deaf speakers and dysarthric speakers. *American Annals of the Deaf,* 1968, **113,** 134–146.

145. Ingram, D. Phonological rules in young children. *Papers and Reports on Child Language Development, Committee on Linguistics, Stanford University,* 1971, **3,** 31–50.

146. Irvin, B. E., & Wilson, L. S. The voiced-unvoiced distinction in deaf speech. *American Annals of the Deaf,* 1973, **118,** 43–45.

147. Irwin, O. Infant speech: Consonantal sounds according to place of articulation. *Journal of Speech and Hearing Disorders,* 1947, **12,** 397–401.

148. Jakobson, R. C., & Halle, M. *Fundamentals of language.* S-Gravenhage, The Netherlands: Mouton and Co., 1956.
    Early statement of "distinctive features" of speech by two prominent scholars in linguistics.

149. Jakobson, R. C., Fant, G. M., & Halle, M. *Preliminaries to speech analysis: The distinctive features and their correlates.* Cambridge, Massachusetts: Massachusetts Institute of Technology Press, 1969.
    Fundamental up-to-date treatment of "distinctive features."

150. Jeffers, J. Formants and the auditory training of deaf children. *The Volta Review,* 1966, **68,** 418–423, 449.
    A broad and simplified explanations of vowel formants. Frequencies of the second formants of the English vowels and diphthongs are listed for men, women, and children. Presents a simplified idea of the frequency capabilities required of both hearing aids and listeners in order for any particular vowel or diphthong to be reproduced and perceived fairly completely.

151. Johansson, B. The use of the transposer for the management of the deaf child. *International Audiology,* 1966, **5,** 362–371.

152. John, J. E., & Howarth, J. N. The effect of time distortion on the intelligibility of deaf children's speech. *Language and Speech,* 1965. **8,** 127–134.

153. Johnson, D. Communication characteristics of a young deaf adult population: Techniques for evaluating their communication skills. *American Annals of the Deaf.* 1976, **121,** 409–424.

154. Joiner, E. Our speech teaching heritage. *The Volta Review,* 1948, **50,** 417–422.
    Contains practical information about teaching speech from the point of view of an experienced teacher of the deaf whose approach is strongly analytical, stressing conscious, precise control of the articulators.

155. Jones, C. "Deaf voice": A description derived from a survey of the literature. *The Volta Review,* 1967, **69,** 507–508, 539–540.

156. Jones, S. J., & Moss, H. A. Age, state, and maternal behavior associated with infant vocalizations. *Child Development,* 1971, **42,** 1039–1051.

157. Kantner, C. E., West, R., & Wise, H. S. *Phonetics* (Rev. ed.) New York: Harper and Brothers, 1960.

A basic reference and textbook for an introductory phonetics course. Includes phonetic transcription and analysis of phonemes, with particular attention to shades of differences in pronunciation resulting from coarticulation.

158. Kaplan, E. L. The role of intonation in the acquisition of language. Doctoral dissertation, Cornell University, Ithaca, New York, 1969.

159. Kaplan, E., & Kaplan, G. The prelinguistic child. In J. Eliot (Ed.), *Human development and cognitive processes*. New York: Holt, Rinehart, and Winston, 1971.

160. Kellogg, W. N. Communication and language in the home-raised chimpanzee. *Science,* 1968, **162,** 423–427.

161. Kelly, J. C. *Clinician's handbook for auditory training* (2nd Ed.). Washington, D.C.: The Alexander Graham Bell Association for the Deaf, 1973.
A workbook of exercise material for use with adults and older children in conjunction with other habilitation materials.

162. Koenigsknecht, R. A. An investigation of the discrimination of certain spectral and temporal acoustic cues for speech sounds in three-year-old children, six-year-old children, and adults. Doctoral dissertation, Northwestern University, Evanston, Illinois, 1968.

163. Lach, R., Ling, A. H., & Ship, N. Early speech development in deaf infants. *American Annals of the Deaf,* 1970, **115,** 522–526.

164. Ladefoged, P. *Elements of acoustic phonetics*. Chicago: University of Chicago Press, 1962.
Just what the title says. No math required.

165. Laubach, F. C., Kirk, E. M., & Laubach, R. S. *The new stream-lined English series: Teachers' manual*. Syracuse, New York: New Readers Press, 1971.

166. Laurentine, M. The speech program at St. Joseph Institute for the Deaf. *The Volta Review,* 1964, **66,** 459–463.

167. Lehiste, I., & Peterson, G. E. Transitions, glides, and diphthongs. *Journal of the Acoustical Society of America,* 1961, **33,** 268–277.

168. Lenneberg, E. H., & Long, B. S. Language development. *Psychology and the Handicapped Child* (U.S. Department of Health, Education, and Welfare). Washington, D.C.: U.S. Government Printing Office, 1974, No. (OE) 73–05000, 127–148.)

169. Leshin, G. (Ed.), Pearce, M. F., & Funderburg, R. S. *Speech for the hearing impaired child*. Tucson, Arizona: University of Arizona, Department of Special Education, College of Education, 1974.
Suggests specific techniques.

170. Levitt, H., & Nye, P. W. (Eds.). *Proceedings of the Conference on Sensory Training Aids for the Hearing Impaired.* Washington, D.C., 1971.

A conference of engineers, speech scientists, electroacousticians, psychoacousticians, and educators of the deaf.

171. Levitt, H. Sensory aids for the deaf: An overview. In C. P. Smith (Ed.), *Conference on Speech Communication and Processing.* Air Force Cambridge Research Laboratories, Cambridge, Massachusetts, AFCRL-72-0120. Special Report No. 131, 1972b.

172. Levitt, H. & Resnick, S. Speech reception by the hearing impaired: Methods of testing and the development of new tests. *Scandinavian Audiology Supplement,* 1978, **6,** 107-130.

173. Levitt, H., Stromberg, H., Smith, C., & Gold, T. The structure of segmental errors in the speech of deaf children. *Journal of Communicative Disorders,* 1980, **13,** 419-442.

174. Liakh, G. S. Imitation of articulatory movements and of sound production in early infancy. *Neuroscience Transactions,* 1969, **8,** 913-917.

175. Liberman, A. M. The grammars of speech and language. *Cognitive Psychology,* 1970, **1,** 301-323.

176. Liberman, A. M., et. al. A motor theory of speech perception. *Proceedings of Speech Communication Seminar, 1962.* Stockholm, Sweden: Royal Institute of Technology, Transmission Laboratory, 1963.

Argues for a theory that the perceived distinctiveness of a phoneme is tightly linked to the listener's associating the acoustic signal with the articulatory movements appropriate for the phoneme.

177. Lieberman, P. *Intonation, perception, and language.* Cambridge, Massachusetts: Massachusetts Institute of Technology Press, 1967. (Monograph #38.)

Analysis of some linguistic aspects of intonation. Discusses in detail the breath group as both a physiological and linguistic event. Presents a theory of the development of intonation in the very young infant. Examines critically concepts which assume the existence of pitch phonemes in ladder-like levels. Chapter 9 is a critical survey of some fairly recent writings (1892-1965) about the linguistics of intonation.

178. Lieberth, A. K. Functional Speech Therapy for the Deaf Child. In *Deafness and Communication,* Sims, D. G., Walter, G. G., & Whitehead, R. L. (Eds.), Baltimore, MD: William & Wilkins, 1982, 245-257.

179. Ling, D. An auditory approach to the education of deaf children. *Audecibel,* 1964, **13,** 96–101.
A unisensory approach.

180. Ling, D. & Sofin, B. Discrimination of fricatives by hearing impaired children using a vibrotactile cue. *British Journal of Audiology,* 1975, **9,** 14–18.

181. Ling, D. *Speech and the Hearing-Impaired Child: Theory and Practice.* Washington, D.C.: Alexander Graham Bell Association for the Deaf, 1976.

182. Ling, D. and Ling, A. *Aural Habilitation.* Washington, D.C.: Alexander Graham Bell Association for the Deaf, 1978.

183. Ling, D. *Teacher/Clinician's Planbook and Guide to the Development of Speech Skills.* Washington, D.C.: Alexander Graham Bell Association for the Deaf, 1978.

184. Ling, D. *Cumulative Record of Speech Skill Acquisition.* Washington, D.C.: The Alexander Graham Bell Association for the Deaf, 1978.

185. Lisker, L., & Abramson, A. S. Some effects of context on voice onset time in English stops. *Language and Speech,* 1967, **10,** 1–28.

186. Locke, J. L. Questionable assumptions underlying articulation research. *Journal of Speech and Hearing Disorders,* 1968, **33,** 113–116.

187. Locke, J. L. The child's acquisition of phonetic behavior. *Acta Symbolica,* 1971, **2,** 28–32.

188. Locke, J. L., & Locke, V. L. Deaf children's phonetic, visual and dactylic coding in a grapheme recall task. *Journal of Experimental Psychology,* 1971, **89,** 142–146.

189. Locke, J. L., & Kutz, K. J. Memory for speech and speech for memory. *Journal of Speech and Hearing Research,* 1975, **18,** 176–191.
Suggests ways in which subvocalization may aid recall, including motor and acoustic encoding. An echoic store provides additional recall support if subjects rehearse vocally.

190. Ludlow, C. L. & Hart, M. O. (Eds.). Proceedings of the Conference on the Assessment of Vocal Pathology. *ASHA* Report 11. Rockville, MD: American Speech and Hearing Association, 1981.

191. Lyon, E. *The Lyon phonetic manual.* Rochester, New York: American Association To Promote the Teaching of Speech to the Deaf, Circulation of Information #2, 1891.

192. MacNeilage, P. F., & DeClerk, J. E. On the motor control of coarticulation in CVC monosyllables. *Journal of the Acoustical Society of America,* 1969, **45,** 1217–1233.

Investigated the effects of intrasyllable context on tongue movements in the speech of a normally-hearing person. Used cinefluorograms and electromyograms to observe activity of the tongue muscles. Found that motor control of a later syllable component was always influenced by the identity of an earlier component of the syllable, and that motor control of an earlier syllable component was almost always influenced by the identity of a later component. Includes considerable theoretical discussion.

193. MacNeilage, P. F., & Sholes, G. N. An electromyograph study of the tongue during vowel production. *Journal of Speech and Hearing Research,* 1964, **7**, 209-232.

194. Madison, C. L., et. al. Speech-sound discrimination and tactile-kinesthetic discrimination in reference to speech production. *Perceptive Motor Skills,* 1971, **33**, 831-838.

195. Magner, M. E. Beginning speech for young deaf children. *The Volta Review,* 1953, **55**, 20-23.

196. Mahshie, J. J. *Laryngeal behavior of hearing-impaired speakers.* Doctoral dissertation, Syracuse University, 1980.

197. Malmberg, R. (Ed) *Manual of phonetics.* Amsterdam, Holland: North Holland Publishing Co., 1970.

A scientific and current treatment of phonetics. The subjects include the linguistic basis of phonetics; acoustical foundations of phonetics; the functional anatomy of the speech organs; the auditory basis of phonetics; the psychological basis of phonetics; statistical methods in phonetics; the speech communication process; analysis and synthesis of speech processes; mechanism of the larynx and the laryngeal vibrations; the articulatory possibilities of man; radiographic, palatographic, and labiographic methods in phonetics; prosodic phenomena; phonology in relation to phonetics; phonotactic aspects of the linguistic expression; phonetics and linguistic evolution; phonetics and sociology; phonetics and pathology; and phonetics in its relation to aesthetics.

198. Markides, A. The speech of deaf and partially hearing children with special reference to factors affecting intelligibility. *British Journal of Disorders of Communication,* 1970, **5**, 126-140.

199. Martin, J. G. Rhythmic (hierarchical) versus serial structure in speech and other behavior. *Psychological Review,* 1972, **79**, 487-509.

200. Martony, J. Visual aids for speech correction. In G. Fant (Ed.), *Proceedings of the International Symposium on Speech Communication Ability and Profound Deafness, Stockholm, Sweden, 1970.*

Washington, D.C.: The Alexander Graham Bell Association for the Deaf, 1972.

201. Mavilya, M. *Spontaneous vocalization and babbling in hearing-impaired infants.* Doctoral dissertation, Teachers College, Columbia University, 1969.

202. McClumpha, S. *Cinefluorographic investigation of velopharyngeal function in selected deaf speakers.* Master of Arts thesis, University of Florida, 1966.

203. McElroy, C. W. *Speech and language development of the preschool child.* Springfield, Illinois: Charles C Thomas, 1972.

204. McGarr, N. S. and Harris, K. S. Articulatory control in a deaf speaker. In I. Hochberg, H. Levitt, and M. J. Osberger (Eds.), *Speech of the Hearing Impaired: Research, Training, and Personnel Preparation.* Baltimore, MD: University Park Press (submitted, 1981).

205. McGinnis, M. A. *Aphasic children: Identification and education by the Association method.* Washington, D.C.: The Alexander Graham Bell Association for the Deaf, 1963.

    Detailed exposition of the principles and techniques of what in the present book we have called the Association Phoneme Unit Approach.

206. McReynolds, L. V., & Houston, K. A distinctive feature analysis of children's misarticulations. *Journal of Speech and Hearing Disorders,* 1971, **36**, 155–166.

207. Menyuk, P. The role of distinctive features in children's acquisition of phonology. *Journal of Speech and Hearing Research,* 1968, **11**, 138–146.

208. Menyuk, P. *The development of speech.* Indianapolis: Bobbs-Merrill, 1972.

209. Merklein, R. A. A short speech perception test for severely and profoundly deaf children. *The Volta Review,* 1981, **83**, 36–45.

210. Miller, G. A., & Nicely, P. E. Analysis of perceptual confusions among some English consonants. *Journal of the Acoustical Society of America,* 1955, **27**, 338–352.

    Summary of research which analyzed the kinds of consonant confusions that normally-hearing listeners tend to make in listening to speech in noise and distorted by deletion of various frequencies. The task of the listeners in this experiment was somewhat analogous to the task faced by hearing impaired persons receiving normal speech. The experimenters grouped their test consonants according to similarity in the features of voicing, nasality, affrication, duration, and place of articulation. Confusion matrices provide a basis for inferring which of these features are likely to become equivocal under various conditions of signal to noise ratio and frequency loss.

211. Miller, J. D. Directions for research to improve hearing aids and services for the hearing-impaired. *A report of Working Group 65, NAS-NRC, Committee on Hearing, Bioacoustics, and Biomechanics.* Washington, D.C.: National Academy of Science, 1972.

212. Moll, K. L. Velopharyngeal closure on vowels. *Journal of Speech and Hearing Research,* 1962, **5**, 30–37.

Using cinefluorographs of normally-hearing speakers, the variations in velopharyngeal closure in vowels as a function of the context of the vowels were measured. Concluded that the low vowels exhibit less closure than the high vowels; that vowels adjacent to /n/ exhibit incomplete closure, with the vowels preceding /n/ having less closure than those following /n/; and that there are no significant differences between the effects of various non-nasal contexts on vowel closure, but there is a tendency for less closure on isolated vowels than on vowels in non-nasal consonant contexts.

213. Moll, K. L., & Daniloff, R. G. Investigation of the timing of velar movements during speech. *Journal of the Acoustical Society of America,* 1971, **50**, 671–684.

Investigates coarticulation in the speech of normally-hearing persons by cinefluorographic observations of movements of the velum during spoken sentences. Found that where velum movement is required for the articulation of a phoneme, the velum may start to move toward the required position several syllables in anticipation of the actual production of the phoneme. The authors discuss a theory of coarticulation which they think may explain their findings.

214. Monaghan, A. The need for a school to have a philosophy of teaching speech. *The Volta Review,* 1958, **60**, 386–391.

215. Monsen, R. B. A Usable Test for the Speech Intelligibility of Deaf Talkers, *American Annals of the Deaf,* 126, **7**, 1981, 845–852.

216. Monsen, R. The production of English stop consonants in the speech of deaf children. *Journal of Phonetics,* 1976, **4**, 29–42.

217. Monsen, R., Engebretson, M., and Vemula, R. Some effects of deafness on the generation of voice. *Journal of the Acoustical Society of America,* 1979, **66**, 1680–1690.

218. Moog, J. S. Approaches to teaching pre-primary hearing impaired children. *Bulletin: American Organization for the Education of the Hearing Impaired,* 1973, **1**(3), 52–59.

219. Moog, J. S., & Kozak, V. J. *Teacher Assessment of Grammatical Structures.* St. Louis, MO: The Central Institute for the Deaf, 1982.

220. Moores, D. F. Neo-oralism and the education of the deaf. *Exceptional Children,* 1972, **38,** 377–384.
    Cites rejection of teaching speech by simple sound/letter relations even with fingerspelling. Mentions briefly a "concentric" method of teaching speech which concentrates initially on a limited number of sounds for 42 letters.

221. Morkovin, B. V. Organic and inhibitory factors of speech production disturbances in children with hearing disorders. *Report of Proceedings of the International Congress on Education of the Deaf and the 41st Meeting of the Convention of American Instructors of the Deaf, 1963.* Washington, D.C.: U.S. Government Printing Office, 1964, 726–734.

222. Morkovin, B. V. Language in the general development of the preschool deaf child: A review of research in the Soviet Union. *ASHA: Journal of the American Speech and Hearing Association,* 1968, **10,** 195–199.
    Discusses research of the Moscow Institute of Defectology directed toward developing the speech, language, intellects, and personalities of deaf children. References are listed, although the research itself is not described. Among the facets of the MID's approach which the author discusses are: fingerspelling, used to launch little deaf children into language, but eventually to be replaced by lipreading and speech; an enriched environment of child-center experiences in which both verbal and nonverbal communication are encouraged; and formal classes in which lipreading, articulation, grammar, etc., are taught.

223. Morse, P. A. The discrimination of speech and nonspeech stimuli in early infancy. *Journal of Experimental Child Psychology,* 1972, **14,** 477–492.

224. Moskowitz, A. I. The two-year-old stage in the acquisition of English phonology. *Language,* 1970, **46,** 426–441.

225. Mowrer, D. Transfer of training in articulation therapy. *Journal of Speech and Hearing Disorders,* 1971, **36,** 427–466.

226. Nakazima, S. A comparative study of the speech developments of Japanese and American English in childhood: The reorganization process of babbling articulation mechanisms. *Studies in Phonology,* 1970, **5,** 20–36.

227. Nash, J. *Developmental psychology: A psychobiological approach.* Englewood Cliffs, New Jersey: Prentice-Hall, Inc., 1970.

 Proceeds from a description of the biology of human development to a discussion of the environment's interaction with this biological basis. Of particular interest is the treatment of critical periods in development, early stimulation, development of the capacity for learning, and development of communication and cognitive processes.

228. New, M. C. Speech for the young deaf child. *The Volta Review,* 1940, **42,** 592–599.

 Describes the "natural" approach to teaching speech used at the Lexington School. Presents the year-by-year objectives and some of the teaching procedures of a curriculum which from the very beginning uses whole words and flowing language to stimulate nursery-age children to communicate orally with natural rhythm and natural language. Precise articulation is developed through perfecting the pronunciation of whole words and phrases, and only later through conscious control of individual elements. Contrasts this with programs which concentrate first on perfecting the speech of individual elements.

229. New, M. Color in speech teaching. *The Volta Review,* 1942, **44,** 133–138, 199–203.

230. Nickerson, R. On the role of vision in language acquisition by deaf children. In L. Liben (Ed.), *Deaf Children: Developmental Perspectives.* New York: Academic Press, 1978.

231. Nickerson, R. S. Characteristics of the speech of deaf persons. *The Volta Review,* 1975, **77,** 342–362.

232. Niemoeller, A. F. Acoustical design of classrooms for the deaf. *American Annals of the Deaf,* 1968, **113,** 1040–1045.

233. Nober, E. H. Vibrotactile sensitivity of deaf children to high intensity sound. *Laryngoscope,* 1967, **77,** 2128–2146.

234. Northcott, W. H. (Ed.) *The hearing impaired child in a regular classroom: Preschool, elementary, and secondary years.* Washington, D.C.: The Alexander Graham Bell Association for the Deaf, 1973.

235. Northern, J. L. and Downs, M. P. *Hearing in Children.* Baltimore, Maryland: Williams & Wilkins, 1974.

236. Norton, S. J., Schultz, M. C., Reed, C. M., Braida, L. D., Durlach, N. I., Rabinowitz, W. M., & Chomsky, C. Analytic study of the Tadoma method: Background and preliminary results. *Journal of Speech and Hearing Research,* 1977, **20**, 574–595.

237. Numbers, M. E. The place of elements in speech development. *The Volta Review,* 1942, **44**, 261–265.

Argues strongly against the teaching of isolated, discrete articulation elements. Favors basing the teaching of speech on the teaching of whole syllables, with the elements taught as movements within a specific, indivisible syllable or word context. Discusses speech breathing and rhythm, and explains the releasing and arresting functions of consonants.

238. *Oral sensation and perception: Proceedings of a symposium.* Springfield, Illinois: Charles C. Thomas, 1969.

239. Owens, E., Talbott, C., and Schubert, E. Vowel discrimination of hearing-impaired listeners. *Journal of Speech and Hearing Research,* 1968, **11**, 648–655.

240. Oyer, H. J. *Auditory communication for the hard of hearing.* Englewood Cliffs, N.J.: Prentice-Hall, Inc., 1966.

241. Panagos, J. M., Quine, M. E., & Klich, R. J. Syntactic and Phonological Influences on Children's Articulation. *Journal of Speech and Hearing Research,* 1979, **22**, 841–848.

242. Parker, A. The laryngograph. *Hearing* (The Royal National Institute for the Deaf), 1974, **29**, 256–261.

243. Pascoe, D. Frequency responses of hearing aids and their effects on the speech perception of hearing-impaired subjects. *Annals of Otology, Rhinology and Laryngology,* 1975, **84.**

244. Perkins, W. H. *Speech pathology: An applied behavioral science.* St. Louis, MO: Mosby Press, 1971.

A "behavioral science" approach to speech pathology for the beginning student, logically organized and built around questions frequently raised by students and others. A good synthesis of ideas on the development of speech. Good bibliography.

245. Peterson, G. E., & Barney, H. L. Control methods used in a study of vowels. *Journal of the Acoustical Society of America,* 1952, **24**, 175–184.

246. Peterson, G. E., & Shoup, J. E. A physiological theory of phonetics. *Journal of Speech and Hearing Research,* 1966, **9**, 5–67.

Draws together the definitions, assumptions, and concepts about speech and the physiological mechanism for producing it which, in the authors' opinion, are required for accurately, completely, and unequivocally describing any speech sound in any language in terms of the physiological events and conditions necessary for the production of that sound. A set of universally applicable symbols for phonetic notation is defined by being arrayed in charts which list the physiological parameters of speech as identified by the authors. Includes much philosophy about theoretical models of highly complex systems such as a phonetic system.

247. Peterson, G. E., & Shoup, J. E. The elements of an acoustic phonetic theory. *Journal of Speech and Hearing Research,* 1966, **9**, 68–99.

A definition of the acoustical characteristics of speech and a summary of the relationships of these characteristics to physiological phonetics and descriptive phonetics.

248. Peterson, G. E., & Shoup, J. E. Glossary of terms from the physiological and acoustical phonetic theories. *Journal of Speech and Hearing Research,* 1966, **9**, 100–120.

An alphabetically arranged summary of definitions from related references by same authors.

249. Phillips, J. R. Formal characteristics of speech which mothers address to their young children. Doctoral dissertation, The Johns Hopkins University, Baltimore, MD, 1970.

250. Pickett, J. M. (Ed.) Proceedings of the Conference on Speech-Analyzing Aids for the Deaf, Hearing and Speech Center, Gallaudet College, Washington, D.C., 1967. *American Annals of the Deaf,* 1968, **113(2)**, 116–330.

This issue is devoted to the proceedings of a 1967 conference on speech-analyzing aids for the deaf. A substantial portion of the issue is concerned with the use of instruments to transmit information about speech to the hearing impaired and aimed at the development and improvement of their speech. The following papers may be of particular interest to teachers of the deaf.

250.1 Pickett, J. M. Sound patterns of speech: An introductory sketch, 120–126.

This paper describes and classifies the phonemes of English in terms of some of their acoustical features.

250.2 Liberman, A. M., Cooper, F. S., Shankweiler, D. P., & Studdert-Kennedy, M. Why are speech spectrograms hard to read? 127–133.

A discussion of the major theoretical difficulty in displaying speech visually. The paper emphasizes the complexities of the interrelationships of phonemes with their contexts.

250.3 Stewart, R. B. By ear alone, 147–155.

Points out some of the difficulties a listener encounters in analyzing and transcribing the speech of deaf children. Discusses some of the characteristics of speech which must be taken into account in making judgments about speech quality.

250.4 Børrild, K. Experience with the design and use of technical aids for the training of deaf and hard of hearing children, 168–177.

Briefly describes and comments on the usefulness of speech training devices using visual displays which have been tried out at a school for the deaf in Denmark. These include "S" indicators and indicators of pitch, loudness, and spectrum.

250.5 Risberg, A. Visual aids for speech correction, 178–194.

Discusses theoretical reasons why visual display devices should be useful for teaching speech. Describes the following instruments which have been used in his laboratory: a spectrum indicator, a fricative indicator, an "S" indicator, an intonation indicator, a rhythm indicator, and a nasalization indicator. An experiment to test the teaching value of an "S" indicator is reported.

250.6 Martony, J. On the correction of the voice pitch level for severely hard of hearing subjects, 195–202.

Discusses the association of involuntary pitch changes with particular phonemes and the use of a visual pitch indicator by deaf children to help them improve their voices.

250.7 Stark, R. E., Cullen J. K. Jr., & Chase, R. Preliminary work with the new Bell Telephone visible speech translator, 205–214.

Summarizes the results of use of "visible speech" to modify abnormally high pitch, incorrect tuning, excessive nasalization, and articulation of hearing impaired children and adults. Suggestions for teachers who might use a visible speech device are offered.

250.8 Pronovost, W., Yenkin, L., & Anderson, D. C. The voice visualizer, 230–238.

250.9 Phillips, N. D., Remillard, W., & Bass, S. Teaching of intonation to the deaf by visual pattern matching, 239–245.

250.10 Cohen, M. L. The ADL sustained phoneme analyzer, 247–252.

250.11 Pickett, J. M., & Constam, A. A visual speech trainer with simplified indication of vowel spectrum, 253–258.

250.12 Ling, D. Three experiments on frequency transposition, 283–294.

Reports experiments designed to test the value of hearing aids which transpose speech into the low frequencies available to many deaf persons.

250.13 Guttman, N., & Nelson, R. An instrument that creates some artificial speech spectra for the severely hard of hearing, 295–302.

The authors report on a hearing aid which adds low frequency energy to phonemes which might otherwise be inaudible because they normally consist mostly of high frequencies.

250.14 Kringelbotn, M. Experiments with some visual and vibrotactile aids for the deaf, 311–317.

251. Pickett, J. M. Some applications of speech analysis to communication aids for the deaf. *The Volta Review,* 1971, **73,** 147–156.

A description of several tactual and visual speech aids.

252. Pickett, J. M., & Pickett, R. H. Communication of speech sounds by a tactual vocoder. *Journal of Speech and Hearing Research,* 1963, **6,** 207–222.

Discusses results of speech perception tests when the speech signal was analyzed into 10 frequency bands of energy, each of which was presented as vibrations to a different finger of the "listener's" hands. All 10 vibrators had a frequency of 300 Hz, but each differed from the other in vibration amplitude according to the energy distribution among the various frequency bands of the original speech.

253. Pickett, J. M. *The Sounds of Speech Communication: A Primer of Acoustic Phonetics and Speech Perception.* Baltimore, Maryland: University Park Press, 1980.

254. Pike, K. L. *The intonation of American English.* Ann Arbor, Michigan: The University of Michigan Press, 1945.

255. Pitman, J. Can I.T.A. help the deaf child, his parents, and his teacher? In *Proceedings of the International Conference on Oral Education of the Deaf.* Washington, D.C.: The Alexander Graham Bell Association for the Deaf, 1967, 514–542.

The father of the Initial Teaching Alphabet argues that it should be used in the teaching of deaf children, including infants. He suggests that World I.T.A., rather than standard I.T.A., would be more suitable, because the world version provides some information about stress and about vowel neutralization.

256. Pollack, D. *Educational audiology for the limited hearing infant.* Springfield, Illinois: Charles C Thomas, 1970.
The principles and procedures of acoupedics, a comprehensive program of auditory training for teachers, clinicians, and parents.

257. Pollack, I. Within-and-between-modality-correlation detection. *Journal of the Acoustical Society of America.* 1974, **55**, 641–644.

258. Potter, R. K., Kopp, G. A., & Green, H. C. *Visible speech.* New York: Van Nostrand, 1947.

259. Poulos, T. H. Improving the intelligibility of deaf children's speech. *The Volta Review,* 1952, **54**, 265–267.

260. Poulos, T. H. A speech improvement program in a large residential school for the deaf. *The Volta Review,* 1962, **64**, 405–408.

261. Preston, M. S., Yeni-Komshian, G., Stark, R. E., & Port, D. K. Certain aspects of speech production and perception in children (Abstract). *Journal of the Acoustical Society of America,* 1969, **46**, 102.

262. Prosek, R. A., & House, A. S. Intraoral air pressure as a feedback cue in consonant production. *Journal of Speech and Hearing Research,* 1975, **18**, 133–147.

263. Pugh, B. Clarifying speech problems for the deaf. *The Volta Review,* 1963, **65**, 15–21.

264. Rebelsky, F., & Hanks, C. Fathers' verbal interaction with infants in the first three months of life. *Child Development.* 1971, **42**, 63–68.

265. Reilly, A. P. Syllable nucleus duration in the speech of hearing and deaf children. Doctoral dissertation, City University of New York, New York, NY: 1979.

266. Risberg, A. A critical review of work on speech analyzing hearing aids. *The Volta Review,* 1971, **73**, 23–32.

267. Rockey, D. *Phonetic lexicon.* New York: Heyden and Son, Ltd., 1973.
A compilation of monosyllabic and some disyllabic words arranged according to their phonetic structure. A good source for drill and test material.

268. Roeser, R. J., & Downs, M. P. *Auditory Disorders in School Children: The Law, Identification, Remediation.* New York, N.Y.: Thieme-Stratton, Inc., 1981.

269. Ronnei, E. C., & Porter, J. *Tim and his hearing aid* (Rev. ed.). Washington, D.C.: The Alexander Graham Bell Association for the Deaf, 1965. (Spanish edition also available.)
A young boy learns to use a hearing aid.

270. Ross, M. and Lerman, J. A picture identification for hearing-impaired children. *Journal of Speech and Hearing Research* 1970, **13**, 44–53.

271. Ross, M. and Calvert, D. R. Guidelines for Audiology Programs in Educational Settings for Hearing Impaired Children. *American Annals of the Deaf,* 1976, **121**, 346–350.

272. Ross, M., & Calvert, D. R., Guidelines for Audiology Programs in Educational settings for Hearing-Impaired Children, *The Volta Review,* 1977, 79, **3**, 153–161.

273. Ross, M. & Giolas, T. G. (Eds.), *Auditory Management of Hearing-Impaired Children.* Baltimore, MD: University Park Press, 1978.

274. Rothman, H. An electromyographic investigation of articulation and phonation patterns in the speech of deaf adults. *Journal of Phonetics,* 1977, **5**, 369–376.

275. Round Hill Round Table. In defense of the Northampton Charts. *The Volta Review,* 1942, **44**, 487.

276. Sander, E. K. When are speech sounds learned? *Journal of Speech and Hearing Disorders,* 1972, **37**, 55–63.

277. Schour, I., & Massler, M. The development of the human dentition. *The Journal of the American Dental Association,* 1941, **28**, 1153–1160.

278. Schubert, E. and Owens, E. CVC words as test items. *Audiological Research,* 1971, **11**, 88–100.

279. Schulte, K. Speech production—the capacity of communication-systems structuring speech for the deaf. Proceedings of the International Congress on education of the Deaf, Tokyo, Japan: 1975, 76–83.

280. Shunhoff, H. F. (Ed.). *The teaching of speech and by speech in public residential schools for the deaf in the United States,* 1815–1955. Romney, W. Va.: West Virginia Schools for the Deaf and the Blind, 1957.

281. Sheppard, W. C., & Lane, H. L. Development of the prosodic features of infant vocalizing. *Journal of Speech and Hearing Research,* 1968, **11**, 94–108.

282. Sher, A. and Owens, E. Consonant confusions associated with hearing loss above 2000 Hz. *Journal of Speech and Hearing Research,* 1974, **17**, 669–681.

283. Sherrick, C. E. The art of tactile communication. *American Psychologist,* 1975, **30**, 353–360.

284. Shoup, J. E., Lass, N. J. and Kuehn, D. P. Acoustics of Speech. In *Speech, Language, and Hearing,* Vol. I, Lass, N. J., McReynolds, L. V., Northern, J. L. & Yoder, D. E. (Eds.), Philadelphia, PA: W. B. Saunders Company, 1982, 193–218.

285. Silverman, S. R. Tolerance for pure tones and speech in normal and defective hearing. *Annals of Otology,* 1947, **56,** 658–678.

A summary of studies that dealt with the mapping of thresholds of discomfort and pain in listening to loud sounds.

286. Silverman, S. R. Teaching speech to the deaf: The issues. *The Volta Review,* 1954, **56,** 385–389, 417.

This paper summarizes and explains the issues in some important areas of disagreement among those who believe in teaching speech to the deaf. The areas of disagreement which are discussed are: fundamental attitudes toward speech (For everyday communication? As a second language? . . .); Sensory approaches (Visual? Auditory? . . . One? Many? . . .); Orthography systems (Northampton? IPA? . . .); Basic units of speech (Elements? Syllables? Words? . . .); Evaluation of teaching (By oral reading? In real-life situations? . . .).

287. Simmons, A. A. Teaching aural language. *The Volta Review,* 1968, **70,** 26–30.

Stresses that in the education of young deaf children speech and language must not be separated from each other. What needs to be taught initially is oral-aural communication, not precise speech and precise language. Urges teachers to use multi-word phrases, not single words. Emphasizes the information-carrying significance of prosody and maintains that prosody is the first aspect of language to develop in hearing children and should be the first aspect developed in deaf children.

288. Simmons-Martin, A. The oral/aural procedure: Theoretical basis and rationale. *The Volta Review,* 1972, **74,** 541–551.

289. Sims, D. G., Gottermeier, L., & Walter, G. G. Factors contributing to the development of intelligible speech among prelingually deaf persons. *American Annals of the Deaf,* 1980, **125,** 374–381.

290. Slis, I. H., & Cohen, A. On the complex regulating the voiced-voiceless distinction II. *Language and speech,* 1969, **12,** 137–155.

291. Smith, C. Residual hearing and speech production in deaf children. *Communicative Sciences Laboratory Report* #4. New York City University of New York Graduate Center, 1973.

292. Snow, C. E. Mother's speech to children learning language. *Child Development,* 1973, **43,** 549–565.

293. Stark, R. E. Teaching /ba/ and /pa/ to deaf children using real-time spectral displays. *Language and Speech,* 1972, **15,** 14–29.

294. Stark, R. E. (Ed.) *Sensory capabilities of hearing-impaired children.* Baltimore, MD: University Park Press, 1974.

Proceedings of a workshop of speech and hearing scientists and workers on speech of hearing impaired children dealing with the needs and capabilities of children for whom auditory and nonauditory aids were being designed. The topics included sensory capabilities, perceptual and cognitive strategies, and language processing.

295. Stark, R., Tallal, P., & Curtiss, B. Speech perception and production errors in dysphasic children. *Journal of the Acoustical Society of America,* 1975, **57,** Supplement 1, 524.

An abstract of studies demonstrating that dysphasics who failed to discriminate between speech sounds which incorporate brief duration acoustic cues also failed to produce such speech sounds correctly.

296. Steele, J., Binnie, C., and Cooper, W. Combining auditory and visual stimuli in the adaptive testing of speech discrimination. *Journal of Speech and Hearing Disorders,* 1978, **43,** 115–122.

297. Stetson, R. H. Contributions of teachers of the deaf to the science of phonetics. *The Volta Review,* 1943, **45,** 19–20; 54–56.

A historical note about some of the contributions which teachers of the deaf have made to the sciences of speech and hearing since Melville Bell produced his system of Visible Speech in 1867. Focuses on the ideas of those who emphasized that the dynamic nature of speech makes the syllable rather than the single element the more useful unit on which to base the teaching of speech to deaf persons.

298. Stetson, R. H. *Motor phonetics.* Amsterdam, Holland: North Holland Publishing Co., 1951.

299. Stevens, K. N., & House, A. S. Perturbation of vowel articulations by consonantal context: An acoustical study. *Journal of Speech and Hearing Research,* 1963, **6,** 111–128.

300. Stevens, K. N., & Klatt, D. H. Role of formant transitions in the voiced-voiceless distinction for stops. *Journal of the Acoustical Society of America,* 1974, **55,** 653–659.

301. Stevenson, H. W. *Children's learning.* Englewood Cliffs, New Jersey: Prentice Hall, Inc., 1972.

A recent research-based treatment of children's learning. Of particular interest are Chapters 4 through 10 concerned with language and learning and Chapter 19 on perceptual learning. The role of reinforcement is analyzed as it influences learning in various task contexts.

302. Stewart, R. B. By ear alone. *American Annals of the Deaf,* 1968, **113,** 147–155.

303. Stoner, M. The development of early speech with emphasis on the synthetic method. *The Volta Review,* 1955, **57,** 15–17.

304. Stratton, W. D. Intonation feedback through a tactile display. *The Volta Review,* 1974, **76,** 26–35.

305. Subtelny, J. D. Speech Assessment of the Adolescent with Impaired Hearing. In *Deafness and Communication,* Sims, D. G., Walter, G. G., & Whitehead, R. L. (Eds.), Baltimore, MD: Williams & Wilkins, 1982, 156–176.

306. Suchman, R. G. Visual impairment among deaf children. *Archives of Ophthalmology,* 1967, **77,** 18–21.

307. Sweet, M. E. The association method for aphasics: Its application to the deaf. *The Volta Review,* 1955, **57,** 13–15.

308. Swets, A., & Elliott, L. (Eds.). *Psychology and the handicapped child.* Washington, D.C.: U.S. Department of Health, Education and Welfare, 1974.

309. Tervoort, B. Speech and language development in the normal and hearing impaired child (Dutch). *Gehoorgestoorde Kind,* 1973, **13,** 77–87.

310. Thomas, W. G. Intelligibility of the speech of deaf children. *Report of Proceedings of the International Congress on Education of the Deaf and the 41st Meeting of the Convention of American Instructors of the Deaf, 1963.* Washington, D.C.: U.S. Government Printing Office, 1964. (Document 106, 245–261.)
Evaluates the effects on the intelligibility of the speech of deaf children of three factors: the kind of speech materials; whether or not the listener could see the speaker; and the previous experience of the listener with deaf children.

311. Todd, G., & Palmer, B. Social reinforcement of infant babbling. *Child Development,* 1968, **39,** 591–596.

312. John Tracy Clinic. *Teaching speech to the profoundly deaf. Study guide for the film series.* Los Angeles, CA: The John Tracy Clinic, 1970.

313. Travis, L. E. (Ed.). *Handbook of speech pathology and audiology.* New York: Appleton-Century-Crofts, 1971.
A massive reference work of more than 1300 pages containing much fundamental information on speech production. The bibliographies are impressively extensive.

314. Trehub, S. E., & Rabinovitch, M. S. Auditory-linguistic sensitivity in early infancy. *Developmental Psychology,* 1972, **6,** 74–77.

315. Urbantschitsch, V. *Auditory Training for Deaf Mutism and Acquired Deafness*. Translated from original German text of 1895 by S. Richard Silverman. Washington, D.C.: Alexander Graham Bell Association for the Deaf, 1982.

316. Utley, J. *What's its name?* Urbana, Illinois: The University of Illinois Press, 1950.
A workbook designed for parents and teachers of preschool and primary age hearing impaired children. Auditory training album. Records to accompany *What's Its Name?*

317. van Uden, A. Instructing prelingually deaf children by the rhythms of bodily movements and of sounds, by oral mime and general bodily expressions: its possibilities and difficulties. In *Report of Proceedings of the International Congress on Education of the Deaf and the 41st Meeting of the Convention of American Instructors of the Deaf, 1963*. Washington, D.C.: U.S. Government Printing Office, 1964, 852–873.

318. van Uden, A. New realizations in the light of the pure oral method. *The Volta Review*, 1970, **72**, 524–536.
Discusses some of the major points of the "Maternal Reflective Method" which is used to teach speech and language at Sint-Michielsgestel School for the Deaf in the Netherlands. Among the features of the program are: the goal is oral conversation, starting in childhood; all sensory channels are used; teaching is through conversations in which the teacher corrects and expands the children's own utterances; diaries of conversations are kept; great attention is paid to developing natural intonation and speech rhythm, especially accent groupings, based on the rationale that a feel for natural speech rhythm will help constrain a child into using correct language.

319. van Uden, A. *Dove kinderen leren spreken (How children learn to speak)*. Rotterdam, Holland: Universitaire Pers Rotterdam, 1974. (Summary in English.)

320. Vegeley, C. Monitoring of monosyllabic words by deaf children. *Report of Proceedings of the International Congress on Education of the Deaf and the 41st Meeting of the Convention of American Instructors of the Deaf, 1963*. Washington, D.C.: U.S. Government Printing Office, 1964. (Document 106, 735–748.)
Evaluation of the intelligibility of deaf talkers' speech by the deaf speakers themselves and also by normally-hearing listeners.

321. Venezky, R. L. English orthography: Its graphical structure and its relation to sound. *Reading Research Quarterly,* 1967, **2,** 75–105.
Concepts about spelling which lead to regular relationships between the pronunciation and spelling of English words, many of which would ordinarily be considered hopelessly irregular. The author's insight into the regular patterns apparently embedded in the complex of spelling-meaning-pronunciation was aided by a computer-assisted analysis of 20,000 common English words. Inspires respect for the learning and skill of the ordinary reader who can, with reasonable correctness, pronounce new words that he encounters in his reading.

322. Vivian, R. M. The Tadoma method: A tactual approach to speech and speech reading. *The Volta Review,* 1966, **68,** 733–737.
A teacher at Perkins School for the Blind tells how the Tadoma method is used with deaf-blind children. Describes commonly used positions of the hands on the face. Offers suggestions about stimulating awareness of vibration and developing tactual sensitivity and tactual skills. Lists some exercises to build ability to imitate the muscular movement of others. Briefly discusses some procedures for teaching speechreading and speech production.

323. Voelker, C. H. An experimental study of the comparative rate of utterance of deaf and normal hearing speakers. *American Annals of the Deaf,* 1938, **83,** 274–284.

324. Vorce, E. *Teaching speech to deaf children.* (The Lexington School for the Deaf, Education Series, Book IX.) Washington, D.C.: The Alexander Graham Bell Association for the Deaf, 1974.
Organization and methods of the speech program at Lexington School for the Deaf, New York.

325. Walter, B. Dynamic and formal elements in the teaching of spoken language to deaf children. In A. Ewing (Ed.), *The modern educational treatment of deafness.* Manchester, England: Manchester University Press, 1960, 45/1–45/6.

326. Waterson, N. Child phonology: A prosodic view. *Journal of Linguistics,* 1971, **7,** 179–211.

327. Watson, T. J. Auditory training and the development of speech and language in children with defective hearing. *Acta Oto-Laryngologica,* 1951, **40,** 59–103.
Directed to participants in an audiology course, most of whom were otologists and audiologists. The auditory training program to which the author devotes most of his discussion is aimed at training pro-

foundly deaf children to use their residual hearing to master the prosodic features of speech and as an adjunct to lipreading. Broad goals and activities for nursery, primary, and post-primary programs are outlined.

328. Webster, J., & O'Shea, N. Current developments in auditory speech discrimination tests for the profoundly deaf at NTID. *American Annals of the Deaf,* 1980, **125,** 350–359.

329. Webster, R. L. Changes in infants' vocalizations as a function of differential acoustic stimulation. *Developmental Psychology,* 1972, **7,** 39–43.

330. Wedenberg, E. Auditory training of severely hard of hearing preschool children. *Acta Oto-Laryngologica,* 1954, Supplement 110.

331. Weiner, F. F., & Ostrowski. A. A. Effects of listener uncertainty on articulatory inconsistency. *Journal of Speech and Hearing Disorders,* 1979, **44,** 487–493.

332. Weiner, P. S. Auditory discrimination and articulation. *Journal of Speech and Hearing Disorders,* 1967, **32,** 19–28.
    A survey of published research which bears on the question of whether or not presumably normally-hearing persons who make articulation errors in their own speech also tend to make errors in distinguishing among the speech sounds spoken by others. Discusses a number of the variables which affect this relation.

333. Whetnall, E., & Fry, D. B. *The deaf child.* London, England: William Heinemann, 1964.
    An exposition of the development of communication in deaf children emphasizing an early auditory approach.

334. Whetnall, E., & Fry, D. B. *Learning to hear.* London, England: William Heinemann, 1970. Washington, D.C.: R. B. Niven, Ed.

335. Whitehead, R. L., & Barefoot, S. Some aerodynamic characteristics of plosive consonants produced by hearing-impaired speakers. *American Annals of the Deaf,* 1980, **125,** 366–373.

336. Whitehead, R. L., & Barefoot, S. Air flow characteristics of fricative consonants produced by normally hearing and hearing-impaired speakers. *Journal of Speech and Hearing Research* (in review).

337. Whitehurst, M. W. *Auditory training for children.* (Rev. ed.) Armonk, New York: Hearing Rehabilitation Co., 1966.
    Graded lessons from very simple to difficult.

338. Willemain, T. R., & Lee, F. F. Tactile pitch feedback for deaf speakers. *The Volta Review,* 1971, **73,** 541–553.
    Describes a device which pokes different fingers of a speaker's hand

to signal him that his pitch is too high, too low, or satisfactory. A hypothesis to explain the cause of unnaturally high pitch in the speech of the deaf is offered.

339. Wilson, D. K. *Voice problems of children.* Baltimore, Maryland: The Williams and Wilkins Co., 1972.

340. Winitz, H. *Articulatory acquisition and behavior.* New York: Appleton-Century-Crofts, 1969.

A book attempting to "bring articulation, as studied by the speech pathologist, within the mainstream of present-day psycholinguistic thought." Methods and models of descriptive linguistics, instrumental phonetics, and learning theory related to articulatory behavior and correction.

341. Wolfe, W. D., & Goulding, D. J. (Eds.) *Articulation and learning.* Springfield, Illinois: Charles C Thomas, 1973.

342. Yale, C. A. Dr. Bell's early experiments in giving speech to the deaf. *The Volta Review,* 1927, **29**, 293–295.

Describes an experiment that Alexander Graham Bell conducted at the Clarke School for the Deaf in the belief that knowledge of the articulation positions of individual speech elements would result in better speech. The experiment involved vocal gymnastics and voiceless practicing of the mechanical actions of speech, without actually speaking. Tells of Bell's training a very deaf girl to sound the eight notes of the musical scale and to sing a tune.

343. Yale, C. A. *Formation and development of elementary English sounds.* Northampton, Massachusetts: Metcalf, 1938.

The Northampton Charts and their rationale. An accompanying explication of each sound on the charts describes the production of the sound and gives suggestions on how to elicit it from a deaf child.

344. Zaliouk, A. A visual-tactile system of phonetical symbolization. *Journal of Speech and Hearing Disorders,* 1954, **19**, 190–207.

Concerned with labeling each phoneme, with both pictures and hand cues, to show the articulator positions and movements for the phoneme and also to indicate the tactile information which production of the phoneme generates. Lists finger and hand placements for doing this. Presents a system for diagramming phonemes, and offers a phonetic alphabet in which the symbols are pictographs of the articulators and also suggest tactile information.

345. Zeiser, M. L., & Erber, N. P. Auditory/vibratory perception of syllabic structure in words by profoundly hearing-impaired children. *Journal of Speech and Hearing Research,* 1977, **20**, 430–436.

346. Zimmerman, G., & Rettaliata, P. Articulatory patterns of an adventitiously deaf speaker: Implications for the role of auditory information in speech production. *Journal of Speech and Hearing Research,* 1981, **24**, 169–178.

347. Zipf, G. K. *The psycho-biology of language: An introduction to dynamic philology.* Cambridge, Massachusetts: The Massachusetts Institute of Technology Press, 1965.

A book of fascinating insights and theories about speech and language approached through statistical analysis. For example, Chapter III, "The Form and Behavior of Phonemes," after a clear and interesting discussion of the concept of phoneme, builds and ties together a complex of theories about the frequency of occurrence of phonemes and words, the complexity and effort of production, and phonological evolution. First published in 1935, the present edition is enhanced by an introduction by G. A. Miller in which he puts much of Zipf's theorizing into perspective.

348. Zubek, J. P. (Ed.) *Sensory deprivation: Fifteen years of research.* New York: Appleton-Century-Crofts, 1969.

A review of research of sensory deprivation. Most of the research reviewed involved contrived laboratory situations using normal adult subjects. Does not enter the realm of deafness and only fleetingly alludes to the effects of sensory deprivation on children. Nevertheless, a central idea to which the bulk of the book points— that sensory stimulation is important for the maintenance of effective functioning—is of interest to those concerned with the education of the deaf.

Index